IN THE FACE OF CHALLENGE

IN THE FACE OF FACE OF CHALLENGE

PERSEVERANCE IN SALES

Frank Lodewick

All models and photos copyright © Frank Lodewick
www.franklodewick.com

First published in 2019 in Melbourne

ISBN 978-0-6482812-8-3

A catalogue record for this book is available from the National Library of Australia

Edited by Joanna Yardley at The Editing House

Typeset, logo and cover design by Grapefish, Voorschoten, the Netherlands
Cover photograph: rosephotos.com.au

This book uses anecdotes to enforce the meaning behind the relevant chapter. Some names have been omitted or changed to protect individual privacy. Every effort has been made to trace (and seek permission for use of) the original source of material used within this book. Where the attempt has been unsuccessful, the publisher would be pleased to hear from the author/publisher to rectify any omission.

Acknowledgements

This book wouldn't have been possible without all the amazing people who supported me after my accident.

A special thanks to the ambulance officers, nurses, doctors, surgeons, therapists, social workers, general practitioners, dentists, and other medical specialists in Sydney, Australia. I'm incredibly lucky to live in a country with such high quality medical systems and specialists who work day and night to help people. You will read about some of these specialists in this book.

I will always be thankful for their extraordinary dedication to my recovery.

For Esther, who taught me never to take things for granted.

Preface

It is often said that the sales profession can be the hardest high-paying job or the easiest low-paying job. Both extremes – and everything in between – bring challenges. When you find yourself in a challenging patch behind target, the additional scrutiny from your manager will make it more demanding and stressful. When you're kicking goals, the money coming in can make it all seem worth the stress, until the new financial year resets the numbers and you're back at zero. Wherever you find yourself in your sales career, you will have learned that your profession is one of the most demanding career paths one can follow.

In this book, I will help you develop the skills that your sales trainer, typically, won't teach you. These are soft skills that will help you stay motivated to keep going with your chin up and with your eyes on the ball. These are the skills of perseverance.

What this book *is* about

This book is about the 'sales mindset' you need to increase your sales productivity in the face of setbacks. I want to help you, the sales professional, to develop skills and practices that will allow you to better deal with the daily stressors that sales throws at you. How do you keep motivated after 20 reach outs led to zero meetings? How do you deal with the constant rejection, the reality of 20–30% win rates, and the many, many disappointments that come with the job? How do you *not* give up, but actually become *more motivated* to succeed?

The focus of this book is to highlight the crucial skills with which everybody around you somehow assumes you were born. The practices I share help build perseverance in sales; some will work best when adopted across the whole sales team, but you can also apply them at an individual level.

What this book *is not* about

If you're looking for yet another book on solution selling, insight selling, SPIN, command of the message, or any other variant of a sales methodology, this is not it. This book will not guide you on sales strategy, quota setting, negotiating, or other 'hard skills' that will convince your customers to sign. Instead, I focus on you, the sales professional. I will help you stay motivated to keep going, and keep you mentally and physically healthy in your demanding sales role.

Who this book is written for

This book is specifically written for sales professionals who want to increase their sales success in a healthy way that gives them more joy. Whether you are new to sales or have been in sales for many years, my goal is to give you proven practices to strengthen your sales mindset. I have written this book on a foundation of 20 years of software (on premise and Software as a Service (SaaS)) sales experience and have provided many practical examples based on the typical challenges and structures of SaaS sales teams. Still, this book can be used by any professional in a B2B sales environment:

- Sales reps, account executives, area sales managers or any other role that focuses on hunting.
- Customer success managers, account directors, account managers or other farming roles.
- Solution consultants, solution architects, pre-sales engineers or any other role supporting the sales lead to close deals.
- Business development managers, sales development managers, market development managers, marketing managers or any other role helping to develop pipeline for sales.
- CEOs, sales managers, sales directors and any other sales leaders managing a team of individual contributors like the ones mentioned above.
- Startup founders, company owners, or individual contractors who regularly have to sell their ideas.

A note on acronyms, abbreviations and other 'sales' talk

Like most departments in business, the sales department is infected with the Corporate Acronym Plague (CAP). Often, we freely use acronyms without being clear on what they really mean. In particular, people like to throw around complex terminology to show off their supposed expertise and in-depth understanding of the business. This creates environments where people are afraid to ask the 'stupid' questions that could reveal their limited grasp of the complexity/technology/process/industry/interface/application/whatever.

In a sales environment, if you admit to not knowing something, you are assumed to have a lack of confidence or some other weakness that could hinder your ability to deliver; therefore, sales teams are awash with intimidating corporate speak that is counterproductive.

In this book, I will keep the use of acronyms to a minimum. Often, companies use different variations with the same meaning. To ensure we're clear on what I mean, here is a list of acronyms you will find.

- AE: account executive. The sales professional who takes an opportunity, qualifies it and brings it all the way to a close. Also called sales representative, sales rep, area sales manager and business development manager.
- ARR: annual recurring revenue. The value of the contracted recurring revenue components of your term subscriptions normalised to a one year period.
- APAC: Asia Pacific i.e. the region compromising South East Asia and the Pacific (Australia, New Zealand and surrounds). In some companies, APAC covers the whole of Asia, e.g. East Asia (China, Taiwan, Korea, and Japan) and North Asia (Russia). Japan is often separated, leading to more abbreviations like JAPAC and APJ.
- BDR: business development representative. This role is focused on the early stages of opportunity finding ('prospecting'). They can be inbound or outbound or a combination. Also called SDR, sales development representative, and MDR, market development representative.

- **B2B:** business to business. A sales cadence where a business sells to people in another business. As opposed to consumers, B2C.
- **CSM:** customer success manager. The role in a SaaS company responsible for the managing of existing customers. Often, they're tasked to upsell or cross sell even though they tend to not be trained as sales people.
- **CMO:** chief marketing officer.
- **CRM:** a customer relationship management system like Salesforce, Microsoft Dynamics, or HubSpot.
- **EMEA:** Europe, Middle East, Africa. Some companies draw the geographical territory line at India; if it's included in EMEA, EMEAI is the result. Others include Russia in their EMEA territory.
- **IPO:** initial public offer. The process of offering shares of a private corporation to the public in a new stock issuance.
- **KPI:** key performance indicator. An agreed upon metric that demonstrates how a company, team, or individual is achieving business objectives.
- **NDA:** non-disclosure agreement.
- **PS:** professional services. The teams that are responsible for implementing products in software companies.
- **QBR:** quarterly business review. A sales meeting in which the past quarter is reviewed, and actions for the next quarter are agreed upon. Some companies call it a Quarterly Sales Review (QSR).
- **ROI:** return on investment. A performance ratio that aims to measure the return of a particular investment, relative to the investment's cost.
- **RFP:** request for proposal. A document that solicits proposals by a company interested to procure new software or services.
- **SaaS:** software as a service. This is a subscription-based service to use technology online.
- **SC:** solution consultant. The technical product specialist for a SaaS product who often gets involved at demo or scoping stage. Also called pre-sales consultant.
- **SKO:** sales kick off. The annual event to kick off the start of the financial year.
- **SPIN selling:** a sales methodology focused on four areas of prospect questioning: situation, problem, implication and need/pay off.
- **UI:** user interface. The visual space where interactions between humans and the software occur.
- **USP:** unique selling proposition. A distinctive element of a company's offering that sets it apart from its competitors.

Contents

Introduction

This is not a typical book about sales. As you'll soon read, I experienced a life-threatening accident a couple of years ago. I use the story of my recovery as a backdrop to share what I have learned about perseverance, and how those lessons can be applied to sales. The book is structured as follows:

- Chapter 1: the story of my near-death experience that was the catalyst for writing this book.
- Chapter 2: the paradigm shift that is required in sales. Perseverance is a crucial skill for us, yet it is not something we are trained in.
- Chapter 3: the importance of determining your True North (why you are in sales). You'll learn that the typical throwaway answer *'for the money'* is the least effective motivation to stay determined when things go wrong.
- Chapter 4: the importance of creating the right circumstances for the brain to be productive. You'll learn how to change behaviours that are counterproductive to developing perseverance.
- Chapter 5: how to let go and free up time to focus on the right activities, including the practices suggested in this book.
- Chapter 6: the importance of finding perspective. When you're behind target, and stressed out: how do you remain calm? Learn how to stay completely committed to winning a deal, without being dragged down by negative events.
- Chapter 7: the all-important practice of planning things. How to apply planning in day to day sales, including the planning of smaller activities like an outbound call, the creation of a proposal or the delivery of a presentation.
- Chapter 8: how tracking your progress can help you develop more determination to keep going.
- Chapter 9: how the people around you play a major role in the development of your perseverance.

I have also endeavoured to make this a very practical book. Within each chapter, I include:

- A summary of my research into a particular skill, so you can understand the context and appreciate how it relates to our world of sales.
- A list of **Perseverance Promotors**. These are practical tips and exercises you can apply in your daily sales role. Some are simple, eye-opening questions that will help you strengthen your ability to persevere straight away, others are more elaborate activities that require brain energy and time to help you properly develop and embed perseverance.
- A list of what *not* to do. There are the **Perseverance Destroyers**. This list highlights the common habits within sales organisations that hamper the development of perseverance. *They (unintentionally) make our jobs harder.* Being aware of these counterproductive activities will help you change them or change how you deal with them.

A note on the Perseverance Promotors and the Perseverance Destroyers.

I have kept these lists simple and practical. Developing perseverance is an individual creation. Choose the practices that work for you, make them your own, and find a way to incorporate them into your daily routines.

To help you develop the practices and behaviours discussed in these chapters, you can download my *Perseverance in Sales Workbook* at www.franklodewick. com/books. This PDF provides more than 50 practical examples, exercises, models, and prompters that you can print and hang near your desk to constantly remind yourself of the practical tweaks that lead to more perseverance.

Alternatively, you can develop your own system of making notes and jotting down ideas specific to your situation. Without this, you're likely to forget most of the tips I provide. A few pages have been left blank for notes at the end of the book.

Chapter 1: Crashing down

Calling Sydney home

I always thought I could handle setbacks well. I counted myself lucky that I had a mindset that helped me pull through hard times, and cope with disappointment and challenges along the way. That all changed when I crashed face first onto a beach from a height of ten metres (30 feet). Or rather, it was in the two years that followed. Two years of operations, rehabilitation, physiotherapy and dental work peppered with setback after setback on a physical and mental level I had never experienced before.

Funnily enough, that crash happened just when my sales career had reached a new height: work had never been so good. Life, in general, couldn't have been much better. My wife, Elvira, also a Dutch native, and I had moved to Dee Why Beachw, north of Sydney, ten years earlier. We had been on several business trips to Australia and were both drawn to Sydney: the stunning city, the multi-cultural population, the amazing beaches, the beautiful mountains, the warm climate, and the mix of Asian and European cuisine.

The plan was to stay in Sydney for five years, then venture back into the wider world. Little did we know, that our initial excitement for Sydney would develop into a deep love that changed our fundamental feelings about further travel. We still took every opportunity to vacation aboard but after a few years of living in Sydney, the enthusiasm was for coming home – to Sydney.

Going up

At the time of my accident, I was working for an awesome SaaS company. Headquarters were in San Francisco but I was the first sales rep on the ground in Australia. Even with 10 years' of sales experience under my belt when I was recruited, the first few years in that role were a hard gig. No one knew the company, the product served a need that was still evolving in a less mature market, and the concept of SaaS was relatively new in Australia. Half of the sell was to convince customers that storing data into the cloud was the way of the future – not a common belief back then. I found myself evangelising more than selling, with lots of opportunities that didn't go anywhere.

I only made 80 percent of target the first year, which added a lot of pressure to my slowly developing pipeline. The second year was even worse. Cheaper competitors had landed in Australia and benefited from all that evangelising I had been doing, or at least that's how it felt. I had worked so hard yet the results weren't there. At the start of the third year – the moment where you're supposed to be pumping your fist and running out of the door to find new customers – I became down on myself. I was demotivated. While my track record from the years prior had been good, I questioned if I were the right guy for this trailblazing challenge. I doubted whether I could even get close to target. In those first few months, the thought of resigning hung above me every time I faced even the smallest of setbacks.

I had to climb out of that hole. In 2012, I had a renewed energy and decided to give it another go. I'll explain how that happened later. I closed the year at 101 percent of target. This was just enough to start 2013 with the right level of confidence to get out there and win some deals. At this point, we had built a foundation of happy customers, many of whom were well-known Australian corporations like Flybuys, Telstra and Qantas. In our small market in Australia, people started to talk and that worked in our favour.

I wanted to hit it out of the park in 2013. I felt I needed to make up for the first few years. It had been demotivating to watch US reps be praised at Sales Kick Off (SKO) for closing huge deals with large companies, of which we had so few in Australia. I wanted recognition for my hard work too. I wanted the acknowledgement that I could do it. No, I *needed* it. I didn't need to show *others* I could do it, I needed to show *myself* I could do it. I had to get my old sense of self back. So, I gave myself a target to make up for those first couple of meagre years and to regain my confidence. I envisioned myself standing on stage at SKO in 2014, as the sales rep who had sold more than anyone else in absolute dollar numbers. I wanted to prove to myself that those years of hard work had been worth it – I wanted to be No.1 globally.

The year started well. I made 100 percent of my annual target at the close of Q2 in June. Some of those deals had been years in the making. My hard slog had also created the perfect foundation to venture into South East Asia. I was familiar with that part of the world having spent five years in Singapore prior to our Sydney arrival. Still, I wasn't sure if markets like Singapore, Malaysia, Indonesia, Thailand and the Philippines were ready for what the company was offering.

In Q3 of 2013, I went on numerous trips to Singapore, Kuala Lumpur and Bangkok and immediately received confirmation of the market's readiness. Deals came in quickly. Our pitch had resonated, and since our competitors hadn't made the move yet, there were some big deals up for grabs. I got to 200 percent of my annual target by the end of Q3 – our strategy to focus on South East Asia was paying off. I spent most of October and November in Asia. The desire to be No.1 kept me focused: this would be the year I would claim that spot.

But something else was happening. I couldn't sleep anymore. I was exhausted at the end of every day. I would fall asleep quickly but wake two hours later and lay awake till sunrise. Initially, I blamed jet lag so I decided to go on longer trips to limit the constant changes in time zones. When this didn't work, I went to see my doctor, Dr Susan, who warned me of the impact stress was having on my body. I admitted that I had been stressed in the years before, but with 200 percent of my target already done, I wasn't convinced that stress was the cause of my troubled sleeping patterns. After all, that desire to be No.1 was simply a voluntarily committed stretch goal. In my mind, stress had to come from external expectations, not from my own personal motivations.

By the end of that year, my lack of sleep made it hard for me to think clearly. I had developed such an irregular sleeping pattern that I couldn't rest in my own bed. I would wake in the night and become stressed about all the things I still had to do to keep my pipeline progressing. It felt counter intuitive because I was already twice over target and in reach of becoming the No.1 rep globally. Yet, I still stressed out. Dr Susan told me to take it easy. But I couldn't. I was on such an adrenaline high; I had to push even harder.
And I did.

In November, on what turned out to be my final trip for a while, I closed another deal in KL. It got me to 253 percent of target and easily put me in the No.1 position globally. However, when I returned to Sydney on Saturday 23 November, I was exhausted. I hardly slept that night. Sunday was the same. My brain was complete fog. After another restless night, I decided to work from home on Monday. We only had the weekly sales call that morning, and my priorities were limited to updating our CRM and preparing handover documents for the last deal I closed.

By noon, I realised nothing productive was going to come out of me. A strong southerly wind was forecast to come in that afternoon and that meant only one thing, kitesurfing. I'd been kitesurfing for many years and lived for the thrill of the big jumps – my speciality. 'Frank's stress release valve', my wife called it, and it was the main reason we chose to live near the beach. Whenever I got stuck or stressed out, a couple of hours on the water would be the big reset that put things into perspective again. And that was exactly what I needed that afternoon.

Crashing down

When I got to the beach it was already windy. In fact, it was too windy. The ocean was white from gusts rolling in from the south, and dark clouds hugged the horizon in the far distance. My initial reaction was to give it a miss. Kiting in windy conditions can be fun, but too much of it can be dangerous. Sometimes, it's just not really worth it. It looked messy. Then again, I had been kiting for nearly twenty years and (surely) would be able to handle it. With all the excitement and restless nights, I struggled to think straight. I hung around for an hour trying to make up my mind. In the end, I convinced myself that it was going to be ok. All my worries and stress seemed to dissipate when I changed into my wetsuit and pumped up my kite. I launched my kite and walked into the Pacific Ocean until the cold water was hip high. I laid back, slid my feet into my kiteboard, slowly let the kite pull me out of the water, and ... that's all I remember.

The helicopter that took me to the hospital

My kite buddies, who had also arrived on the beach, told me what happened months later. Further upwind, another kiter had launched. He was a beginner and became overpowered by the unusually strong winds. Just before I entered the water, he lost control of his kite and dropped it in the waves. When I launched my kite, I hadn't seen him floating my way. I kited for a few minutes without having any idea of what was about to happen. His kite was crumbled up by the waves and floated into my path, or rather, his lines were, and they were suddenly wrapped around my ankles.

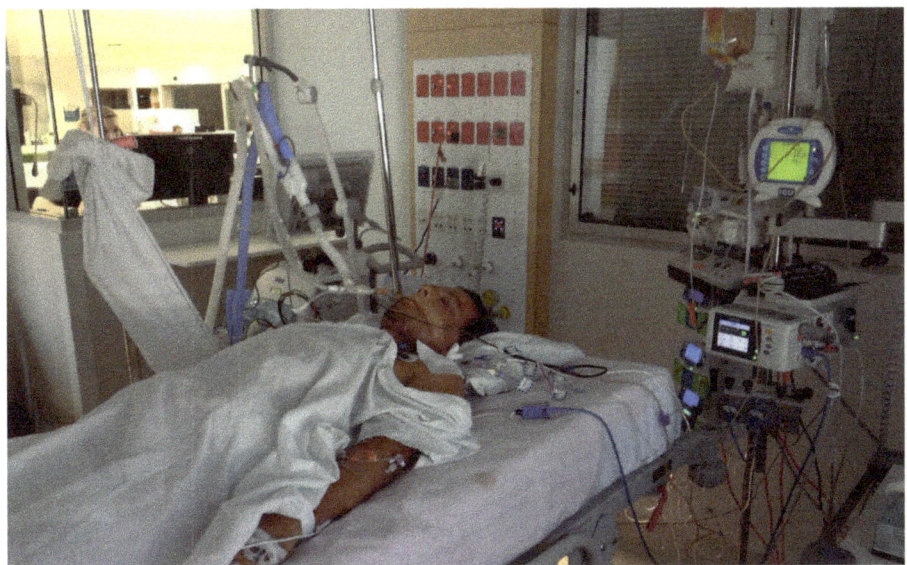

Hooked up to machines in ICU

I should have pulled the *quick release*; it's a safety system that completely disconnects the kite. It would have let go of my kite, putting me out of (most of the) danger. But I didn't. Instead, I tried to get the lines away from my ankles. This would have been impossible as the pull of my own kite put too much tension on them. I didn't hear my kite buddies scream to pull the quick release. Then a wave rolled over the other kite, opening it up and letting the wind launch it again – with me in it. It all happened within a few seconds. I was wrapped in a kite high above the water, with my own kite violently getting out of control. The winds pushed us closer to shore. The other kiter was being dragged through the pounding waves, and I was hanging high above the water. When the other kiter reached the beach, he did what both of us should have done straight away and pulled his quick release. His kite, with me still in it, flew higher, causing me to lose control of my own kite.

My kite slammed down onto the beach. The outgoing tide had turned the beach into a concrete-like plain and the loud sound of the kite smashing onto it startled people all along the beach. A few seconds later, I followed as I crashed face first onto the beach. 'It sounded like that loud wet smack when some 300-pound guy hits the mat after a failed attempt of pole vaulting', said one of the other kiters many months later.

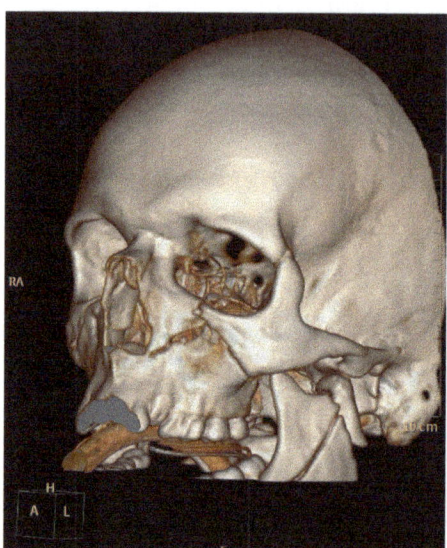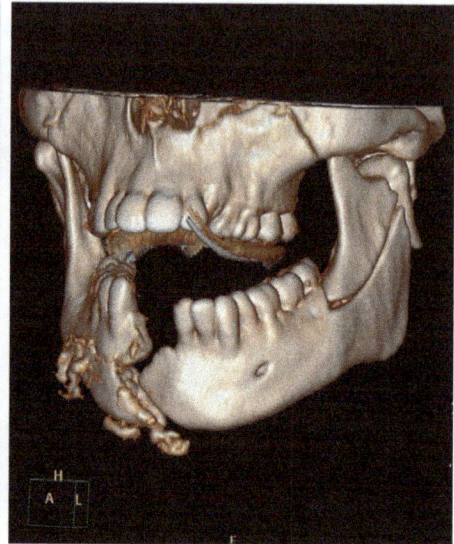

X-rays of my face reveal the damage

An emergency helicopter flew me to hospital where scans revealed I had broken my face into seven pieces – each floating freely in a mess of skin and blood. My right eye had sunk into the cheekbone, and a piece of my lower jaw poked through the skin. My pelvis had snapped off my spine, resulting in one of my legs sticking out ten centimeters more than the other. My right wrist was completely shattered. A lot of my teeth were either missing or broken, and a couple of my ribs were cracked. Another set of scans revealed an even more disturbing injury: a haemorrhage of the brain. My brain had smashed the inside of my skull so severely, it swelled. I was in an induced coma in the Intensive Care Unit (ICU) for two weeks in the hope the swelling would dissipate.

During my two months in hospital, the continuous flow of ups and downs was relentless; it was a gruesome roller-coaster of good and bad news that challenged Elvira (my wife) as much, if not more, than it challenged me. By the time I came out of the coma, my face had mostly been reconstructed. However,

I needed further operations, so for a month, I was restricted to breathing via a machine attached to a hole in my oesophagus (windpipe). My progress was slow. A deep vein thrombosis (a blood clot) that formed in my right leg sent me back to the ICU. My right eye socket was replaced with a titanium one. They attached my pelvis back to my spine with a screw 15 centimeters long. One of the operations on my wrist caused nerve damage that required more operations. More screws, too.

When I was finally discharged, I had lost 10 kilos, but gained a total of 47 screws, 11 titanium plates and a shiny new eye socket.

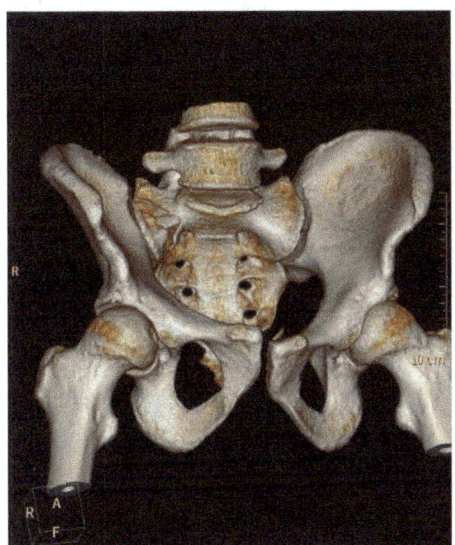 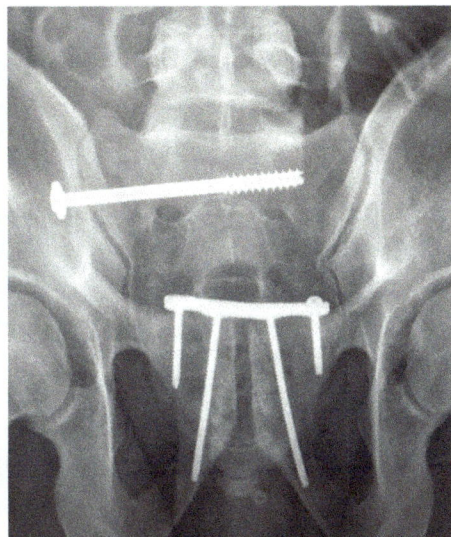

My pelvis before and after the operations

Scrambling back up

The ups and downs would continue for a full two years. That's how long it took for me to recover fully and to regain my health and strength. It was a relentless journey filled with pain, setbacks and uncertainty, but also with accomplishments, progress, and eventually, success. At some level, it had similarities to the sales profession. I needed to be mentally strong and remain positive and confident. As a patient, the outcome I was striving for once I came out of the hospital was determined by my mindset, my willingness to stay on course, my motivation to keep going, my resilience to deal with disappointments along the way, my drive, my grit – my ability to persevere.

After 15 years in the sales profession, I intuitively knew that my challenge was not just physical rehabilitation. It wasn't just about healing bones, building muscles and hoping for the best outcomes after yet another operation. My key driver to persevere towards a successful outcome was my mindset. And throughout my recovery, it was indeed this perseverance that doctors, surgeons and physiotherapists would comment on. They told me that most patients wouldn't have reached such a great outcome. Sure, plain old luck played a huge part in limiting the damage. If I had fallen at a slightly different angle, I would have broken my neck. If I had fallen on rocks rather than hard sand, I would have cracked open my skull and not survived. If the pelvis had broken in a slightly different way, I would have been in a wheelchair. If that blood clot wasn't discovered, it could have travelled to my heart or lungs preventing blood flow. Luck may have saved my life but it wasn't luck that helped me recover. How I tackled my recovery was rather unusual, they said. Patients normally don't have such a methodical approach, they said.

This intrigued me. While I knew that my mindset and approach to deal with unexpected setbacks was fundamental for my chances of success, it was the one topic that was not addressed in my many sessions with surgeons, doctors, dentists and physiotherapists. In the medical world I encountered, there was no real framework or resource available to help patients deal with setbacks. Medical practitioners focus on the physical side. You are left to your own devices to stay mentally strong. You somehow have to develop perseverance and a positive mindset on your own accord. This isn't easy and is proven by the fact that a third of Intensive Care Unit survivors fall into depression.[1] Their ability to recover physically gets hampered by their mental state. Nietzsche said it wrong. What doesn't kill you, doesn't make you stronger – you need more for that.

After I was discharged from hospital, Dr Susan took over. For that two-year period, we would meet monthly for a checkup to address complications that popped up relentlessly. Whenever a blood test or scan led to another complication, Dr Susan would explain what was happening and lay out my options. She would advise me on what follow-up specialist to see and what medicine to take, and she guided me back into work. I started with half a day a week, then a couple of half days a week, then eventually back to full time. Her no-nonsense approach of prioritising health over work made me want to cling to her even after I had fully recovered. I was disappointed when she said my checkups were coming to an end.

When it was time for my final consultation, I bought Dr Susan a bottle of champagne to thank her for her guidance. With the humility that all medical professionals in Sydney seem to have, she blushed uncomfortably and said I shouldn't be thanking her. She said that I should thank myself because it was my determination that led to my unusual and amazing outcome. This time, I couldn't keep my opinion to myself. 'In the last two years, every single doctor or specialist who played a part in fixing me up, said it was important to have perseverance and determination to come out strong after such trauma. Yet none of them provided suggestions to help with that,' I countered. 'The reality is that I struggled. I had setbacks that pushed me into dark places and made it hard to keep going. If my perseverance helped me, why doesn't the medical system teach this to patients?'

From her reaction, I could tell this was a realisation that wasn't new to her. She stared at her desk for a few seconds, pushed her reading glasses lower down her nose, and looked me in the eye. 'No, we don't generally help patients develop their mental resilience or motivation. We just don't have the bandwidth so we focus on repairing the body. When we see patients struggle, we organise psychological treatments or prescribe antidepressant medication, but that's reactive, not proactive. Unfortunately, our industry is more focused on treating symptoms rather than preventing them in the first place.' She took her glasses off her nose and started cleaning them. 'Do you do that in your corporate sales job? Does your company have frameworks or methods to help deal with setbacks proactively, so you stay motivated when things go wrong?'

That question struck me like a thunderbolt. My criticism for the medical system was equally valid for the sales profession. As I had experienced in the years before, we don't help people deal with their lack of motivation or confidence after setbacks. We don't have frameworks to help sales people stay motivated. Why don't we equip ourselves to deal with the unavoidable high level of stress and disappointments we'll be experiencing in sales? Why do trainings focus on hard skills like discovery, presenting, negotiating or convincing customers we can help them? Why do we never address soft skills that we need *to help ourselves*? Because, contrary to what we like to believe about ourselves, sales people are not super confident beings. We're just like anyone else. We have our insecurities, self-doubts and dark periods in which we question our abilities and feel inadequate. We might be better at hiding those insecurities, but that doesn't mean we have an effective coping mechanism.

It's worth it when you're winning sales but when you're facing setbacks, it can take a huge toll on your mindset. In reality, adversity will play a big role in the path to your success. *In sales, it's not about knowing how to win, it's about knowing how to lose.*

Onwards and upwards

In the years after I crashed onto that hard sand, I started researching these topics. I read dozens of books, signed up for courses in resilience, positive intelligence, and mindfulness, and met many people who devote their careers to positive psychology. I learned that in the last fifty years, there has been a huge amount of progress in the research of positive psychology, neuroscience, cognitive psychology and other performance sciences.

Martin Seligman is the first name I came across when I started doing my research. Born in 1942, he's an American psychologist who became known as the grandfather of positive psychology. Seligman's early research focused on trauma survivors: he wanted to understand how trauma affected people's mental health. His research led to an interesting insight that changed his field of study and has since been referred to as Seligman's Bell Curve. He found that if you plot the number of survivors of trauma on a graph to show how they fared after that trauma, a small percentage, on the left side of the curve, developed the mental disorder Post Traumatic Stress Disorder (PTSD). They struggle with the adversity they have encountered. A large group of people (the middle of the curve) came out moderately ok. They somehow got their lives and mental health back to what it once was.

However, Seligman was more interested in the right side of that bell curve. The side that represented a small percentage of trauma survivors who flourished. They actually *came out stronger*. Rather than focusing on mental *illness*, Seligman devoted his career to mental health. What do people who come out stronger do, and how can we bolster people's mental health with those insights? How can we get more people to flourish?

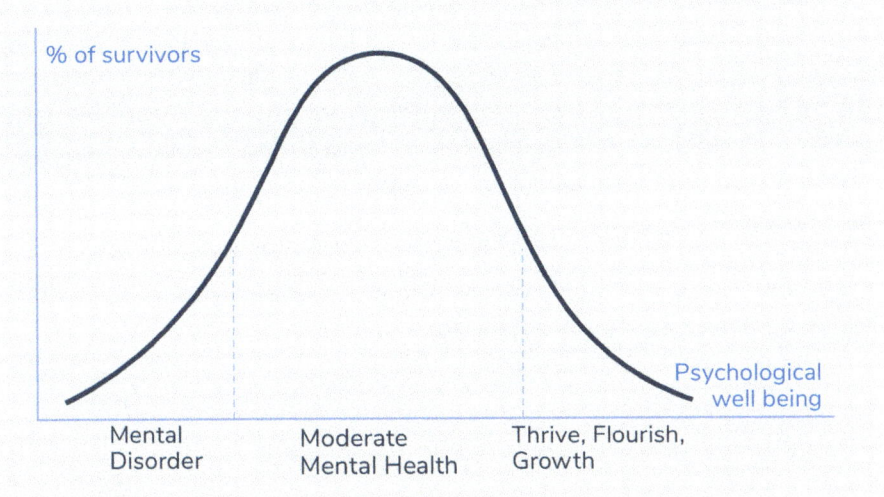

Seligman's Bell Curve

Many researchers have joined him on this journey. In the past two decades, many books have been written on positive psychology, resilience, grit, happiness, wellbeing, and what motivates people. These research-led insights are slowly making it back into the real word, including business and management. But for all the advances science has made in studying how humans behave and deal with setbacks, not much has been translated into specific practices for sales professionals. Instead, we have to make do with the popular assumption that sales people are 'tough and determined individuals'. We expect sales professionals naturally to have determination to keep going; we believe they're born that way. We don't question it. We don't talk about it. When we lose a deal, or things go wrong, we look at each other awkwardly and throw around platitudes like 'ah well, onwards and upwards' or 'keep on keeping on!'.

We need more than meaningless morale boosters. We need to learn from the research and apply it in our daily sales activities. What should we do when we face setbacks in sales? After my accident, I set out to discover the answer.

Clearly, having done all that research does not make me a behavioural psychologist: I'm still a sales guy. But I approached everything I learned from all these very smart people with one simple question: how can we apply this in sales? I learned that while I intuitively applied a few practices that got me to that successful recovery, I also did a few things wrong. Yes, I managed to scramble back from a life threatening accident, and did pretty well in sales, but if I knew then what I now know, I would have done better. I would have recovered quicker and used less energy. I would have held my chin up higher when things went wrong. I would have sold more with less stress and would have slept better. I would have freed up more time and achieved the same. I would have shared less negative energy with my colleagues and Elvira every time I lost a deal.

I would have achieved more with a calm mindset and a smile on my face. That's what I hope this book will do for you.

Chapter 2: The department of habits

How did we get here?

There are many people across the globe who make a living selling things. In most economies, one in eight people, in the workforce, is in sales. This would bring the total number of sales people to a staggering 375 million worldwide. However, not all of these are in B2B sales; numbers from government bodies like the United States Department of Labor show that of the 15.8 million people in 'sales and related occupations', around 7 million are not in 'retail'.[2] While it's hard to get statistics for our profession, it is safe to assume that the B2B sales workforce adds up to over 100 million people globally.

Whatever the number, there are two characteristics that make our crew different from other professional groups. Ok, *at least* two. First of all, chances are you didn't really choose to be here. You never actively decided to pursue a career in sales. It just happened. Before you started working, you probably thought lowly of sales as a profession. Sales people are smooth talking, pushy people who seem to have a bit too much confidence as they jam their foot in the door. That's not you, so that's not a career you ever aspired to follow. Yet, here you are. You may have started your sales career as a business development rep, doing the hard and thankless job of cold calling. Maybe your gig in the call center extended and slowly evolved from activity KPIs to revenue targets. Maybe you were a product specialist or solution consultant who was so good at dealing with customers that you were asked to take on a sales role. Or maybe you decided to start working for yourself and now have to go out and knock on doors to convince clients to pay for your products or services. Whether or not you chose to be on this path, you're here – you're in sales.

And your path was not unique. A survey among hundreds of sales people in 2017 found that nearly half had not originally intended to enter the sales profession.[3] Assuming that these findings are representative of the whole profession, half of the readers of this book somehow, somewhere, and for some reason, ended up in sales.

The second characteristic that makes us different has to do with our education. In the lead up to your professional life, it's unlikely you went to sales university. You didn't do a Masters of Sales or a Bachelor of Business Development. Whether you're from the US, the UK, Europe, APAC or South America, chances are the educational foundation you received did not focus on building the skills and expertise you are expected to leverage in your current role.

Your colleagues outside sales who are a programmer, IT Manager, HR manager, accountant, or legal counsel all attended schools and universities that thoroughly prepared them for their desired career direction. They knew what they wanted to become and invested for years to meet the expectations from prospective employers. For instance, employers looking to hire software engineers typically require programmers to hold at least a bachelor's degree in a field such as computer science, mathematics or information systems. Some jobs even call for a master's degree. These people consciously chose their profession and readied themselves through years of study.

I have a friend who works in the legal department of a global manufacturing company, as a general counsel. He spent five years doing a Bachelor in Business Studies (BA). Then he spent two years getting a Bachelor in Law (LLB) followed by two years getting his Diploma of Legal Practice. His first job, in his chosen profession, was a two-year traineeship with a solicitor's firm. And it didn't stop then. He has since been required to take regular exams to stay abreast of the developments is his field. He can't apply for certain roles in his field if he doesn't have the right certificates that show his expertise.

Before Elvira started her first job in marketing, she had done a four years' Master of Marketing Study at a university, followed by a two-year postgraduate course abroad. Today, she'd have the option to update her skills and knowledge through a Masters of Marketing or specialised courses on Marketing Analytics, Digital Marketing or Social Media Marketing. Depending on where she'd want to take her career in marketing, these are required specialisations without which, she'd have little chance of being hired. It is widely accepted that we need to teach professionals marketing skills that help corporates fill the top of the funnel. Without marketing, there is no positioning, no awareness, and no interest in whatever product or service a company has to sell.

When it comes to sales, we somehow have different standards. For the sales profession, these educational pathways *don't exist*. Universities do not run post-graduate programmes in sales. There are no formal qualifications like those of a programmer, HR professional, accountant, legal counsel or marketer. None of our educational years produced a diploma in the very task we're supposed to succeed in today: selling.

Luckily, the education system is slowly changing, at least in the US. A very small number of universities are now offering trainings specific to sales. But it still doesn't add up. Even though 50 percent of US graduates end up working in sales at some point in their career, less than 5 percent of all US universities teach sales as a topic.[4] To this day, the lack of formal qualification quietly under-appreciates the fundamental skills required for successful selling. *Oh wait*, I hear you think, *what about my two-day SPIN selling course?*

Sales training

The sales training industry has been around for over 50 years. As selling has evolved, sales methodologies like AIDA (Awareness, Interest, Desire, Action), Strategic Selling, SPIN Selling, Solution Selling, Value Selling, Target Account Selling (TAS), the Challenger Sale, Insight Selling and numerous other methodologies have been 'invented' and are typically marketed as the best thing since sliced bread. Some required new sales processes and collaboration structures, while others were merely a polished version of a previous methodology. All of these methodologies were designed to increase sales productivity and allow B2B sales teams to scale more efficiently.

What they didn't give us, however, was a common sales standard. There is no commonly accepted sales accreditation that pops up on job descriptions; although, this doesn't stop you from proudly listing your two-day SPIN course on your resumé. There simply is no agreed industry standard on sales: not on how to do sales, and not on how to teach sales. You might start your career with a company that swears by Solution Selling but in your next job, SPIN, Value Selling, Challenger or some other 'new and improved' formula is the go. As sales professionals, we have never had an educational sales framework impressed on us the way it has been with marketers, coders or accountants. We have been left to our own devices to create something out of all that works for us. We let these practices blend into one exotic soup that somehow seems to work for us at an individual level. Our peers might end up with their own – different – ways that work for them. In other words, *the sales department is the department of habits.*

Most *other* training systems can at least agree on a couple of standards created by National or International Standard Organisations. In finance, General Accepted Accounting Principles are the standard worldwide for bookkeeping. The European Aviation Safety Agency created strict guidelines for the Airline

Transport Pilot Licence (ATPL). In education, a Postgraduate Certificate in Education (PGCE) is set by the National Board for Professional Teaching Standards in the United States and recognised by any institution hiring professionals in that space. Even marketing has the International Institute of Marketing Professionals (IIMP), which 'develops and advocates international standards within the marketing field to be recognised on a global level'.

We don't have this. There is no International Institute of Sales Accreditation or Generally Accepted Sales Principles. Instead, sales professionals build their skills on the job, on a combination of models and practices that somehow have worked for them. Would that be an acceptable outcome in finance? Would we let legal counsels just decide to work with whatever model they favour? Would we let accountants or marketers just mess around with what they learned at a Massive Open Online Course?

Maybe one day we'll have a more formal way to accredit the teaching and testing of these skills. The sales training industry is more than willing to help us with that. Just google 'sales training' and be amazed by the amount of small and large organisations spruiking their services. They're super keen to help you and get you to pay a lot of money in return. Over and over again.

Ebbing who?

In 1880, Hermann Ebbinghaus revealed what he called the Forgetting Curve. It's based on a simple notion that 'people easily forget'. There have been numerous follow-up studies (including one this decade) that have proven his thesis to still be valid. It's based on a pretty simple notion: people easily forget.

Exact numbers differ per study, but the curve is nonetheless consistent. Within one hour of a training, people will have forgotten, on average, 50 percent of the information with which they were presented. Within 24 hours, that memory leak increases, on average, to 70 percent. Within a week, people begin forgetting an average of 80 percent of what was taught.[5] This has nothing to do with intelligence. It's more of a protection mechanism of the brain. Survival mechanisms have trained the brain to be selective as to how to spend energy and attention to store information. The brain isn't built to absorb all that information for long. It's not the sponge to which we figuratively refer. It can easily get overwhelmed but has built-in protections to cope.

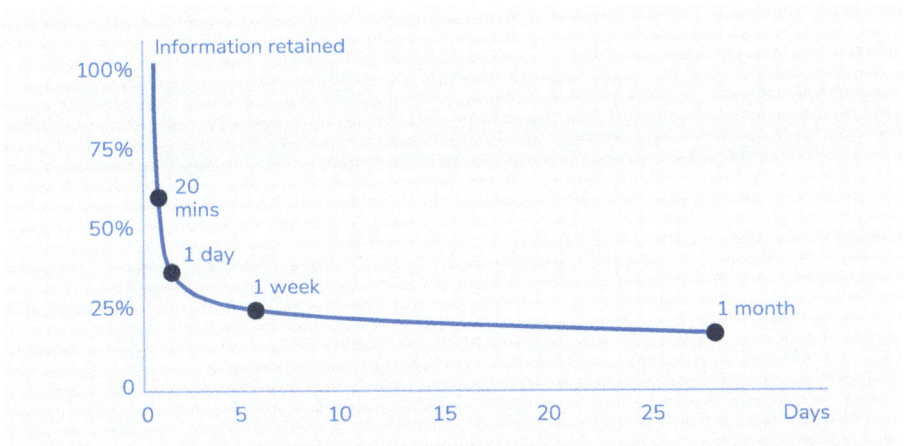

Hermann Ebbinghaus' Forgetting Curve

If you have ever sat through a sales training, this wouldn't surprise you. You experience several 'aha moments' on the first day and make plans to apply certain learnings when you get back to work. By the time that happens, however, you'll find yourself doing your work mostly the same way you did before the course. There is a billion dollar sales training industry that thrives on leaving behind 20 percent of what they promise to deliver. Of course, what can stop this drop is *repetition. Repetition. Repetition.* The more you repeat the message, the more it will stick. While your sales training provider is more than happy to help you with that, the reality is that your available time doesn't allow for it. You have to get out there and sell. You don't have time to be trained continuously. This, of course, is the reason why other professions have agreed to require multi-year studies before you start your career, rather than multi-day courses during your career.

So why then, do we keep on investing in two-day sales trainings? Unfortunately, there is another depressing answer: *because that's the way we've always done it.* Someone created a line item in the budget for sales training, and that line item effectively determines *the way we do things around here.* This logic carries into Sales Induction Programs, Sales Kick Offs, and Quarterly Business Reviews. Your Global Sales Enablement Manager is going to do what they did last year: a set of trainings cramped into the three-day global Sales Kick Off or Bootcamp. Everybody flies back to their own territory and by the time the jet lag and hangover have worn off, the majority of the training has been forgotten. Sales professionals show up on Monday and pick up their work routine like nothing happened.

The rise of bite-sized digital courses (eLearning) tries to improve on this by offering a steady and manageable set of courses that can be digested by participants in a better way. The intention of the concept is great. The eLearning courses are cheap and logistically easy to roll out at scale. But they often lack the personal interaction that makes the trainee completely engaged. As a result, sales professionals do not give the online courses the attention they deserve. It becomes a must-do exercise that sits at the bottom of their priority list, only to be upgraded after their manager starts sending angry emails. Then, when it's time to do the course, the training participant is too distracted trying to get a proposal out of the door, or doing some other multi-tasking activity (more on that later) that prevents any information from 'sticking'. As we know from The Forgetting Curve, much more is needed to accomplish this. We need hands-on, real world application of knowledge to produce the right behaviours. And to change habits, we need repetition, repetition, repetition.

Whatever way you look at it, sales professionals are not just in a career they didn't chose, they also haven't been equipped to deal with the many challenges that come with their jobs. To allow us to survive in these hard circumstances, we have created individualised *habits* formed through on-the-job learnings in different companies with different methodologies and sales strategy-specific practices. Plus a tiny amount of information *that stuck* from several short training courses. Some of these habits are good. Some are not. Due to the lack of certification frameworks, we'll never know which ones fall in what category. When we win deals, we can't put our finger on what went well, specifically. When we lose deals, reasons are even more nebulous. We develop a gut feel around what works and carry on propagating our habits. Then we take these habits into our next role at a different company, where we're asked to work with a different sales methodology with different definitions and practices. Our survival mechanism kicks in and tells us to be selective and not deviate from what we think has worked in the past. The end result is an even more convoluted set of practices.

The sales profession's scorecard

At this point, you might shrug your shoulders and tell me I'm exaggerating the problem. We shouldn't be too worried. We can do this. We're in *sales*. We are stubborn individuals who just don't give up. We are never-say-die spirits who just keep going at it. Doors get slammed in our faces, phone calls remain unanswered, LinkedIn requests are ignored, and emails are never responded to, yet our strong backbone ensures we remain positive and keep smiling. We're determined to never give up. Right?

Let's look at our scorecard and review a few key factors that showcase how we're really faring as a profession.

Win rates

There's only one indisputable metric that shows how well we're all doing in sales: our win rate. And in B2B sales, average win rates are very low. On their blog, CRM provider Salesforce says that 13 percent of leads convert to opportunities and in turn, only 6 percent of opportunities lead to a win. Their competitor, HubSpot, shares similarly depressing insights through an online benchmark tool where you can compare your win rate with the average for your industry. According to their website, the average close rate across all industries is 19 percent.[6] These figures are not very different from what I see when I coach sales teams. Some fare a bit better, around 25 percent. The ones with substantially higher numbers tend to measure their win rate differently: rather than measuring all wins as a ratio to all opened opportunities, they only count the opportunities that reach a certain stage. For instance, they only count opportunities that reached demo stage or proposal stage. This ignores the fact that people worked hard to find those leads and to progress them as opportunities to these stages. They invested time and energy with the hope that the opportunity would turn into a win.

Whatever your definition for win rates, the reality is that in sales you will always have more losses than you will have wins. The *majority* of the deals you will be working on during your sales career, will lead to disappointment. If you're in sales, most of the hours you energetically spent chasing deals actually lead to the non-fulfilment of your hopes and dreams. That's sobering.

Quota attainment

If we're looking for more black and white numbers, average quota attainment has to be next. Quota attainment is the clearest reflection, if not the only one, of how sales professionals perform against what is expected. And unfortunately, the numbers set off more alarm bells. In 2017, insidesales.com researched over 1,100 companies around their sales productivity; one of the topics explored was quota attainment. A not-so-pretty-picture emerged. The number of account executives reaching quota in the US represented just 58.4 percent. For the 28 countries they researched in Europe, an average of 65 percent of reps made quota. Roughly a third of account executives does not get to 100 percent. A third of sales professionals out there do not 'meet expectations'.[7] One-in-three does not close the year with a high-five celebration or a level of satisfaction that gives the confidence and determination to kick it out of the park again next year.

Of course, confidence is an important factor in our ability to succeed and stay motivated. When reps were asked to share whether they *expected* to reach quota, the numbers were even more disturbing. In its 2018 State of Sales research report covering over 2,900 sales professionals, Salesforce found that 58 percent of sales account executives expect to miss quota that year. In the UK, it's even worse: 64 percent of reps don't think they will reach quota. The only country where reps who think they will make quota outnumbers those who don't, is the Netherlands. *Only* 41 percent of reps in my country of birth think they'll miss their quota. The Dutch are an exception, though. In APAC, confidence among reps is lowest. In Hong Kong, 66 percent think they will miss quota; in Singapore it's 68 percent, and in Australia, it's 70 percent.[8] *Less than a third of reps* think they will be successful in reaching quota. That doesn't exactly tally up to a confident, stress-free environment full of optimism and joy.

Attrition
Of course then, a trailing indicator to look at is attrition (or 'employee turnover'). Attrition is defined as the percentage of people who voluntarily or involuntarily leave a company within a year.

In 2017, LinkedIn initiated a substantial study across half a billion (!) members. It found the average attrition for that year was 10.9 percent. As you would expect, those numbers vary per industry, but the range is pretty consistent. Attrition rates in the technology sector including software is 13.2 percent. For financial services it's 10.8 percent, telco is 10.8 percent and healthcare is 9.4 percent. These numbers are across the whole industry (not just the sales department). If you ask HR professionals, numbers of around 10 percent are pretty typical – not necessarily something to worry about.[9]

The department with one of the worst scorecards is the call centre. The International Customer Management Institute pegs the average to be 33 percent.[10] This unattainable number speaks to the challenges this department faces in motivating people whose job is dealing with those who usually only call to complain.

Unfortunately, the attrition rates for the sales profession shows we are in the same boat. The Bridge Group researched hundreds of B2B SaaS Companies and found an average annual attrition rate in sales of 34 percent. In a given year, one in three B2B SaaS sales people throw in the towel. Less than 1 in 10 SaaS companies have attrition rates in sales under 15 percent. At the worst end of town, 12 percent of the SaaS companies surveyed reported attrition to be in excess of 55 percent annually.[11] It's not a challenge that's confined to the world of SaaS companies, either. In 2016, Global B2B research firm Sirius Decisions found that 45 percent of the B2B sales organisations report attrition rates higher than 30 percent.[12]

For all that talk of determination and backbone, sales people are three times as likely to give up and throw in the towel as non-sales people. And this is unlikely to improve. Deloitte's annual research on what drives millennials in the workforce shows some troubling numbers when it comes to loyalty. In 2018, 43 percent of millennials intended to leave their jobs after two years. In 2019, that number climbed to 49 percent. Employed Gen Z workers show even less loyalty with 61 percent saying they would leave in two years if given the choice.[13] While this research does not look into sales specifically, it's safe to say that the sales department will be impacted by these low levels of loyalty with younger sales professionals.

LinkedIn lists jobs for sales representatives in the top three of 'hardest to fill' jobs, globally.[14] Once talent acquisition finds that role, the next stage towards sales productivity, or onboarding, is time consuming and costly. 71 percent of companies take six months or longer for the process of induction, training, and all other activities required to get a sales professional's productivity up to speed. A third of sales organisations take over nine months.[15] Attrition is a very costly part of sales.

Stress in sales

In the USA, 80 percent of workers say they feel stress at work.[16] In Australia in 2019, work-related stress costs businesses $10bln a year.[17] In the UK, stress, depression or anxiety accounted for 49 percent of all working days lost due to ill health in 2016/2017[18] That's 12.5 million days of lost productivity due to stress. Industries where stress rates are highest are in public services like human health, social care, and education. Outside of these industries, the job titles of those jobs with high stress levels are rather generic. People with roles like 'business professionals' and 'media professionals' have the most stress outside of public services. Sales is typically not itemised as a category. What these high stress occupations have in common though is something that represents a unique character of the sales profession: they deal with people. Or more specifically, they are people-centric occupations that bring a high potential for *interpersonal friction*. Dealing with co-workers, bosses and customers is fun, but when expectations aren't aligned, people are also the biggest *source* of stress.

That's why burnout and stress in the workplace have been getting more attention in the media. Numbers, like the ones I shared before, regularly show up in publications and raise the alarm on mental wellbeing, and workplace health and safety. It's good to scratch the surface to understand what's behind that worrying shift. There are some big-ticket topics that represent profound changes that are easy to under-appreciate.

The shift to knowledge work

The first big development has been going on for over 60 years: the shift to knowledge work. Knowledge workers are workers whose main capital is knowledge: software engineers, accountants, design thinkers, consultants, lawyers, sales professionals, and so on. They are white collar workers who create value with their minds. Skill workers represent the other category. They use their skills to produce value, typically through labour-intensive work; they are blue-collar workers. A hundred years ago, 75 percent of workers were considered skill workers who worked on farms, or in factories, or doing other jobs considered labour work. Today, depending on the industry, that number has gone the other way. 75 percent of workers are knowledge workers. In software, finance or IT, that number is 100 percent.

Peter Drucker is one of the most influential management thinkers of our time. Since the 1950s, he had been anticipating this monumental leap to an age where people would produce value with their minds rather than with their muscles. Drucker had been alerting businesses to not underestimate the impact of this shift. Within the 41 management books he wrote, he warned of the fundamental difference in the way knowledge workers needed to 'keep up'. Skills required for labour work don't need to evolve that quickly, he notioned. A truck driver today leverages the same skills they did 10 years ago. Same for an artist, crane worker, factory worker or farmer. Their skills do need to evolve but not at that high a pace. As a result, the window to utilise their learned skills has been much greater. That isn't to say their jobs are safer, particularly with that Sword of Damocles (automation) hanging above their heads. They've simply been able to do their work without the incremental and constant need to re-skill.

Not so for knowledge workers like us sales professionals. Drucker says that for our growing category, the window is a lot smaller because 'Knowledge changes itself. It makes itself obsolete, and very rapidly. A knowledge worker becomes obsolescent if he or she does not go back to school every three or four years'.[19] A software engineer who was top notch five years ago, would be worth a lot less today if he or she had not kept up with the huge amount of changes in the industry. Same for a legal counsel, security specialist, marketing automation solution consultant, or cloud storage sales rep. Knowledge workers need to continuously reinvent, on the job, or through trainings, to ensure their value remains. In many industries, knowledge that's two years old is simply irrelevant. Constant learning is a prerequisite not just to success, but to survival.

The flattening of the organisation

In the search to cut costs and find efficiencies, organisations have been engaging in a flattening exercise by removing layers of middle management. This means that the average sales manager's span of control has increased substantially. In the US, a sales manager manages around 10 to 12 individual sales reps.[20] Even if you're one of the lucky ones to see a span of control of one manager for, say, six sales reps, that doesn't necessarily mean it's a good thing. Particularly in fast growing SaaS companies, where managers are often promoted too quickly. They had a few years of sales success and suddenly find themselves managing a whole sales team, even though they have not gained enough experience to even know 'what good looks like'. As a result, the individual customer-facing sales professional doesn't get much practical support, like how to get to the decision maker or how to keep the conversation at a business level during discovery. The manager simply doesn't know.

Drucker, who passed away in 2005, addressed this tension throughout the later stages of his life. He found that 'Companies today aren't managing their knowledge workers' careers. Instead, you must be your own CEO'.[21] Sales professionals, like ourselves, not only have to take control of where we want our careers to go, we have to ensure we develop the right skills that help us get there. This has been my main driver for the development of the *Perseverance Promotors* and *Destroyers* in the later chapters of this book. We need to take control and strengthen our ability to persevere regardless of our external environment. Our managers are not going to do that for us.

The digitisation of the workplace

Digitisation has made our jobs easier in many ways, but at the same time is one of the main drivers of stress. The European Trade Union Institute has been researching the impact that digital technologies has on the workforce, and even coined a new term for one of the downsides: technostress. In HesaMag #16 *The Future of Work in the Digital Era*, Gerard Valenduc states that 'Technostress refers to work-related psychosocial stress. It occurs when the potential benefits offered by the new digital devices mutate into pressure being put on an employee in the form of explicit or implicit expectations of an employer or colleagues, customer expectations or demands, connectivity problems disturbing normal working routine or when workers become dependent on digital devices, in particular mobile devices such as smartphones or tablets'.[22]

Information overload is at the basis of many of these high-pressure expectations. The average office worker receives around 121 emails a day and sends around 40.[23] Group emails and that productivity killer, cc-emails, explain the difference. Numbers for the channels that beg for more attention and urgency (SMS, Slack, WhatsApp, LinkedIn) are more difficult to find, but whatever their volumes, they only add to the constant distraction coming our way.

Of course, not all of those messages are urgent or even important. But because there are no proper filtering mechanisms, it's up to us to shift through all of them to avoid getting admonished for potentially overlooking them. As Valenduc says: 'This permanent mix of significant and insignificant information characterising the Internet and social media is a source of mental fatigue, as is the need to be permanently accessible and available'. The tools that are making our jobs more efficient are also a driving force for stress. And that's before truly intrusive technologies like augmented reality, smartglasses, and robots supporting collaborative learning are becoming part of our daily work.

Globalisation and nomadism

Geographical boundaries have disappeared; your job can be done by someone in India, the Philippines, or from a town in your own country with a lower cost of living and lower salary expectations. A surge in the global supply of medium-skilled workers fuelled many years of expansion in trade across the globe. And now, another wave is coming. 'In the decades ahead, the main shock to global labour markets will come from the sustained rapid expansion in the supply of high-skill workers – almost all of them from emerging markets,' according to analysis by Bloomberg Economics.[24] This means that competition for our jobs will continue to increase. You have to ensure your value is perceived to be higher than that of the thousands of other people who might be able to do your job – something our grandparents didn't have to worry about.

Sure, there's an upside. Digitisation means we can work from anywhere and reduce long commutes. The downside of that digital improvement could be bigger though. Today, work-life balance is much harder to achieve than it was even five years ago. The (portable) laptop is the default option rather than the desktop. Software as a service and other cloud services allow us to work from anywhere at any time, further blurring the lines we used to have between work and not-work. If we're online, we're effectively in the office. And when we're awake, we are online. Of course, not all of these hours are spent on work-related activities. But while all these digital services have made our lives easier in many ways, most of us simply spend more hours working.

I am a morning person, so I start reading and sending emails from around 7 am. People who hit send on 'the other side of my screen' don't all have that same daily rhythm. I tend to receive replies till around midnight. So, while I'm technically not in the office, I am creating and responding to expectations during a workday that spans over 16 hours. For those of us who work in global companies, those expectations literally form non-stop, 24 hours a day. And while that is typically only an implicit expectation, it does create pressure. There is a growing assumption that we're active throughout this 'extended workday'. Whether we're quickly checking emails before our commute, writing a management report over the weekend, preparing a presentation after we put the kids to sleep, or doing LinkedIn reach-outs on the bus to work, we're working longer. Valenduc says we've become digital nomads, working anywhere, anytime. Our time online makes it harder to switch off when we finally do find the time to not work and enjoy life.

The future of sales

In the last ten years, plenty of players in the sales industry have come out to help us with new technologies and models. The sales tech landscape, consisting of software companies that promise increased sales performance, is booming. By a count in 2019, this included 950 software vendors that sold sales tools for call recording, speech to text, predictive forecasting, social engagement, scheduling and appointment setting and many more.[25]

Of course, the sales training industry is stepping up too. More specialisations are being developed, including social selling, prospecting, qualification, storytelling, negotiation, persuasion, dealing with objection and so on. There are hundreds of sales gurus who offer new school, 'sales 2.0' practices with catchy names that tell you how to use social media, write blogs, go to meetups, or in some other way try to convince you that their new way of selling really is what will get you to crush your target. In the crudest sense, they help you better convince the customer to buy from you and not from the competition. Sales trainings mostly focus on the *convincing skill* needed in our profession. While I'll be the first to review new technologies or sales models to work smarter in sales, I don't think they will resolve the structural problems of the sales profession. They'll make things temporarily bearable, but won't fix the deeply flawed nature of sales, for two reasons.

First off all, these technologies and sales gurus tend to evolve around a recurring promise: there is an easier way to get to your sales target. If you'd only buy their software or book, or sign up to their online content or come to their event, you can make quota without breaking a sweat. After my twenty years in sales, I can tell you that that simply doesn't sit right. There is no silver bullet that miraculously boosts your sales performance. Sales is hard work. Whatever someone promises you, sales is not a ride in the park. Your job, as a sales professional, is hard – one of the hardest in the company. That's why you get paid so well if you reach target. But you need to do the hard yards to get there. You need to pick up the phone and cold call to fill your pipeline. You need to be smart, and find and influence the multiple stakeholders who get involved in your deal at the buyer's side. You need to deal with objections, stay professional, and just keep going at it. There are no shortcuts in sales. That's right ... there is no such thing as an easy way to get to your target. Whoever tells you otherwise is full of BS.

I am not saying these productivity enhancing methods have no merit. There are tools and methods that can help increase your sales success. And that gets us to the second point. Just as they can help you act smarter to win that deal, they can also help your competitor. Just like with your company, your competitors are also investing in sales tech, like predictive forecasting and speech to text analytics. Just like you, they start their year with sales kick off and some new sales training around prospecting, qualification, or negotiation. All of these enhancements merely lift the bar for all of us sales professionals. *The tide rises for all of us.*

To languish or to flourish

Whatever way we look at our preparedness for a career in sales, it's not going to be a walk in the park. A career in sales, regardless of whether it was a deliberate choice or not, will be a rewarding one packaged with a high degree of disappointment and stress. Sales is a balancing game of success and failures, unfairly tilted to the latter. A career in sales requires you to be able to deal with that lopsided reality. *Again, a career in sales is not just about knowing how to win. It's also about knowing how to lose.*

It's about finding motivation to keep going. It's about feeling energised and upbeat, even when that big Q4 deal shows signs of wavering. It's knowing how to deal with setbacks, big and small. It's about persevering in the face of every challenge. And that's a topic we don't normally discuss much in sales. The topic of 'resilience', a term that has found mainstream media and reached other departments, hasn't made it to the agenda of our QBR yet.

'Resilience' stems from the Latin word Resili, which technically means 'to spring back, or 'to rebound'. The common use of the term has gone beyond this elasticity principle though. Resilience is not just about bending back to the original shape, it's about coming out stronger so that we're better prepared for the next potential hit. Angela Duckworth confirms that idea in her book *Grit: The Power of Perseverance and Passion* (2017). 'You can grow your grit from the inside out', she says. Additionally, Sheryl Sandberg, the Facebook COO who unexpectedly lost her husband, wrote a book to share her lessons learned on the harrowing journey that followed. The book called *Option B: Facing Adversity, Building Resilience, and Finding Joy* (2017) is co-authored by organisational psychologist Adam Grant, a leading expert in finding motivation and meaning, and in it, the pair share certain things you can do to better deal with adversity and setbacks. They share the notion that you can develop these skills. Sheryl articulates this as follows: 'It is not about having a backbone. It's about strengthening the muscles around our backbone'. The next chapters will help you do exactly that.

Chapter 3: Find your True North

Out of control

For me, coming out of a coma wasn't like what you see in the movies. I didn't suddenly wake up, and, after a few confusing seconds wonder what had happened or what day it was. Instead, it was a long, drawn-out process in which my brain floated in a grey area between being offline and online. Clarity came in waves of energy that slowly made me more aware of where I was. Those waves then resided, and I fell back into periods of unconsciousness for who knows how long. Ketamine, one of the pain killing and sedation medications used in intensive care, played an unfortunate role in this tidal process. Other popular names for this drug are the Horse Tranquilliser and Special K.

The powerful drug is indeed used by veterinarians to sedate big animals like horses, but it's also used in ICUs as a human anesthetic. Ketamine impedes the brain's sensory connection to the body. It stops the brain from receiving pain signals, or any signals for that matter, without impacting the respiratory system. Autopilot functions like breathing, heart rate and digestion are not switched off; however, inject enough Ketamine into someone's system, and they're 'out'. In my case, the anesthetist needed to apply double the dose someone of my size and weight would normally receive. My brain simply kept fighting to stay online, and it took more Ketamine to help it surrender. The complications of this brings us to the second nickname, Special K. Ketamine can lead to serious hallucinations. People in club scenes across the world have embraced the drug (in a less powerful powder form) for that reason. Ketamine distorts your perception of what's happening around you, which I assume can be fun if you're in good spirits.

I wasn't, though. As I slowly came out of the coma, the mental alarm bells that had been muted for weeks, became louder and louder. When I was awake, I tried to make sense of why I couldn't move or talk, or why my eyes didn't work. But then I'd fall into unconsciousness again, only to wake up in a different room with different people and muffled sounds around me. Ketamine didn't allow my brain to piece this all together in a rational manner. Instead, it came up with horrible interpretations of what these strangers in blurry white coats were doing to me. It concluded that I had been kidnapped and tortured. In my mind, they were clearly out to hurt me. I was completely helpless and had no say as to what was happening to me.

The hallucinatory effects of the cocktail of these scary environments, the drugs, and falling in and out of consciousness created the worst nightmare I had ever had. However, unlike a regular nightmare, this one kept going. Not just for hours, or even days, but for a time that never seemed to end. There was neither daylight, sunshine or the sound of birds to indicate a new day. Instead, there were machines that steadily beeped, sometimes with alarming intensity and constant noise from people coming and going. For the longest time, not one external signal represented the slightest hint that the nightmare would soon come to an end. It seemed everlasting. Later, I would be able to appreciate just how long it lasted – a full three weeks. Three weeks of being completely out of control with no say or influence to make it stop.

It wasn't exactly a fight for survival – I simply couldn't do anything. I felt like I was lying on the floor, defenseless, and everyone around me was hitting me and kicking me, non-stop. In the moments when I was awake – if that's what you call it – I had developed a level of distrust that I would keep to myself even when I became more clear-headed. Speaking out would only make it worse, I feared. Besides, my jaws had been wired together to prevent me from speaking. Or, rather, to prevent me from moving my jaw, which had carefully been screwed back together. That explanation didn't make much sense to my battered mind, nor did it matter. I had no intention of confronting my abductors. A laminated A4 poster of the alphabet lay on my bed. I used this to communicate with the nurses by pointing to the letters. Since my eyesight was very poor, it took minutes to even get a single word out. Elvira was by my side for most of the time; I recognised her voice, which sounded worried and tired. I feared that if I had told Elvira what really was happening when she wasn't around, the nurses would hear me. Or maybe they would find the scrambled notes she made to decipher my alphabetic transmissions.

Five weeks into my ordeal, my jaw was unwired. That same day, just after the nurses and doctors finished their morning review of my situation, I gathered the strength to tell Elvira what really had been happening. She was shocked. I tried to calm her down and begged her to keep her voice down. Seeing the fear in my eyes, Elvira carefully started prodding for examples and details of my accusations. 'They did something with my eyes and burned my hand,' I told her. 'They cut my legs open. They wired my jaws shut, and put this tube down my throat so I can't speak'. As details poured out, Elvira started to make sense of what was happening. She climbed onto the hospital bed with the diary she had been keeping. Over a period of a full day, she walked me through the tumultuous events that had happened in the month before. She talked about the accident, the many operations on my hand, legs and face, and spoke about the nurses and surgeons involved. Doctors who came in to shine lights in my eyes were testing my reflexes, she told me. And nurses jammed needles into me to administer medicines or measure my blood. That tube that went all the way into my stomach was a feeding tube. The horrible thing that disappeared into a hole under my Adam's apple was a breathing tube because oxygen couldn't get passed the swelling in my face. Even after she explained the reason for all these painful interventions, it still didn't make sense to me. My brain simply couldn't cope. When I asked her for a mirror to properly understand her explanation of the tubes in my face and neck, she changed the topic. It made me wonder why.

It took a long time to for my erratic thinking to stop. Even when I was put on much lighter painkillers, I kept experiencing hallucinatory episodes. Certain moments would yank me back into a very suspicious state where I refused to talk. One day a nurse walked in with a deep voice that I clearly recognised from one of the torture sessions on my hand. The heart monitor started beeping crazily, which only made it worse. It was late in the evening and Elvira was already on her way home. When the nurse left, I texted Elvira to come back and rescue me. She did. She drove all the way back to convince me that I was in safe hands, and only left after I fell asleep.

Looking back, even though I didn't understand, I did have this automatic drive to keep going. Again, it wasn't so much a fight for survival, it was a fight to get out of there. Obviously, the logical thing to say is that no one likes being in hospital, so of course I wanted out. It wasn't that rational though, it was a drive, a motivation that came from deep within me. It was a primal drive to not be helpless, to not let others decide what they were going to do to me, to not be dependent on others, however well their intentions. I had a fundamental need to stay in control.

What motivates us in sales?

It was more than plain competitiveness that kept me believing I would become the No.1 sales rep. There was a much deeper driver that allowed me to persevere in the face of all the setbacks over my years in sales. The frightening memories of that primal fight for control in the hospital made me go deeper and uncover my true motivation. As my mental wounds healed, it slowly dawned on me. The fundamental motivation to stay in control during those months in hospital wasn't actually that foreign to me. In fact, it was more of an extension of what had always kept me going, just at a much more intense level.

It wasn't so much the 'being No.1' that I cared about. It was the increased sense of control that would result from me reaching such a goal. If I'd reach my target and show everyone I could do this, I simply had a bigger control over my destiny. I'd have less scrutiny of my daily activities; I'd be able to decide what to focus on and what to de-priortise; and I would have more of a say in what I'd do the year after. That's what kept me going. That was my True North in the lead up to the accident.

For you, the sales professional, it's important to unwrap your motivation to persevere. You need to understand what drives you, or what should be driving you. Your core motivation says a lot about the intensity of your determination. *The Why behind any action determines not only the direction of your actions, but also its firmness.* The more you are driven by a clear Why, the stronger your ability to scramble back up when things don't go your way.

The reality is that we don't often stand still long enough to explore the Why of a sales professional. Non-sales people often assume we're in sales for the money. There are two reasons for this. First, why else would we deal with all that stress and disappointment? Second, why else do we get paid so well? This notion is partially based on the way popular media characterises sales people. The Wolf of Wall Street, Glengarry Glen Ross, Boiler Room and other populistic depictions of our profession all enforce that snake-oil stereotype of dishonest human beings whose main motivation is financial gain, with no regard to damage done to others. The last scene of their storyline tends to involve a sweaty insider wired with a microphone triggering an FBI raid on the sales villain. Not exactly the poster children that present our profession as an aspirational and credible career path.

Likewise, companies that purely motivate their staff by focusing on profit or their share price, don't tend to do well in the long run. We all know how the 'money hungry' likes of Enron and the Lehman Brothers ended up. And for those corporates driven by greed who seemingly still seem to succeed, we must question the definition of success. They burn out their workforce, alien-ate their customers and eventually pay the price.

Of course, sales professionals with such attitudes don't last long nowadays. Transparency, another upside of digitisation, means our customers and managers will see through bad intentions very quickly. Yes, money can be good in sales but we should be careful not to make that a reason to be in sales. While it might have played a role in getting us into sales, money cannot be the driver that keeps us going when things don't go well. This sounds counterintuitive because the *Reward and Punishment* theory has been around for years. This theory, also referred to as *Operant Conditioning*, assumes that behaviour is determined by rewards or punishment that results from achievement. If a child is promised use of the iPad after he cleans his room, he's more motivated to do that job. If he touches a hot stove, and gets burned, then he's motivated to avoid that behaviour. This theory, which stems from the early 1900s, has been fundamental to a lot of management theories. In fact, the foundations of sales have been built on it. If you promise a sales guy commission, then he'll try to sell more. If you want quick results, and create a SPIF, sales people will steer their actions accordingly.

In sales, people for whom money alone is the motivator are often referred to as being coin-operated. Money can be a reward that motivates, but it is not a driver that builds long term perseverance. Of course, you need to pay the bills, and financial gain for you and your family is a good thing, but if you're in sales purely because of the commission check, you're not making it easy for yourself. In his book, *Drive: The Surprising Truth About What Motivates Us* (2011), Daniel Pink explains why. Pink refers to research originating from the 1970s, when Edward Deci (a well-known Professor of Psychology at the University of Rochester) wanted to find out what motivated students. Deci was primarily interested in understanding the impact of motivation on students' overall wellbeing. Deci tracked the students after they finished their studies and ventured into the real world. He found that students who were motivated by the accumulation of wealth or status, and attained goals they set for themselves, '... reported levels of satisfaction, self-esteem, and positive affect no higher than when they were students. In other words, they'd reached their goals, but it didn't make them any happier. What's more, graduates with profit goals showed increases in anxiety, depression, and other negative indicators – again, even though they were attaining their goals'. Deci's research showed us that monetary motivation doesn't make you happier, instead, it makes you anxious.

Pink explains that people who are intrinsically motivated, however, find reward in the behaviour itself. For example, with Wikipedia, Firefox, Linux and other open source initiatives, thousands of people free up time in their busy lives to help develop or improve such software without expecting any external rewards. Such intrinsic motivation, Pink says, leads to more perseverance, because 'People who are intrinsically motivated in their actions are not easily disturbed by external events'.

So what is behind intrinsic motivation? Pink breaks it down into three elements: autonomy, mastery and purpose.

Autonomy

Autonomous motivation, or the drive to be self-directed, involves behaving with a full sense of volition and choice. Clearly, this was the driver that kept me focused when I came out of the coma. Not being autonomous was a horrible state to be in. My desire to be autonomous fueled my motivation to get out of that hospital. But as I discovered, that same drive kept me going in sales as well. It keeps all of us going. We want to have control over our actions and the sense of control represents that intrinsic reward. The opposite of autonomy is controlled motivation. This means behaving with the experience of pressure and demand toward specific outcomes from forces perceived to be external to the self. We don't want someone else telling us what to do. It feels good to be the master of our destiny and that represents a motivation by itself. Remember those poor call centre workers? One reason their attrition rate is so high is that they have very limited autonomy. They can't choose what customers they talk to; when they pick up the phone, they have to deal with whatever is thrown at them. Not only does their boss 'physically' see what they are doing, he/she measures the duration of calls and can even listen in. It's a role with minimal autonomy – an accountant has more freedom.

For many sales professionals, it is this autonomy, this freedom, which motivates them more than the money. Sales is one of the few jobs that allows you to do well while keeping a high level of autonomy. As long as you make your number, you're ok. Your boss will have other problems to prioritise, which means you can be self-directing around how you fill in your day. For me, that freedom was the key that originally attracted me to sales. Straight after my studies, I just couldn't see myself sitting in an office all day. Travelling to customers, being in different cities every week, and having freedom on the road all day, were key reasons I opted for a job in sales. And the more I became used to that autonomy, the more I needed it. I just wasn't consciously aware and let it be masked by other motivations, like making money and being No.1.

Sure, there were downsides. Being on the road by myself was often lonely. I couldn't develop relationships with my peers, who were hardly in the office either, which meant I couldn't bounce ideas off of others. Sales can be a lonely job, which can slow down our learning curve. Most of all, the isolation makes it hard to address the downside of sales we talked about before. And, as you know from your friends outside of sales, there's no such thing as a stress-less corporate job anyway – everyone has to deal with stress. There are company restructures and downsizings, acquisitions that suddenly make roles or whole departments redundant, changes in strategic directions that make product lines obsolete or move work to other parts of the world. But at least in sales, we have that autonomy to better deal with these changes. We're at the pointy end of the company and can see what's working and what isn't. Often, we can see change coming before anyone else. And if all goes wrong, we can go on interviews or 'network' without having to come up with excuses.

It's this autonomy that made me decide to 'demote' from sales manager to sales rep ten years into my career. I wanted more control; I wanted to have a greater say in how I would spend my day. It was also a key driver to start working for myself, as a sales coach, after my accident. I can choose my own clients and determine my own utilisation, independent from what others tell me to do. Of course, the people who pay my salary (my clients) are my boss(es), but I have the highest sense of autonomy and that keeps me going in tough months when the money doesn't provide much motivation.

That 'roaming' freedom was also key in my life. I was one of the first people to pick up kitesurfing in 1998, just before my first sales job. Kitesurfing is a pretty fickle sport, you're dependent on wind strength, wind direction, waves, and the natural elements. You need to be ready to drop everything when the wind picks up. In sales, I could do that. I could plan my days around the wind forecast. If the wind was good, I simply blocked out an hour or two to get out on the water and accepted more evening work to make up for it. This autonomous arrangement played a big role in my ability to persevere.

Mastery

Mastery reflects our urge to get better at something that matters to us. People are driven by progress and the intrinsic confirmation that what they did today was better than what they did yesterday. Legendary psychologist, Mihaly Csikszentmihalyi, devoted his career to this topic and relays his findings in his book, *Flow: The Psychology of Optimal Experience* (2008), where he describes 'flow' as the optimal experience where you are so absorbed in what you are doing that you stop being aware of yourself and your problems, and enter an automatic state. If you are in flow or 'in the zone', you perform at optimal levels and lose your sense of space and time. In his research, which spans half a century, he refers to extreme sportspeople to illustrate people who are 'in flow'. Here, he quotes a rock climber: 'You are so involved in what you are doing [that] you aren't thinking of yourself as separate from the immediate activity. You don't see yourself as separate from what you are doing ... The purpose of the flow is to keep on flowing, not looking for a peak or utopia but staying in the flow. It is not a moving up but a continuous flowing; you move up to keep the flow going. There is no possible reason for climbing except the climbing itself; it is a self-communication.'

These colourful snippets were truly eye opening to me. They helped me understand why kitesurfing had played such a huge role in my life, and why I needed it to be able to deal with the stress that came with my sales career. Whenever I was stuck on a problem, I had that deep-rooted urge to kite. And once I was on the beach and launched that kite, a relaxation and calmness came over me. The hell with it. I stepped into the liquid world and I took charge. And every time I did it, I got better at it. I wasn't a risk taker either. I was the opposite. I needed to be in control, and being on the water dealing with the elements by myself gave me exactly that. As Csikszentmihalyi says: 'What people enjoy is not the sense of being in control, but the sense of exercising control in difficult situations. It is not possible to experience a feeling of control unless one is willing to give up the safety of protective routines. Only when a doubtful outcome is at stake, and one is able to influence that outcome, can a person really know whether she is in control.'

I couldn't come up with a better way to sum up sales. In sales, it's completely up to us to grab something that's challenging and, in our own way, make something out of it. That is motivating in itself, regardless of the outcome. We are the master of our destinies and even if what we do doesn't lead to a win, the journey is ours. Every time we have a shot at an opportunity, we can try new techniques, and see what works and what doesn't. That gives us joy and keeps us going.

Purpose

I only need to drop one name to let you appreciate the impact that purpose has on perseverance. Nelson Mandela. Here's a man who stood up for equality and justice. A man with strong values and beliefs around the unfairness of apartheid. A man with convictions so strong that he devoted his life to fighting apartheid and changing the world. At a young age, Mandela started to speak out against racism. He joined the African National Congress (ANC) at the age of 24 and was arrested after he helped organise a three-day strike for workers. He was sentenced to life imprisonment and spent the following 27 years in jail. All those years that he could have spent with his wife and kids, Mandela, instead, spent them locked up on a desolate island kilometres from the mainland. The deprivation and isolation, the many friends who died due to the brutal apartheid regime, the poor nutrition, the uncertainty of his health and future, none of it would budge Mandela. After his release at the age of 71, rather than giving up his plight, he kept fighting. He became president of the ANC, and a couple of years later was South Africa's first democratically elected President. Mandela got knocked down many times, but each time, he brushed himself off and kept going. Most of all, he came out stronger. He did change the world. He had so many reasons to give up, but his determination kept his chin up. Why? Because he was driven to change the world and fight the injustices from the apartheid movement. He made that his life purpose.

On the other end of the seniority spectrum, we have another name that oozes perseverance. Malala. Malala Yousafzai grew up in the Swat Valley in Northwest Pakistan, where the local Taliban had banned girls from attending school. She started speaking out against this, and at the age of 11 wrote a blog to fight for equal education for girls and boys. After taking an exam at the age of 15, she was shot in the face by a Taliban gunman on the bus on her the way home. Luckily, she survived that ordeal, and man, did she come out stronger. She now lives in the UK and is an activist for female education with a worldwide audience. She wrote a book, *I am Malala: The Girl who Stood up for Education and was Shot by the Taliban* (2013); she is a recipient of the Nobel Peace Prize (2014), and does speaking engagements across the globe to create awareness of her plight. Like Mandela, at the heart of her determination is her drive for equality. That's more important to her than anything in life.

Clearly, our setbacks pale in comparison to those of Mandela and Malala. We don't all deal with such bigger-than-life challenges. However, the purpose that feeds our motivation at work can come from anything that is meaningful to us.

The easiest way to illustrate this point is by introducing you to three brothers: John, Richard and Rob. The three brothers are working on the construction of an elderly home, as brick layers, in San Francisco. The brothers have exactly the same job. They physically perform the same activities on a daily basis. It's the mental side that sets them apart.

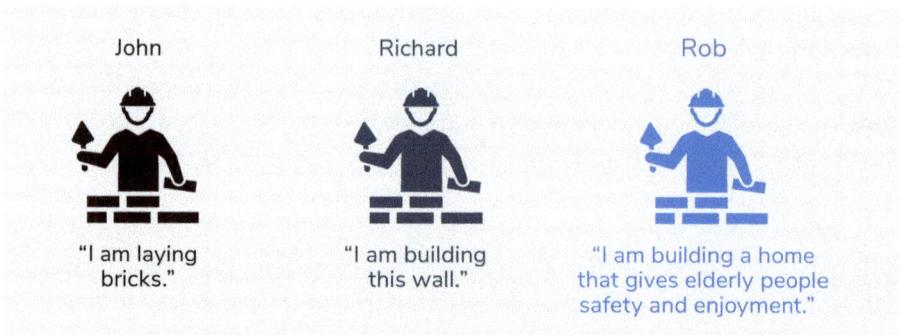

Same work, different purpose

When we ask John what he's doing for work, his answer is straight forward: 'I am laying bricks'. Richard, on the other hand, has a slightly bigger view of his role when he says: 'I am building this wall'. Rob, the third brother, looks at his job with a different lens altogether: 'I am building a home that gives elderly people safety and enjoyment'. Now, imagine the brothers face a setback. A small earthquake topples over the wall. The three brothers must face the fact that they're back to square one. Who do you think is most motivated to pick up his tools and start building again? Who's most likely to persevere? Clearly, it'll be Rob. Rob has found a meaningful purpose in the work he's doing, and as a result, will have an edge over John and Richard.

Bringing this reasoning into the corporate world doesn't require that much of a stretch. Which accountant would be more motivated to persevere? Peter, who says he's just entering numbers? Harry, who helps ensures accurate financial reporting, or Steve, who says he plays a role in safeguarding the financial stability of the company?

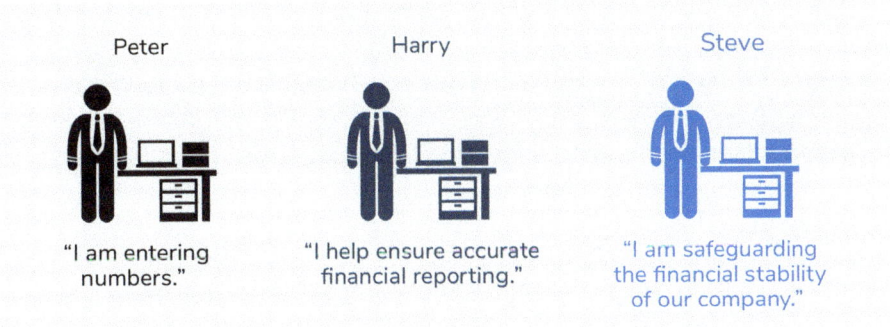

Peter	Harry	Steve
"I am entering numbers."	"I help ensure accurate financial reporting."	"I am safeguarding the financial stability of our company."

Same work, different purpose

Purpose in sales

As sales professionals, we can find meaningful purpose that will strengthen our perseverance. In her book, *Selling with Noble Purpose: How to Drive Revenue and do Work That Makes You Proud* (2012), Lisa Earle McLeod writes about a study she conducted for a major biotech company. The company's management wanted to determine what behaviours separated top sales people from average sales people, and see how they could learn from those behaviours. What McLeod found surprised everyone. Top performing sales professionals had a *sense of purpose* that did not evolve around money or any other selfish motivation. Instead, top performers were driven to help others. 'The salespeople who sold with noble purpose – who truly wanted to make a difference to customers – consistently outsold the salespeople who were focused on sales' goals and money,' she writes.

On a sales call to a local hospital, a sales rep from the above biotech company was approached by an elderly lady who recognised her company's name badge. She had been prescribed the company's drug to help with her lack of energy to even leave the house. From the moment she started taking the drug, she was able to travel and visit her grandkids. She had the energy to get on the floor and play with them. She wanted to thank the sales rep for giving her back her life. That off-the-cuff conversation, in the hallway of a hospital, made a profound impact on the rep, who told McLeod: 'I think about that woman every day. If it's 4:30 on a rainy Friday afternoon, other sales reps go home. I don't. I make the extra sales call because I know I'm not just pitching a product. I'm saving people's lives. That grandmother is my higher purpose'.

Spurred by this anecdote, McLeod did more research and kept coming to the same conclusion: *sales professionals driven to make a difference to customers outperformed those who were not.* While psychologists might find this a bit of an open door, the sales profession, with its commission-focused culture, has been built on the notion that money is the main driver for motivation and sales success. It is such a fundamental aspect of sales that non-sales people tend to assume that all sales people are purely in it for the money, and that such motivation is an ugly necessity for corporate success. Other research found this common notion to be wrong. A ten-year study by Millward Brown Optimor, *Stengel Study of Business Growth* (2011) found that companies who put improving people's lives at their centre, outperform the market by a huge margin with growth rates triple that of their competitors. And improving people's lives isn't limited to drug companies, any company can articulate the value of their offering in the context of how it improves people's lives. And they should. As McLeod writes, 'When you know that your job matters to people, you come alive. Your frontal lobes light up, and you have greater access to problem solving, language, and empathy'.

My purpose

Interestingly enough, when I read that section of McLeod's book, something clicked for me. The way she elevated the purpose of sales – the Why – made me realise that I had not given it much thought. But looking back, I unconsciously had actually experienced this very angle already. As you will remember from Chapter 1, I was on the verge of resigning after not making my target, two years in a row, at that SaaS company from San Francisco. We created Marketing Automation solutions: one of the first Software as a Service (SaaS) offerings in the industry. Marketing Automation helped B2C marketers create data driven campaigns online and through email and mobile messaging, so they could target consumers with the right message, at the right time, through the right channel. Now that the likes of Adobe, Marketo, Salesforce, and HubSpot are well engrained in B2C and B2B businesses, I am sure this explanation makes sense to you. But in 2009, it wasn't so straight forward. Educating the less mature market in APAC was fun but also frustrating as it would lead to long sales cycles and small dip-the-toe-in-the-water deals. For me, it was a case of high effort and low return, particularly from a financial perspective. And while I never saw myself as a coin-operated sales guy, I felt that not reaching my target meant I was failing. So I contemplated no longer persevering, and resigning instead.

During a conversation with a colleague, I shared my frustration of feeling useless. I had worked my ass off for two years, and wasn't successful. Sure, we were making progress in growing our APAC footprint, but I wasn't making my sales target. I felt I was failing, I told him. This colleague wasn't in sales, and his response came from a different and refreshing angle. He reflected on the deals I already closed and said, 'Our customers are already experiencing how our software helps them run their marketing more efficiently and that will lead them to grow revenues, get promoted, and talk to others about us. As long are we're improving our customers' business, we're improving their careers, and lives too. We're changing the way our industry works. Isn't it exciting to be part of that?'

This planted a seed. I wasn't fully convinced but, deep down, I felt we were on to something. It initially felt awkward to shift from numbers-driven success to improving-lives success. Our sales trainings had never put too much emphasis on this angle; it was all about positioning value in terms of business success. I hadn't put much value on the success it brought for people's careers. But it made sense: if a marketer decided to invest in our solution, and as a result would meet the business goals, surely, that could only be a good thing for that marketer's future. So I reached out to my counterparts in the US, not to ask how much more revenue our software had created for our customers, but to ask how many marketers, who favoured our solution, had been promoted. Had their decision to purchase our SaaS solution created career opportunities as a result? And if so, what did that mean for them?

How purpose helped me sell

These questions didn't lead to clear answers straight away. Most of the reps I talked to were intrigued, but didn't have the answers. They had already moved on to the next deal and didn't have the time to track careers of people they sold to before. So I reached out to the CSMs, who dealt with customers after the rep stepped away. That led to some really promising insights. CSMs confirmed that many of the marketers who had stuck their neck out and favoured our solution, ended up doing well in their career. In fact, *career progression* was a key talking point for the CSMs who developed close ties with our customers. Naturally, possible promotions were dependent on marketers reaching KPIs that were driven by business goals like increasing revenue or reducing cost. That was the main value of our solution to the business, but to the marketer who bought it from us, these personal motivations were as, if not more, important. While it made a lot of sense, it also felt like I uncovered two hugely important and untapped insights.

First of all, our structure of decoupling hunting from farming had many advantages, but it prevented the hunters from being able to appreciate the impact they made on customers. Even if the CSM organised case studies or press releases to celebrate our success with a new customer, those stories weren't about the impact we made on the people. The PR or legal teams that had to approve the case studies had beat all 'colour' out of the stories. Secondly, our sales methodology and training told us to focus on business values like return on investment (ROI) or in other words, how much more money a company was going to make after deciding to buy from us. Uncovering personal drivers was an element of the discovery phase, but it didn't get much attention. There definitely weren't any blue prints for personal drivers in the way we had them for business drivers. We were clearly missing out. Not only could we create more motivation with the hunters, we could expand their talk tracks to incorporate real stories around the impact we made on people.

It didn't take much effort to incorporate 'career progression' into my sales messages. Straight away, I realised it resonated. In meetings, people would sit up and clearly showed interest every time I went into a colourful account of what we had done for 'people like them'. My sales pitch became a lot more authentic and people-oriented. I noticed the energy in the room changed whenever I would illustrate what our solutions could mean for the prospect's career and life. They would lean in and ask more questions, and divulge more of their pains, too.

One such prospect was Emma. She was the type of career hungry marketer who was determined to become CMO. In every meeting we had with her and her team, we talked about the impact our solution would have on their personal jobs. Emma decided to go with us, even though our competitor was half the price. She built a case with her management to invest in our solution, spent three times as much as she did before, and backed that up with ROI models our teams had developed. It paid off from an ROI and career progression perspective. Emma was promoted to head up the whole marketing team and to this day sees her decision to invest with us as a key enabler. *Knowing this has helped me built perseverance when I faced setbacks.*

That line of thinking around how our offering could help the very people I sold to uncovered more valuable insights around personal drivers. It wasn't just careers I helped improve. I improved lives too. One prospect, Ron, told me he just had twins. He was struggling to leave the office in time as the incumbent solution was cumbersome to use. He had to do a lot of manual work to upload data and assets and double check things before he could run his marketing campaigns. Before, I would have missed out on this opportunity to focus on how our solution would improve his life. I would have created a ROI model that would have shown how the reduction in hours spent would have led to a lower Total Cost of Ownership. But now, I found myself passionately talking about the not-so-sexy features of our solution that would help him automate much of his work so that he could go home earlier and take care of his newborn twins. Sure, we had to prove what 'more efficient marketing' would mean to Ron's company's bottom line, but I simply left that to Ron. He had truly bought into our offering because of what it would mean to him and his family. Ron had a big personal vested interest that I simply made a point of emphasising, and he did the rest. Not only did we win that deal with zero discount, I only spent half of the time and energy to close it compared to other deals.

Over time, I found myself becoming more enthusiastic about our offering. It became easier to talk about its merits when I had personal stories to back it up. I became more convincing as I talked to prospects about Emma and Ron, and others we had helped. These stories were more real than the case studies coming from headquarters. No one really cares about the ROI that our customer Verizon got, or the cost reduction Wells Fargo booked. These were colourless and faceless stories that my competitor had, too. But my stories were about how we helped *people*.

The message resonated because it was authentic. It wasn't some sales script I rattled off; it was true and verifiable. I soon developed a bank of stories around how our solution had improved the lives of our customers and made sure to steer reference calls to that fact ('Just call Ron, he'll be glad to talk to you'). Our customers all had their own stories around how we impacted their personal lives, which they could articulate with great colour and detail. For me, it was a fun driver to pitch because I really believed in it and found myself sharing animated stories with anyone who wanted to listen.

I began using the angle of 'improvement in life' in my recruitment. Rather than telling candidates for sales roles that they could make a lot of money, my main message would focus on how they would be developing skills that would enhance their careers. Selling SaaS in APAC wasn't going to be easy, but it would help them push their sales skill to a higher level. A guy I hired seven years ago still remembers how I told him I couldn't give him the base salary he wanted, but that taking the role would make him a better sales professional, which would set him up for life. That was the promise he bought into, and that was what made him determined to stick around when he struggled to make his target the first year. He's still there as the longest serving sales rep who consistently beats his target.

Most of all, the purpose that I uncovered made me more enthusiastic and motivated to sell. Sure, it didn't shield me from setbacks, but having this higher purpose gave me a conviction that brought extra levels of energy to deal with them. Having this purpose made it possible for me to persevere. I became the No.1 sales rep worldwide, two years after I nearly resigned, selling twice as many deals as the No.2. I couldn't have done that without my new-found view of Why I was selling.

Perseverance Promotors

1. Define your True North

My motivation will not be the same as yours, and what keeps your colleagues and friends going might not be the same either. Don't complicate it by thinking you're just in it for the money. Spend some time defining what motivates you about your role. Work out what it is in terms of autonomy, mastery and purpose that gets you out of bed. What accounts or people do you find interesting? What specific skills can you improve on this quarter? And how does what you sell help other people? Think it through, and write it down. Go one step further and work out the long-term vision of True North for your sales career. You'll be surprised about what you find deep down inside; it is likely to be a mixture of drivers around autonomy, mastery and purpose. My workbook has a simple template for both exercises.

2. Find your release

Most well-paying jobs don't allow you to balance work with your hobbies, or life for that matter. In sales, that's not easy either, but at least we can autonomously decide our priorities and sometimes sneak out to step away from life in the office. Leverage that. Find a hobby that gives you the ability to master your skills. Take note of an interesting insight that Csikszentmihalyi writes about in *Flow*. 'What we found was that when people were pursuing leisure activities that were expensive in terms of the outside resources required – activities that demanded expensive equipment, or electricity, or other forms of energy measured in BTUs, such as power boating, driving, or watching television – they were significantly less happy than when involved in inexpensive leisure'. Sports that involve big toys generally require less attention and as a result produce less memorable rewards. Instead, hobbies like climbing, surfing, running, gardening, dancing, knitting and yoga help you become more in flow, which strengthens your resolve to persevere.

3. Go climbing

After my accident, I picked up indoor rock climbing. My initial aim was to physically strengthen and test myself, but I soon learned that the mental side of climbing is what really allowed me to flourish. Climbing is a mental sport. And as long as you use ropes, it's a sport where you can safely test the boundaries and learn that your mind is often wrong when it keeps telling you that you can't do it. Learn how overstepping the boundaries of your comfort will help you control your mind and build confidence that you can do more than you think.

4. Talk to customers

In a perfect world, your company has bought into the importance of purpose. Your management's messaging is about how your offering helps to improve the lives of your customers. The reality will be different for the majority of us. You will have to uncover the Why (the purpose) of what you sell independently, from the ground up. Find out how your offering has impacted your customers' lives.

Get buy-in from the CSMs so they know why you're talking to their customers. Pick three customers and offer to buy them a coffee. Don't just focus on the decision makers, go after the end users too – find your Ron. Find something of value to offer in return for 30 minutes of their time (like a 3rd party white paper, an intro to another customer, a conference pass, an inspiring book). Tell them you are proud they are a customer of your company. Ensure you have no other motivation; don't try to sell them something. Your goal is to learn.

Ask these questions to uncover how your solution has improved their lives:

- Has your work changed since you bought our solution?
- How have we helped you become more efficient?

- Think back to before you worked with our solution, what were you doing then that you are happy to stop doing now? (For example, have activities shifted from laborious manual work to more strategic work?)
- What has this meant for how you spend your day in the office? How does this impact you personally?
- How has our solution helped you reduce stress?
- How has that impacted you and your family?
- Are there things you can now do that make life easier? Can you give me some specific examples?

You will find themes that help you see the bigger picture of what selling your product delivers to other people. You can use these insights to sell more. Group them in a simple one-pager and write the customer's name next to each one. You want to be able to tell your prospects, 'Ron, who works a couple of blocks away from you, told me that since he bought our solution he ...'

Practice the pitch on your friends and you'll see that even though they aren't interested in your product, they want to hear about those personal stories.

5. Talk to CSMs

It's always best to go to the source and talk to customers directly. Sometimes, this is not practical and the Customer Success Manager is your source. If you find they don't have detailed insights, see if you can coach them. It'll develop their perseverance too.

Questions to ask:

- How does your customer define success from a business perspective? What about the personal perspective?
- Is the decision maker looking for a promotion? Have they told you the KPIs that will make that happen?
- In your quarterly reviews, what gets the most attention? What makes your customer happy?
- Have they told you how our solution has improved things? Any specific anecdotes around how things used to be?

- Are there any specific features your customers rave about that you think we don't emphasise enough?
- What's the power or dynamic from the end users? How much of a say do they have in the roadmap of activities? What drives them?

6. Change your focus towards purpose

If you're a sales manager running regular sales meetings, don't just focus on the numbers. Create a culture where there's a steady emphasis on the impact you are making on people's lives.

Here are a few things you could do:

- Create a Google doc called 'Customer Career Progression' and make it part of a CSM's KPIs to log promotions your customers have experienced since they signed up with you. Link the LinkedIn profiles of your actual customers in the document and let the CSM write a brief synopsis of the role your solution played in that promotion.
- During your weekly sales call, go through that list and celebrate the addition of a new promotion as hard as you celebrate the closing of a new deal. If your sales culture involves ringing a bell whenever you close a new deal, expand that practice by ringing that bell whenever a customer gets promoted.
- During QBRs, invite real customers to come and tell you how your solution has improved their business and their lives.
- Invite customers for your Friday social event, and create a Q&A session where SDRs and AEs can ask what they like most about your solution. Ask them how you should pitch your solution to get people like them to respond to your outreaches. Ask for personal angles, not business angles, as per the questions listed above.
- Create a Customer Story Library. This could be a simple Google sheet where you list your customers and snippets of their personal stories. You will find recurring themes, so group them accordingly. If you already have something in place for your Sales Playbooks, with business impacts or use cases, expand it to reflect the personal themes. Add the LinkedIn profile pictures of your customers to make the stories come alive.
- Give the AEs and CSMs a KPI to find three customer stories every quarter to present during QBR.

- Expand your training to cover these customer stories. Test your reps on their ability to articulate the value of your solution based on the training coming from sales enablement, but insist they need to 'weave in' these customer stories. Don't make them rely on impersonal case studies, insist they tell real stories with real names. They only need to master three.

- Create prospecting dinners where you invite two recently promoted customers and five prospects. Set the scene that this is a networking event sponsored by you – you like to advance people's careers. Have one or two of your own people there, preferably a senior exec and a CSM. However hard it is, resist inviting sales people. The customers will do the selling.

- During Sales Kick Off, it's common to invite customers to stand up and talk about how awesome your solution is for their business. Keep doing that, but also ask them to outline how it has changed their personal lives.

- See if you can convince management and marketing on the power of being able to articulate a story around purpose. Start with how it helps you sell more, but slowly bend it to what really matters: your ability to motivate your sales teams. While it makes more sense to start with this one, the reality is that most organisations' DNA doesn't make this an easy change to implement top down. Use all the initiatives above to build your case from the bottom up.

- Don't let this definition of purpose be hijacked by some HQ committee tasked to create a vision or mission statement for the company. These tend to end up being meaningless platitudes filled with jargon that won't motivate your salesforce. Keep it specific to your sales people as it will increase their drive and performance before the HQ committee has even been able to agree on a name for their initiative.

7. Find joy in nailing a presentation

This was a big factor in keeping me focused on my goal to reach the No.1 rep spot. I used a good storyline and a template from HQ that I had adjusted to incorporate personal snippets. I had done a lot of presentations by then and found myself trying to do better every time. 'Better' for me was telling the story without slides. I would remove some slides and rely on the spoken word. Realising that the audience was more engaged only heightened my motivation to become better at storytelling. Even when I knew it was 'only' the first presentation of a 6-months sales cycle, it gave me the most joy. Mastering the skill became the win, and this became the fuel to keep going.

8. Talk to your friends

Whenever you feel demotivated and wonder why you're in sales, talk to friends who aren't. Ask them what their day is like, and see if that sounds appealing to you. This reality check will help you realise that the autonomy we have in sales, and the exciting things we get to do and learn about on a daily basis, is what makes sales such an awesome career.

9. Take a sabbatical

Stepping away from your hectic job, now and then, will help you discover your drive. Read. Travel. Meet people in different industries and learn what drives them. It's important to broaden your horizon particularly if you're surrounded by coin-operated sales people. It's not money that makes the world go around, it's people who are driven by autonomy, mastery and purpose.

Perseverance Destroyers

1. Don't be sceptical of sales candidates who have taken a sabbatical

There is often an apprehension to hire people who have taken a year off. We should embrace such risk-takers, those who dared to expand their horizons and learn what drives them. They tend to have a motivation that's driven by more than their wallets. Of course, make sure to find out what's behind the sabbatical. If indications are that the candidate sat on the couch watching Netflix all year, I'd be less inclined.

2. Don't just talk about you

I often see sales decks that are more about the vendor than the customer. They offer slide after slide showing their offices, their range of products, quotes from industry sources like Gartner and Forrester about how awesome they are, logos of the customers they serve, maybe even something about their funding rounds, IPO plans or share price. None of this is of interest to the prospect. Instead, a pitch should focus on the prospect's world, the changes you see there, how such changes lead to pains, and how you could help resolve such pains by showcasing how you helped other customers. Once you get your prospect to ask you how big you actually are, and where you have offices and so on, you've earned the right to talk about you. Don't lead with that; it's not about you, it's about how you can help *them*.

3. Don't make your purpose the maximising of shareholder value

You confuse your audience and messaging by telling the sales team your purpose is to increase shareholder value. Even if they have options or shares, the share price is not what gets sales people out of bed. The company's valuation is a longer term lagging indicator that is a result of sales success. Sales professionals need to have perseverance that makes them book that success. There is no increased shareholder value if sales is not motivated to keep going. Create that perseverance first and monetary success will automatically follow.

4. Don't give end-of-quarter sweeteners

You indicate to prospects that you are willing to do better deals towards the end of the quarter. This tells the customer that you're willing to create shortcuts to reach your monetary success; whereas, the customer's interest is their business and personal success. Another side effect of this end-of-quarter-discounting is that customers will remind themselves (and their peers) to wait to sign that expansion or renewal towards the end of the quarter next time around. It's difficult to get out of such spirals to elevate the conversation back to business and personal success, so don't start it.

5. Don't talk about a Close Plan

Never talk about a Close Plan with your prospect. Yes, you definitely need one (more on that later), but the unintentional signal you are giving, simply by referring to it as a Close Plan, is that your goal is to close the deal. But that's not your prospect's goal at all. They want to see business and personal success, which happens (way) after the close. The close is merely the start of that journey. And if you determine your goals, language and actions around that close, as an end point, you are giving the prospect a signal that your goals are not aligned with their goals. Instead, call it an Implementation Plan or a Mutual Success Plan, and don't let the final action be the contract signature. Start with the end, and include activities like First Quarterly Review, Go Live, Pilot, Migration, Integration, Scoping with the Professional Services team, Kick off, Account Activation, Contract signed, Agree on scope, and so on – work backwards. Be confident and agree on a date to publish a Customer Case Study or Success Story. For an example of a Mutual Success Plan, see my workbook. You can get it from www.franklodewick.com/books.

6. Don't use the win report for chest beating

Your win report's template focuses on how awesome your sales team was in closing the deal. While there is some value is letting the winners showcase their success, the real value is in educating the rest of the organisation around what pains and challenges we are resolving for the new customer (again, from a business as well as a personal perspective). A win report should be a reflection of that and not a colourful depiction of who you had dinner with or who you took to a baseball game. That's not why prospects buy from you, so don't spread that old school sales message.

7. Don't limit high achiever rewards to quantifiable goals

Ok, I was driven to become the No.1 sales rep. I wanted to be on stage at SKO. That goal, and the recognition that would follow, motivated me to keep going. I now know this was an extrinsically motivated goal, which played a role in disrupting my sleeping patterns and creating unnecessary anxiety. In hindsight, a more intrinsically driven motivation would have been more sustainable. If you, as a sales manager, only have high achiever rewards for *most sold* or *biggest deal* successes, you're indicating that your definition of success is limited to such metrics – not the end customer. If you really want to single people out, focus on metrics around customer success, and award those who 'helped most customers achieve career progression'. Soon, you'll see that sales people who win these awards are also the ones who close the most deals. That will be a result, not the cause, of their purpose-driven approach.

8. Don't forget to tailor the CEO's internal presentation

In your quarterly 'all hands with the CEO', your proof points of success are often limited to your revenue, profit, or share price. Wrong audience. Your shareholders care about that, and while you should update the internal organisation with the financials, if that's the only thing staff hear from the CEO, it's what they believe is the only thing the organisation cares about. Mix such messaging with customer success stories. Financial success is a lag indicator of customer success.

9. Don't accept a raise as a reason to stay

If you are thinking about resigning, don't let a bonus or raise be the reason to change your mind. It will only give you a short-lasting sugar hit. You'll not only fall back to previous levels of dissatisfaction, you'll feel an extra (extrinsically motivated) obligation to persevere. As we saw before, it's intrinsic motivators that keep people motivated to keep going. Reflect on elements of autonomy, mastery, and purpose in your role to help you reconsider. See if you could get your boss to play around with these levers rather than only with your wallet.

10. Don't de-prioritise your health

Jobs in sales are stressful, and we will always struggle to get our work-life balance right. But we need a sound mind to perform, and it's our responsibility to create the right environment for that. My lack of sleep played a big role in my accident. If I would have been well rested, I would not have gone kitesurfing. I would have assessed the situation differently and decided to wait for safer conditions. Even if I would have gone out, I would have been alert enough to get out of my predicament. Instead, my brain was foggy and I didn't respond quickly. As we'll see in the next chapter, sustaining the brain is not only key in preventing things from spiraling out of control, it's *fundamental* to our ability to persevere.

Chapter 4: Sustain the brain

I never really cared for my brain. I mean, it's not like I didn't care whether I had a healthy, functioning brain- I wanted that. I just never actively cared for it. I cared for my teeth; I would brush them well and regularly get checkups at the dentist. I cared for my weight; I was conscious about what I ate and drank, and would regularly check the mirror to ensure I stayed in shape. I cared for my heart and blood, and once a year had a checkup to ensure my stressful life-style wasn't taking too much of a toll. I even cared about my looks, and would spend a couple of hundred bucks a year on haircuts.

But I never cared for my brain. I never did anything to actively ensure it was healthy and allowed me to be smart, to make the right decisions, and to be efficient in getting the results I wanted in my private life and in my sales career. I took it for granted. It was one of those organs that sat there and did its thing, like my liver or my stomach. That all changed the first time I 'met my brain'.

Brain, meet Frank. Frank, meet Brain

Or rather, when I saw a 3D scan of it. The day after the helicopter flew me to hospital, the radiologist team took dozens of X-rays and CT scans of my body. Because of the obvious facial fractures, the skull and brain received particular attention. While Elvira was anxiously waiting outside, the donut-shaped machine wilfully hummed as it devoured my broken body. The machine captured hundreds of narrow slices of my brain through X-rays that were later stitched together in a 3D model. It showed my head, with a big lump on top, a mess of bones where my face was, and black pockets of air indicating the sinuses. The brain snugly sat in the midst of all this, safely protected by a thick white band of skull.

The skull was intact, but that didn't mean my brain was unharmed. The sudden stop on the hard sand had made my brain hit the inside of the skull with such a force that it had started to swell. Unlike a swelling on, say, our shin, there's not much room in our skull for the brain to swell. In the confinements of a strong skull, swelling pushes downwards, towards the brain stem. This can be lethal or cause serious permanent damage. Pressure on the brain stem can be so severe that all cognitive function is limited, forcing the patient into a vegetative state. The brain is a sensitive organ, that's why the skull is so strong.

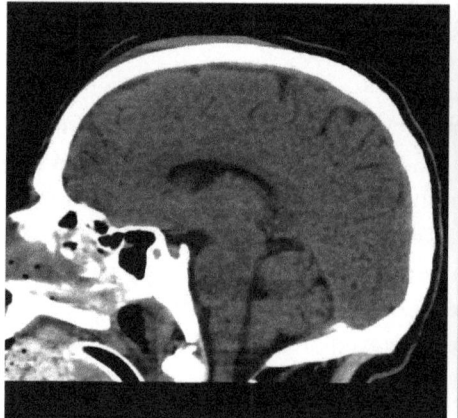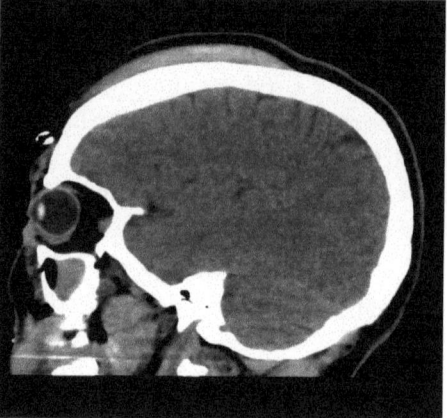

CT scans showing vertical slices of my brain (middle, and right side)

Research is still being done on the effect of repeated brain injuries, like the ones that boxers and rugby players experience, and findings, so far, point to long term negative effects including dementia.

Luckily, none of that was on the cards for me. By the time I was able to see that scan, the swelling had disappeared, and my diagnoses had been downgraded to a severe concussion: a shaking of the brain, which in 80–90 percent of the cases leads to a full recovery. Having said that, the weeks that followed in hospital weren't exactly easy for my brain. I struggled with light and sound, and felt my energy levels drop whenever I had to think. Even a simple question from the nurse took a lot of energy. I'd been lying flat on my back for nearly two months, and in the first month had not been able to use my senses. When I came out of the induced coma, my ear canals were filled with blood, limiting my hearing. My wired up jaws prevented me from talking. I couldn't taste or smell anything either; a common consequence of brain injury.

It was a while before my eyes began working again. Their sensory inputs were limited for the first few weeks when I could only just see the ceiling of the hospital room. In that ceiling, there were two squares. Initially, I couldn't make out what they were, but after a couple of days I realised they were air vents that kept my room ventilated. And when I'd turn my head to the right, I could see two TV screens that showed my heart-rate and other blurry graphs in green and purple. Doctors seemed to turn up in pairs, but speak as one. That double vision stayed with me for two months and demanded a lot of my brain. I became exhausted by looking at things and preferred to keep my eyes shut whenever possible. My brain coped better that way.

Over the next few weeks, my hearing slowly returned; first in one ear, then in the other. Visually, there wasn't much movement to process, apart from when nurses or doctors would lean over my bed. Then came the day that I was ready to sit up straight and have a look around the room I was in. What I remember most from those 'early days' was how every time I made progress and more sensory signals came in, my brain struggled. Every new sensation quickly led to a feeling of 'depleted brain'. I needed to be selective about what sensory inputs to allow. During the day, I used a sleeping mask to minimise input from my eyes. Elvira asked nurses to keep sound levels low. It became a conscious task to manage the energy I was demanding from my brain.

This became tricky when I was wheeled to the surgical theatre, in my bed, for yet another operation on my hand. Bolstered by my newfound ability to explore what was around me, I tried to keep my eyes open while I laid flat in bed – and quickly paid the price. That calm, two-dimensional ceiling I had been looking at until then, was replaced by a three dimensional corridor that zoomed past me. Doors opening. The sound of conversations. Doors closing. Alarms going off. My brain, which hadn't processed such inputs for over a month, drained in seconds like an old iPhone trying to run a hundred apps with Background App Refresh turned on. It simply couldn't cope.

As I slowly recovered, I made a habit of closing my eyes to preserve my energy. I couldn't join conversations for long, particularly the ones that required complicated thinking, like planning ahead. My contribution to the world around me was limited by simply nodding or shaking my head. And whenever I did have enough brain capacity to do something, I could only do one thing at a time. Multitasking, like having a conversation while processing visual sensory signals, was not an option. My brain literally would lose all its energy – within seconds. It took another couple of months for my brain to be on 'full battery' again.

There were other experiences during these months that later would lead to a deep, conscious interest in the brain. One of them had to do with my physical nerves: the cable-like bundle of fibres that spread throughout the body. Nerves provide pathways for impulses to the brain and nervous system. They relay sensory signals: feeling pressure, pain and temperature, as well as motor signals, which allow us to move our muscles. These signals get processed by certain parts of the brain. For instance, the signals coming from the nerves in the hand are processed in a different part of the brain than those coming from the face, eyes or legs.

The many fractures in my hand, arm and face caused nerve damage across several organs. I couldn't feel much of my right hand after they attempted to reconstruct my wrist. The nerves had been pushed aside during many operations. The nerves around my elbow had been permanently moved ('transpositioned') to avoid damaged areas. This meant that the nerves weren't firing off any signals to the brain – they were 'offline'. This caused a few interesting reactions from the brain, which further deepened my intrigue.

How does the brain deal with impulses?

I am not a neuroscientist, and this chapter is not aimed at getting you up to speed on this complex field of science. Still, it is helpful to understand some of the rudimentary workings of the brain as it can be used to develop perseverance in sales. I've been lucky enough to have had an up-close-and-personal experience with my brain, and my goal is simply to help you appreciate how this beautiful organ works without having to go through an eight-year PhD program (or a visit to the ICU, for that matter). I am sure that as I try to do this I'll oversimplify things in the same way a neuroscientist would when trying to explain sales to their (super-interested) colleagues.

In the media's urge to make this complex area of science exciting for the masses, a great amount of over simplification and misrepresentation has occurred. I am sure that in researching this topic, and in distilling what I learned and how it can be used to develop perseverance in sales, I will make that same mistake. Apologies up front.

The brain consumes around 20 percent of the body's energy levels, even though it only weighs around 2 percent of the body's mass. It needs all that energy to fuel the electrical impulses that neurons employ to communicate with one another. The processing and sending of signals from and towards nerves makes up a large part of that. Impulses coming from different nerves are processed in different parts of the brain. Motor control is done at the mid top, in the frontal lobe. Vision is processed at the back of the brain, in what's called the occipital lobe. Impulses from touch and pressure are managed by the parietal lobe, close to the area where motor control is orchestrated. And while the medical field still needs years of research to comprehend the complexities of the brain, they have found that even within the parietal lobe, different areas take care of touch and pressure signals that originate from different parts of the body. What we 'feel' in our face is processed in a different part of the parietal lobe compared to what we feel from, say, our right arm.

Back to my nerve damage. Signals from certain nerves no longer made it to my brain. But here's the amazing thing: the brain is plastic. Brain plasticity is the brain's ability to modify its connections – to re-wire itself. The brain's many neural pathways can replicate another's function so that small errors in development or temporary loss of function through damage can be corrected by rerouting signals along a different pathway. It can do so, miraculously, without needing much help. Mostly. As my nerves slowly turned on again, I was given exercises to ensure the automatic re-routing of signals happened correctly. One of them was to stroke my face with my left (working) hand while looking at myself in the mirror. Initially, I could feel that in my hand, but not in my face. It's akin to the effects of local anesthetic you'd get from the dentist. My whole face felt numb for months. When the facial nerves started to come back online, the feeling slowly came back. The 'visual aiding' I did during those months, helped train the brain to re-create the new pathways the right way. It 'saw' the motion and concluded that the signals coming in had to come from the part of the face it watched being stroked. Not doing this exercise would have resulted in the brain re-wiring the wrong way.

It mostly worked; it helped heal that intricate system of impulses and processing power into its original state. Except for one small area. As I am writing this five years later, if I touch the right side of my upper lip, it feels like I am touching my right lower eye lid, two inches higher. It's a weird sensation; the nerves there mostly healed fine, except for that little mix up. It's a souvenir that keeps me aware of how delicate the brain is, and it makes me want to learn more about it.

Neuroscience

I soon learned that we actually don't know everything about the brain yet. Scientists and medical experts are still looking for answers around the functioning of the most complex organ of the human body. Neuroscience, the study of the brain and nervous system, tries to find out how it is structured, how it works, how it develops, how it malfunctions, and how it can be changed. Although a huge amount of progress has been made in neuroscience, we still don't really know how the brain works. Research on Alzheimer's and Parkinson's disease are still in early stages; if we don't really know how somethings works, it's even harder to find fixes for it when something goes wrong. For instance, for over a hundred years, it was commonly believed that brain cells (neurons) did not regenerate. All of a human's brain cells get generated in the first three years of our existence, and after that, it's all down-hill. Or so we thought.

But then, at the end of the last century, neuroscientists researching mature monkeys were startled to find out that the cerebral cortex section of the brain does produce brain cells. This excited them because the cerebral cortex is responsible for high-level decision making and learning. The brain can actually regenerate cells in this crucial and high-functioning part of the brain. It's called 'adult neurogenesis'. You probably don't care what they call it and are more interested to learn whether your school teachers were wrong when they said drinking excessive amounts of alcohol would kill brain cells forever. Hold your horses. Neurogenesis has been proven on monkeys, but, as a clear indicator of the complexity of the brain, twenty years later, science still hasn't proved for this to occur in human brains.

Neurotransmitters

Key recent developments in neuroscience focus on what these neurons do. Neurons (the average human brain roughly has 86 billion of them) create and release molecules called neurotransmitters. Neurotransmitters orchestrate how we feel, act and react to all the impulses coming at us. In other words, they are behind our mood, our feelings, thoughts and even our behaviour. In my quest to find out how to develop perseverance, I found that the area of brain chemistry produces some valuable insights. We now know what certain neurotransmitters do, and neuroscience is also finding ways to influence the chemical balance of these transmitters. Let's learn about a few that influence our ability to persevere.

Serotonin

Of all the molecules flowing through our body, serotonin seems to have the biggest influence on our mood. Serotonin is our 'happy neurotransmitter'. It allows us to feel relaxed and happy. It helps regulate mood and social behaviour, and has an impact on the physical working of our body, too. Good levels of serotonin help control appetite and digestion, sleep, memory and sexual desire. Low levels or serotonin are associated with people who have low levels of self-esteem and people with erratic behaviour. People who are depressed also tend to have low serotonin levels. However, scientists still don't know whether such low levels contribute to depression or whether they are the result of it. What is known, however, is that high levels of serotonin help with our general wellbeing. Clearly, feeling good is a key aspect to helping us remain positive and motivated. Having low serotonin levels makes us feel unhappy and less motivated to keep going. Worse, it leads to poor sleeping patterns and increased feelings of anxiety. While it's important to keep in mind that serotonin's role, in many of these symptoms, still isn't fully understood, balancing your serotonin levels impacts your willingness to persevere.

Cortisol

Cortisol is actually not a neurotransmitter, it's a hormone produced by the adrenal glands, which sit on top of each kidney. Cortisol gets created when the brain perceives danger or stress. A boost in cortisol makes you feel alert, focused, energised, and motivated to act. Perceived danger and stress also creates a rush of adrenaline, which increases our heart rate, resulting in more blood flow to the muscles. And that's important, because our muscles need enough blood to generate the required energy if we decide to act on that danger. This fine balancing act is commonly referred to as the 'fight or flight' mechanism and has been crucial to human survival. The sighting of a sabre-toothed tiger would spike cortisol levels and together with that adrenaline rush, allows us to quickly decide what to do (fight or flight?) and act on it (Run! I'd say).

Popular media has been referring to cortisol as the stress hormone. However, as you would conclude from the quick explanation above, this is not just an over-simplification, it can lead to misunderstanding, too. Cortisol is not bad. We need cortisol to keep us alert and to survive. Having said that, too much of it, is not good. In modern life, we don't encounter the same dangers we did when we lived in caves. We don't really need to be in a constant stage of heightened awareness to act on the appearance of a sabre-toothed tiger. At least, not in Sydney. That delicate chemistry that developed in our bodies over millions of years, hasn't adapted to our modern lifestyle. This means that however amazing the working of these hormones is, it doesn't suit our lives today. When we fear we're going to lose a deal, experience rejection or experience any other form of stress, our cortisol levels go up. That's what our delicate hormone production system is designed to do – to be in a state of high alert, so we can 'fight or flight'.

So overall, we need cortisol. But that doesn't mean it's all good news. Back in 1908, psychologists Yerkes and Dodson plotted the impact of stress on human performance levels. They found that initially, the increased level of arousal caused by stress led to an improvement in performance and efficiency. Stress keeps us sharp and focused. It also enhances memory. The arousal state makes things more vivid; we see the scene around us with more detail and, therefore, will remember more of it. However, after a prolonged period of stress, exactly the opposite happens. Sustained periods of high stress *reduce* our performance levels. Too much stress or too long a period of stress is not good for us. This finding was immortalised in what is now called the Yerkes-Dodson curve.

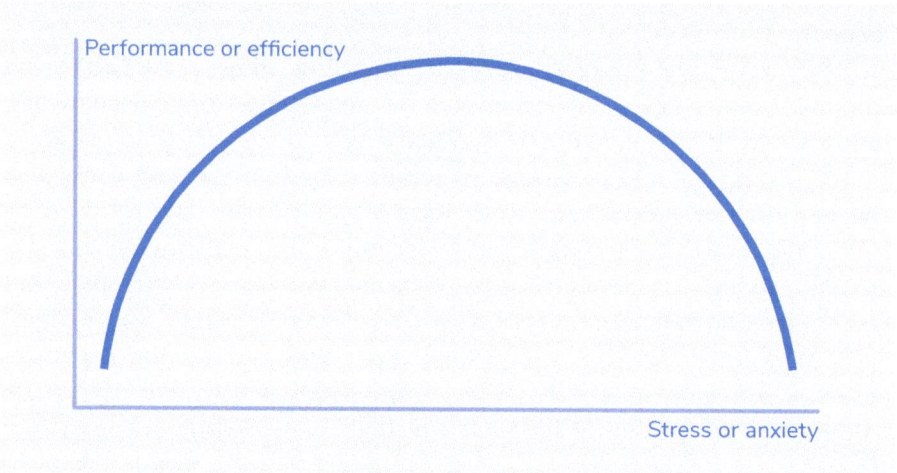

The Yerkes-Dodson Curve showing that stress is good, up to a point

Subsequent research found that cortisol plays a big role in the downward trend of that curve. It turns out that cortisol reduces serotonin, the happy neurotransmitter I described before. This reduction of serotonin makes us less motivated, less able to concentrate, more irritable, and more anxious. To make matters worse, high cortisol levels also impact our sleeping patterns. Too much cortisol keeps the body in a state of constant alertness, making a good night's sleep impossible. When our forefathers knew there was a sabre-toothed tiger lurking around the campfire, a deep sleep wasn't part of the winning formula for survival. Lives were literally at stake. But when you are super pumped to become the No.1 sales rep, and as a result struggle to sleep, the prolonged presence of high cortisol levels work against you. We end up in this negative cycle of working hard, not getting enough sleep, losing productivity and working harder to make up for it. What we need towards the end of our sales quarter is deep sleep, but our survival system doesn't always allow for that.

Dopamine

Although our ability to be on the lookout for danger was one reason we survived as a species, another is pleasure. Humans don't just thrive on avoiding dangers, they are also motivated by rewards. Eating and sex are the most banal forms of such rewards, and popular media has recently broadened the working of dopamine to include all forms of joy like gaming and the gratification from 'likes' on social media. If you Google Dopamine, you'll find ample articles framing it as the 'pleasure chemical'. But while it makes it easier to define the complexities of brain chemistry in easy hype-able terms, this can create misunderstandings, too.

Dopamine is not the chemical that makes you *feel* pleasure. People with depression tend to have low levels of dopamine, but that doesn't mean that inserting dopamine into their system will fix things. In fact, low dopamine levels can still let you experience joy and pleasure. You can still enjoy things even after you take drugs that reduce dopamine levels (as some medicines that treat nausea and vomiting do). What *will* be impacted by low dopamine levels, however, is your motivation to *pursue* things that you enjoy. If you have low dopamine levels, you still will enjoy sex or eating, but chances are you just won't put a lot of effort into seeking it. High levels of dopamine, on the other hand, tend to make us more likely to want that behaviour again and persevere the search for that pleasure. That's why dopamine plays a large part in addictive behaviours. *It is a chemical that plays an important role in our desire to pursue things that could lead to a rewarding outcome.*

Having said that, the goal of this book is to help you get more sales, not sex. Why does Dopamine have such an important impact on our ability to stay motivated in sales? To put it simply, when we encounter an unexpected setback, like the cancellation or rejection of a meeting with a prospect, our dopamine levels plunge. As a result, we're less likely to want to pursue that same activity again. When the outcome of an activity is better than expected, like a prospect saying 'Yes' to a meeting the first time you reach out, we're keener to keep finding more of such prospects, because our dopamine levels spiked. When we lose a deal, our motivation levels drop. When we win a deal, we want more. Dopamine plays a large role in our ability to find motivation and persevere.

Having a prolonged winning streak like I had in those months before the accident elevated my dopamine levels. I wanted more even though I was already over target. I was hooked on dopamine. But just like those who have tried dopamine increasing drugs (cocaine, amphetamines, and Ritalin) have discovered, dopamine also plays a role in regulating sleeping patterns. Dopamine increases feelings of wakefulness, making it hard to fall asleep, or even to hold on to a consistent sleeping pattern. Prolonged high levels of dopamine can create periods of disturbed sleep and serious sleep deprivation – like I experienced towards the end of my successful year. Not sleeping well makes it hard to concentrate or think straight, for instance, to make the right decision to pull your quick release system.

Oxytocin

Known as the 'love hormone', oxytocin is a peptide hormone which plays a role in social relationships. The excitement over the hormone is relatively new. In the 1990s, researchers discovered that breastfeeding mothers can handle psychosocial stress better than bottle-feeding mothers. Their research found that the hormone plays a role in social bonding, sexual reproduction, childbirth and the bonding with the baby. We've since learned that oxytocin increases calmness and general sense of well-being, and decreases anxiety and cortisol levels during socially stressful events. However, researchers in neurology are still trying to fully understand the role the hormone plays in human behaviour.

A particularly interesting area for such research is focused on the health benefits of crying.[26] *Shedding emotional tears seems to release oxytocin.* Which explains that soothing feeling you experience after you 'let it all out'. Such relief is not limited to stressful situations with a bad outcome. Any sustained 'fight or flight' situation that builds up your stress levels, calls for the body to lower cortisol, and crying can help with that. When Theresa May cried when she announced her resignation in May 2019, this helped release all that pent-up stress. And although he 'won' in his 'fight or flight' scenario, the same happened with Barack Obama when, in a tearful speech, he thanked campaign workers after his November 2012 re-election. Such stress needs to come out, regardless of whether the fight is lost or won.

Melatonin

While the medical world doesn't have a 100 percent understanding of what these hormones and chemicals do, and how and by what their production is influenced, sleep clearly is a recurring theme. A poorly or irregularly balanced level of serotonin, cortisol, and dopamine in our body impacts our ability to develop steady sleeping patterns. Sleep scientists are trying to understand what the impact of sleep, or the lack thereof, is on that fine balance of these hormones. Much of this research focuses on another hormone, which regulates biological rhythms such as sleep and wake cycles: melatonin.

Melatonin is produced in the pineal gland, a pea-sized organ found deep inside the brain. The pineal gland is located at the bottom of the two hemispheres of the cerebrum, behind our eyes towards the back of our head. Although it's small, the pineal gland, and the melatonin it produces, play an important role. When darkness falls, melatonin gets secreted to tell our body it's time to sleep. When the body experiences light, melatonin secretion stops, allowing us to wake up. This is one of the causes of jet lag: when a change in the rhythm of exposure to light requires a change in the release of melatonin. It takes a while for the body to adapt and get that cycle balanced so we can sleep well, and feel rested the next day.

Cortisol can upset this cycle. Regardless of whether it's dark or light, cortisol gets released whenever we need to feel alert. Of course, this alertness is good at 7 am after a great night's sleep. It'll make us jump out of bed refreshed and energised to start a new day. But high cortisol levels are of no help at 3 am when we need to rest; we end up stressing about an important presentation the next day. Rather than getting the rest our brain so desperately needs so we can perform well, we spend hours tossing and turning. This won't help us jump out of bed the next morning.

Serotonin helps regulate sleep. Again, research hasn't come to indisputable conclusions, other than there is a link with decreased serotonin and difficulty sleeping. Whenever you sleep poorly, that feeling of grogginess, or foggy brain syndrome is caused by the impact of imbalances of melatonin, cortisol and serotonin. And us sales professionals don't need much further research to know that the general tiredness that follows a poor night's sleep only makes things harder the next day. You become less efficient, struggle to concentrate and don't feel motivated to take on difficult challenges. A lack of sleep hampers our ability to persevere and think straight. This topic deserves a deeper dive.

The importance of sleep

In her book, *The Sleep Revolution: Transforming Your Life, One Night at a Time* (2017), Arianna Huffington provides a couple of eye openers about the importance of sleep. She describes the common lack of appreciation or understanding of how important sleep is, as a fundamental problem. In the 21st century, sleeping well is not seen as a necessity. It's a luxurious 'nice to have' that is the first to go out the door, particularly towards quarter end.

Worse, this lack of sleep is seen as a 'badge of honour', especially in corporate life. We find ourselves bragging about how little sleep we get, like it's something others should admire. We're showing off when we tell our team mates that we were out with a customer till 1 am, and stayed up till 3 am to put the finishing touches on a presentation. We're signalling that we're more committed when we go home at 7 pm, grab a quick bite, and respond to emails till midnight. We think we are a better employee if we only need five hours sleep. Not sleeping much is somehow cool and supposedly reflective of your commitment to your job, and your chance of success.

There is a downward destructive culture in international sales teams, when it comes to sleep. We have early morning conference calls, late nights with customers, and regular trips overseas, which cause jet lag that upsets our sleeping patterns during and after the trip. The default attitude, not just top-down from sales management, but at all levels in sales, is that disturbed sleep comes with the job. If we want to make our targets, we just need to toughen up. The general (typically unspoken) expectation is that closing the deal comes first. Once the deal is done, we can take some time to rejuvenate.

In sales, sleep comes after success. It's your reward *after* results are booked. It's like a commission cheque you'll never cash because once a deal is done (won or lost), there's another deal that requires attention, or a pipeline that needs to be built. Sleep never gets priority in sales. The lack of sleep is just a reality that comes with the job; it's not just because our sales dashboards tell us to focus on more important metrics. This genuine lack of appreciation of the importance of sleep is baked deep into our societies. Research from sleep scientists is too new to change this culture that prioritises hard work over good sleep. Sleep simply is not a topic that ever makes it on the agenda of a sales meeting or a deal review.

We focus on what needs to get done, not on the circumstances that need to be in place to do so in a productive and effective way. Even in 1:1s with managers, sleep is not a topic that gets any attention. And if it does (because someone is getting close to burnout), sales managers are not geared to deal with it. We can help with guidelines on how to qualify an opportunity, we are trained in how to negotiate a deal or how to give a kick-ass presentation. We involve HR when we want to 'put someone on a performance improvement plan' or fire someone. But we don't know what advice to give a team member who has found the nerve to talk about the lack of sleep they are experiencing. We're not trained to recognise the telltale signs of someone who is struggling with the impact of poor sleep. And this poor level of readiness is based on us not being aware of the correct answer to a single, simple question …

How much sleep do we actually need?

I am sure you have them in your team. You might even be one of them. Those (often alpha male-like) sales people who don't see the lack of sleep as an issue. At least, not for them. Maybe other people need more sleep, but these sales tigers are convinced they just don't need that much sleep. They can get away with a couple of hours' sleep a night; they're so busy and important, that really, five is the maximum number of hours their agenda allows for sleep. They focus on closing deals and once a year take a well-deserved break to recharge. For them, sleep definitely comes *after* success but that's nothing we should worry about – presumably because they're anatomically different.

The American Academy of Sleep Medicine put this myth to bed, so to speak. In 2015, they published their findings on the importance of sleep for optimal health and determined that the minimum number of hours of sleep required is seven. Researchers have not found genes or any other anatomical differences that somehow make some individuals need less sleep. In fact, the only thing research is pointing to is the need for more *sleep* depending on age. Babies need 14–17 hours a day, children 9–11 hours, and teenagers 8–10. For adults, it's 7–9 hours.[27] People who claim they can do with less than seven, underestimate the impact of their poor sleep patterns on their body, in the same way that a driver underestimates the impact of a couple of glasses of wine, and in the same way that I assessed the dangerous conditions on the beach and decided to go out and have fun. As I contemplated what to do, I used rational facts like my twenty years of kitesurf experience to convince myself that it would be fine. However, that self-assessment was flawed. The very organ that was doing the assessment, my brain, was not operating at optimal capacity.

What happens when we sleep?

During our awake state, when the brain runs at full capacity, toxic waste proteins accumulate between brain cells. When we sleep, these waste chemicals get cleaned out. Research on mice has pointed to the functioning of the glymphatic system – effectively the brain's plumbing system – that takes care of this maintenance. When we're awake, our brain is just too busy to deal with this maintenance; it gets to that when we sleep. As a result, when we don't sleep enough, this maintenance doesn't happen in full and it impacts our mental awareness, cognitive function, and attention span.

While I'm sure you recognise being groggy after a poor night's sleep doesn't exactly make your day any easier, it's hard to self-assess the impact of bad sleep on your performance. Whenever I slept poorly before a big presentation, or towards the end of the quarter, I couldn't really compare the results of my actions against a baseline. I didn't know if I could have done any better; the results were what they were. It's like the driver who thinks he or she can drive 'just fine' after a couple of beers. They make it home safe and conclude they were operating at 'normal' capacity.

People sometimes ask: what was the worst part of your ordeal? I tend to tell stories about the pain and the operations, but the reality is that the hallucinations were the worst of all. They were a category by themselves and I still struggle to talk about it. Halfway into reading Arianna Huffington's book, when it referred to research on Intensive Care Unit patients in 2014, it became a little bit easier. That research found hallucinations to be a recurring theme in ICUs, and it concluded poor sleep to be the source of it. They found that noise levels in the ICUs were as high as 85 decibels, the noise level of a passing motorcycle. Those noise levels prevent patients from sleeping, which leads to delirium.[28]

For me, it wasn't just the noise during the days and nights in the ICU. The constant beeping and people coming and going continued till the very last night in hospital. Once I was moved to a normal hospital room, the amount of machines I was hooked up to reduced drastically. But because of my critical condition, and regular ongoing operations, the hospital's 'vital signs policy' directed nurses to regularly measure pulse and blood pressure. For the first several weeks, 'regular' meant every four hours. During night time, they didn't wake me deliberately, but the process makes it impossible to stay asleep. The door squeaks open, the light goes on, the inflatable cuff gets velcroed around your arm, the machine pumps it up, uncomfortable pressure builds, the machine starts beeping, and the cuff is ripped off with a loud SSHHHKKRTT. Every single time, it woke me up, even after Elvira asked nurses to use a flashlight rather than the room light. I did not get more than four hours of uninterrupted sleep for many weeks in a row. And after the vital sign policy was loosened, regular noise still continued to prevent me from sleeping. People would walk into my room at any given time of day: nurses, doctors, cleaners, and the lovely lady who brought food. Beeping and alarms from other rooms down the hall would continue throughout the night. It's a well-known fact that the hospital is not a place where people rest. But only since that 2014 research are ICUs slowly taking measures to reduce noise.

Huffington's book also tells the story of New York disk jockey Peter Tripp, who, in 1959, ran a stunt to attract awareness to a charity. During a 'wakeathon', Tripp broadcasted his show from a glass booth at Times Square, non-stop, without sleeping. He kept his show going for nearly eight continuous days – and he paid the price. 'After three days, Tripp became mean and abusive, and two days later he begun to suffer intense hallucinations leading to paranoia.' On the final day, with a paranoia comparable to mine in the ICU, Tripp thought his doctor was an undertaker planning to cart off his corpse.

More recently, the popular TV series *Mythbusters* examined the impact of not sleeping on driving behaviour. In 2012, they put the following myth to the test: *Getting behind the wheel without shut-eye is more dangerous than driving after a couple of drinks.* As you would expect, both Tory and Kari struggled with the impact of alcohol when they did their driving tests, which consisted of 25 laps of monotonous driving around a track, and a more city-like traffic course with turns, traffic lights and parallel parking. When they ran the same test after staying awake for 30 hours, they found the sleep deprivation caused Tory to drive ten times worse. For Kari, his driving was three times more erratic. The myth was confirmed: driving tired equals driving impaired. Similar findings are behind the *Don't trust your tired self* advertising campaigns you see from your national road safety organisations.

Sleep for the sales professional
I am not sure how many deals I have lost due to not sleeping enough. I can't calculate how an extra hour of sleep would increase my productivity or keep me sharp to better negotiate and get a higher order value. And when I discuss the challenge of getting sleep with sales professionals, it's clear that most people are aware of the importance of it. Deep down, we know it's not good to not sleep enough. We do feel more tired, start making mistakes and feel our motivation drop. Our partners or peers start noticing our mood swings, and we say or do things we later regret. Most of us would admit that it's the lack of sleep that is making us do that.

But knowing that doesn't make it any easier. Our sales profession asks a lot from us; it constantly challenges our ability to look after ourselves. In the last decade alone, our ability to stick to eight- or even ten-hour working days is being challenged. Phones and laptops, however convenient they are, make it harder to switch off. Our bosses, and our customers, expect us to answer emails, at whatever time of day and from wherever we are. This increased 'presence' is eating into our time to be away from work and get our brains into lower gears. Even if we're disciplined enough to plan our days to stick to the seven hours of sleep, this sleep tends to be of lesser quality because our brains are still active from checking emails or creating sales presentations.

So rather than going to the source to fix it, many of us find shortcuts. The sleeping pill industry is worth $1.4 billion in the US. That's the combined sales of drugs like Ambien, Belsomra and Lunesta. This number excludes non-prescription, over the counter (OTC) drugs like zzzQuill, Natrol and Unison. If we include the OTC market, total sales of sleeping pills in 2018 were estimated to be $2 billion in the US alone. Additionally, the broader category of sleeping aids (ear plugs, eye pads, anti-snoring aids etc.) gets us to a total value of $30 billion. And this number is expected to grow at alarming rates, not just in the US, but worldwide. As Arianna Huffington states, 'for the drug industry that stands to profit from today's sleep crisis, business is good and the future looks bright'. Of course, these solutions don't focus at the source; they don't create circumstances that allow us to get more sleep naturally.

Luckily, some companies agree that such shortcuts are not the right way to solve the problem. They're taking the connection between sleep and wellness seriously and understand the possible impact lack of sleep can have on productivity. HuffPost (no surprise), Google, Nike, and Ben & Jerry have installed sleep pods in (some of) their offices.[29] Sleep or nap pods are closed off chambers that allow employees to switch off and get a couple of minutes of sleep in the office. Procter & Gamble's offices have a lighting system that helps regulate melatonin so that employees find it easier to switch off in the evenings. Volkswagen even went as far as stopping their email servers from sending emails to some shift workers 30 minutes after their shift, so they could get their minds off work and relax during non-working hours.[30]

The French go even further. They are ahead of the rest of the world when it comes to establishing a legal framework to protect a person's right to disconnect after working hours. On 1 January 2017, a new employment law was introduced which included a chapter titled *The Adaptation of Work Rights to the Digital Era*. *Article 25* creates an obligation with the employer to agree with the employees on what hours they can and cannot contact them outside of office hours. A key goal of this law is to prevent burnout by protecting the worker's non-working hours. Good for them. But unfortunately, as of this moment, France is the only country in the world that has gone this far.

I wonder if this way of disconnecting would work for sales professionals any way. Many of us work in international environments, where the end of our day is the start of someone else's. Even if our local office agrees to limit email or phone communication after 5 pm, it's unlikely we can afford to wait till the next day to respond to an email from legal, sales ops or sales management and let the time zone difference make us lose another day. It's in our interest to sit in on nightly all-hands calls, and stay up to date by dialing in to the weekly sales call, even if it happens after hours. We need to check our emails so we can respond quickly and resolve potential internal roadblocks. In sales, disconnecting from that and picking it up the next day is, often, simply not an option.

What about the elephant in the room? Will our *customers* accept that we don't pick up the phone after working hours? Will they be fine with us taking days to get contract issues resolved or to get discount approvals? Or are they more likely to want to do business with that sales rep who's always responding and can get things organised 'overnight'? Should we even *want* to disconnect? Isn't the sales professional the face of the company, the department that breathes customer centricity, oozes keenness, embodies enthusiasm to help customers, and is more eager to win the customer's business than the competitor? Can we even afford to disconnect or do whatever French people do?

The reality is that sales is a high pressure environment with high expectations. If we want to make target, we need to stay connected. The French solution is not for us. Yet we do have to take care of our brains. We have to find other ways to deal with the stressful challenges we face. We need to find other ways to make sure we sustain the brain, so we stay motivated and can persevere in the face of setbacks. Katy taught me how.

Meet Katy, my speech pathologist

'Yes! Your smile is starting to come back, Frank'. I looked up in the mirror to see Katy raise her fists behind me. 'I reckon in a couple of months, you'll have your smile back. Woohoo!' I looked at myself again, and although the right corner of my mouth was curling up a bit, I wouldn't call it a happy face. But, granted, it curled more than when I first met Katy.

When I was discharged from hospital, I had been referred to Katy. She was my dedicated speech pathologist during those first couple of months. She had completed a four-year bachelor degree in speech pathology at the University of Newcastle and had primarily been working with stroke victims. People who suffer strokes experience a temporary interruption of blood supply to part(s) of the brain as a result of a blocked artery or burst blood vessel. Within minutes, brain cells die, which often is fatal; it's the third leading cause of death. For survivors, it often leads to paralysis to one side of the body. They can't move one arm or leg anymore, and typically end up with a paralysis of the face, too. The muscles on one side stop working, creating a loss of blinking control, and making the mouth droop to the affected side. This tends to bring about slurred speech, which calls for speech therapists like Katy.

At our first meeting in March 2014, she told me she was excited to work with me because I was an unusual case for her. The damage on my face had been severe. What used to be one solid formation of bone had been completely shattered into seven free-floating pieces. My cheekbones had become disconnected from my temples at the side of my face. My eye sockets had broken loose from my cheekbones. My upper jaw had separated; on the scans it looked like upper dentures were loosely floating in my mouth. My lower jaw snapped in two and had torn through the skin at my chin. My forehead was the only part of my face that had not broken.

The only thing I knew when I met Katy was that I couldn't move the muscles in my face much. 'When they did the operation, they cut your face open to get access, and screwed all these bones back together with all those titanium plates,' Katy explained as she stood next to Elvira and I while pointing with her pinky finger on the X-rays she had gathered from my file. I still struggled to look at them and just accepted Katy's explanation. I had seen the X-rays a couple of times, and they didn't look like me. They didn't even look real.

'To get to the bones, they had to push the muscles and nerves away. This can tear them and create damage,' Katy said. 'Sometimes, sharp pieces of broken bone can entrap muscles or cut nerves, but the report from the hospital didn't refer to such complications. It seems like your nerves and muscles were just stretched. That's why you can't smile, Frank.' I had already learned that contrary to what you might think, nerve damage is not always permanent. Nerves can heal themselves; they can regenerate at the pace of one millimetre a day. The nerve that runs from my neck through my chin towards my cheekbones, took half a year to recover. The shorter nerves around my eyes and mouth healed quicker. Hence Katy's excitement. 'I think most of your nerves will grow back. You'll start feeling things again, and will also slowly be able to move your muscles and talk normally. And you'll get your smile back.'

For my face, the scars would prove the big uncertainty. The areas where shattered bone had poked through my skin were rough and angry. Where the surgeons had made incisions to insert the plates, scar tissue was smoother, but there was a lot of it. Eleven plates had been used to piece my face back together. Around and under both eyes, my nose, my ears – a couple of centimetres per incision. To screw my upper row of teeth back to my cheekbones, they had cut my upper lip loose, on the inside of my mouth, under my nose. They did the same for my lower jaw. This provided better access and would limit visible scar tissue and facial deformity. The downside of this 'facial degloving' technique is that it generates scar tissue on the inside of the lips. Scar tissue – the binding together of two parts of tissues – often makes the skin ball up and clump. The skin loses its natural flexibility, which complicates speech even if nerves and muscles regain their function.

Every week, Katy gave me homework. She printed rows of words on A4 pages that I had to read out loud a couple of times a day. I struggled the most with the Ps and the Bs as they require you to close your lips – something I couldn't do for months. *Pebble, Poodle, Remember, Apple and Berries became Wewle, Woodle, Ehremwer, Ahwel and Werries.* As the nerves and muscles slowly came back online, my communication evolved into something more intelligent and comprehensible. Katy asked me to practice simple things that prove impossible unless you can use the ten or so muscles in your mouth properly, for example, drinking through a straw, and blowing up a balloon. 'Also, keep practising that smile in front of the mirror,' Katy instructed me. 'That visual confirmation helps your brain to process the signals from the nerves as they come back online. It's also fun; looking at yourself smiling in the mirror will cheer you up.' Initially, I felt embarrassed to look at my deformed face. My swollen jaw, the droopy right side of my mouth, and the tense scars weren't exactly a comforting sight. But I liked the smiling exercise. I liked that I could see my muscles working. Every week there was more movement and a bigger range.

I started to enjoy those exercises; they had a soothing effect on me. Even if I didn't *really* smile, and all I was doing was merely practising moving my facial muscles, it calmed my state of mind. Or was I imagining that?

What smiling does

When we experience pleasure, we smile. The common, and logical, understanding is that there is a causal link. We smile because we feel pleasure. However, this causality works the other way too. We feel pleasure *because* we smile. In 2012, researchers at the University of Kansas found that manipulated facial expressions influenced the stress response.[31] They found that using the muscles in your face to smile lowers heart rates under stressful conditions, possibly due to a reduced level of cortisol. In case you're skeptical about walking around with a forced smile, here's a brief summary of how they came to that conclusion.

Researchers Tara L. Kraft and Sarah D. Pressman found 169 willing volunteers for a hands-on experiment. To avoid influencing the participants' mood by saying the research was about smiling, Kraft and Pressman devised a cunning plan. They told participants that their research was about multitasking under stress. Participants were asked to hold chopsticks in their mouths in particular ways that prompted various facial expressions. They created three groups: one whose exercise led to a neutral expression, and one whose holding of the chopsticks created a smile. The third group was asked to produce a real smile. This involves the eye muscles as well as the mouth muscles and is referred to as a Duchenne smile. Next, they were asked to do the multitask assignments, which had stressful elements to them like submerging their hands in a bucket of icy water while maintaining the facial expression. Throughout the experiments, the participants' heart rates were measured. Measuring heart rates during the recovery from the stressful events produced some startling findings. The group with 'neutral expressions' had the highest heart rate. 'Chopstick smilers' had lower heart rates, and 'Duchenne smilers' had the lowest. Kraft and Pressman concluded that the act of smiling can reduce overall stress levels, even if it's faked.

Speaking of fake, researchers have also started researching the impact of Botox on processing emotional content. Botox paralyses facial muscles and selectively blocks 'facial feedback': the brain's reception of sensory signals, which confirms that the muscles are moving. In one study, David Havas and colleagues asked participants to read 60 sentences that articulated different emotions (angry, sad, happy). These were presented on a computer screen and participants were asked to press a button on the keyboard to indicate they had finished reading the sentence. Then, they received Botox injections to the corrugator supercilii muscle used in frowning. Participants were asked to do the same reading exercise two weeks later. The researchers were only interested in the brain's capacity to process these emotions; therefore, they measured reading time. They found that after the Botox injections, participants' reading times for happy sentences remained unchanged. However, reading time for angry and sad sentences were significantly longer. They concluded that our ability to process emotional content depends on the (lack of) movement of our facial muscles.[32]

Katy was right: smiling is good for you and your brain.

More than the brain

Of course, it's not just about a healthy brain. You need a healthy body, too. And a healthy body needs a healthy heart. Enough is being written about the impact of physical exercise, good eating habits, and limited consumption of alcohol on the heart. Much of the basis of this comes from American cardiologists Meyer Friedman and Ray Rosenham, who researched heart conditions as far back as the 1950s. They were looking for commonalities in patients who were prone to heart disease, and found that it wasn't just eating habits and genes that determined the likelihood for coronary trouble. People with heart conditions, Friedman writes, demonstrated 'a particular complex of personality traits, including excessive competition drive, aggressiveness, impatience, and a harrying sense of time urgency. Individuals displaying this pattern seem to be engaged in a chronic, ceaseless, and often fruitless struggle – with themselves, with others, with circumstances, with time, sometimes with life itself' (Friedman & Rosenman, 1974).

It was such a ground breaking insight, that the label 'Type A', given to these individuals by Friedman & Rosenman, is still used today. Us sales professionals are likely to recognise ourselves in these characteristics. We might even feel proud about that label. However, if you feel these characteristics describe you, you should approach these traits with care. Your health comes first. Friedman's objective has been to create awareness and help Type A personalities become more like Type B personalities to avoid heart conditions. Type B personalities are just as ambitious but their internal drive provides a steady confidence and security that keeps them healthier for longer. Contrary to what we are led to believe, Type A personalities do not always outperform Type B personalities. What is clear, however, is that they tend to suffer more from the stress that their personality generates. Stress management is key.

Meet Jo, my exercise physiologist

Six months after my accident, I met Jo, an exercise physiologist at Sydney's Northern Beaches. After a four-year bachelor degree, Jo went on to receive a Masters of Clinical Exercise Physiology. She was in her late twenties – and although she admitted she hadn't yet worked with someone who had 47 screws in their body, we clicked straight away. Her fresh enthusiasm and ability to calmly lay out the plan towards recovery were enough to win me over and get me to buy into a journey she said would take two years. We focused on building back muscle and improving range of movement. I was given exercises to ensure muscles that hadn't been used for months were strengthened in a balanced way. As I quickly learned, it's all too easy to focus on rebuilding one muscle while another one is too weak, only to get the weaker one inflamed. The muscles throughout the body are a complex system of interlinked forces – Jo kept reminding me. Having limited strength in the right upper leg can lead to aches in the left shoulder.

After that first year, I told her of my aim to go back to being a busy sales professional. Yes, this would involve spending numerous hours a day behind my laptop at flexible work places, including hot desks, cafes, and airport lounges. I still remember her worried look when she told me of the risks I'd encounter in this next phase. We walked over to *the wall* with the *scary poster:* one of those big illustrations of a faceless body standing straight up with both arms and hands facing out. *The Muscular System*, it read at the top. Bones and joints were drawn in white and the numerous layers of muscles were shown in red. Hundreds of labels pointed at the names of the individual muscles, in confusing Latin names, which to this day I have to Google to recall. Gluteus maximus, gluteus medius, quadriceps fremoris, abductor this and flexor that. What did stick was Jo's warning of what a poor posture would do to a perfectly healthy person with no screws in their body. 'Funnily enough,' she said 'most people I treat haven't had accidents. They're office workers. People who are super stressed out and who, by the time they hit 40, have similar tendon and muscle damage to you.' A slump-shouldered slouch combined with tense muscles can deform your spinal curve, which causes a cascade of other problems. Back pain is the first and obvious one, but longer-term effects include pains elsewhere, impaired digestion, heart problems, reduced blood circulation, and a reduction of the flow of oxygen that your tissues so desperately need.

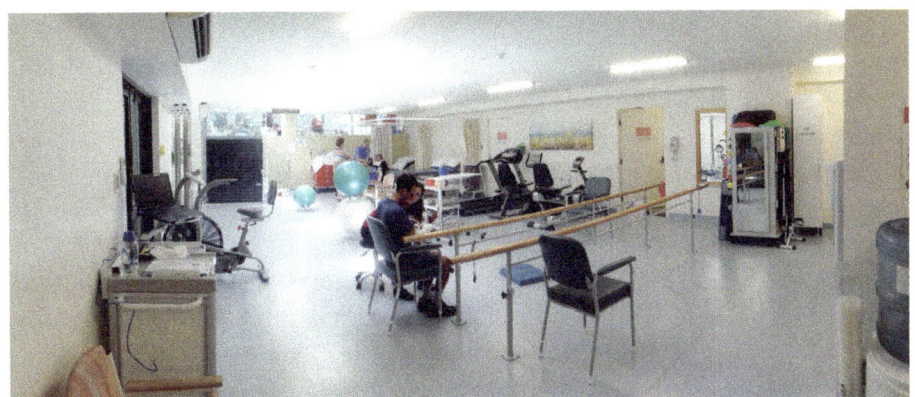
Getting ready for my walking practice

Then, when Jo pulled up her iPad with the scans of my pelvis, legs and arms, it became a lot more personal. We were no longer talking about a faceless man with theoretical problems and Latin labels, we were talking about me. Zooming in on the scans, Jo pointed at the specific joints and muscles that would struggle with my hot desking lifestyle. The glutes (which run over the right side of my pelvis where a couple of pins are screwed in) would weaken, making the pelvis tilt, which would lead to more stress on the lower back. The limited movement in my right hand would lead the left to compensate, putting more strain on a group of muscles there. With all the bone and cartilage damage in my body, I needed to work even harder to avoid long term pain. My muscles and tendons need to be kept flexible; the more tension there was in my body, particularly around the lower back and pelvis, the more aches and pains will build up, Jo explained. 'I tell everyone who walks in here that they only have one body. They can mess up many things in their lives and simply get a new one. But not a body. You only have one body. And for you, Frank, you will need to put more effort in keeping it healthy.'

Sales people are challenged to prevent such injuries. We slump over our laptops from hot desks, cafes, airplanes, taxis and hotels and think we won't pay the price. Until we do.

The paradox of work life balance

Poor habits develop at home, too, particularly around how we spend our free time. Many of us de-stress from a busy day by plonking ourselves on the couch and switching on the telly. Watching TV might feel good, but that's doesn't mean it is. When your brain goes from all that active stressed-out thinking to passive consumption of entertainment that doesn't require much alertness, it releases dopamine. It is effectively telling you 'this feels good, keep doing this, so you can just chill out'. As a result, you develop a pseudo addition – not to *Game of Thrones*, but to the dopamine release it triggers. You're wiring your brain to seek more of it.

The average American spends 2.7 hours per day watching TV. In Australia, that number is slightly less at 2.5 hours. In the UK it's much higher at 3.73 hours per day. These are averages and don't comprise screen time for other 'glowing screens' pastimes like gaming, YouTube, or online streaming services like Netflix and Hulu. Including these makes the numbers even scarier. The average Briton spends around five years of their lives watching live TV. Catch-up TV adds another two years and eight months. And online streaming services adds another two. All in all, Britons spend an average of ten years staring at a screen; that's nearly one-eight of their lifetime.[33]

The problem with passively consuming content from screens is that it won't give you satisfaction that helps build motivation to persevere. The initial relaxation it provides is not followed with a feeling of accomplishment. There's not much mastery in sitting on a couch. You're much more likely to develop a feeling of dissatisfaction after you turn off that screen. And that's a frightful paradox. We work hard, then strive to completely overdo it with a reward based on dull entertainment. That's not re-creation. That is a mindless depletion of energy. It gives us a work-life balance that might be in balance in terms of time spent, but it's not in balance in terms of energy consumed versus energy gained. You'll need to be more considerate to avoid falling into that trap.

Perseverance Promotors

1. Measure your stress levels

The University of Pennsylvania, the home of wellbeing psychologist Martin Seligman, shares a lot of his research and tools. This link will give you access to the *Authentic Happiness Test Center:* www.authentichappiness.sas.upenn.edu/testcenter. It provides several free tests to measure your general happiness, your work life balance, your level of optimism and much more. Angela Duckworth's test to measure grit levels is also on this site. You'll find links to more tests in my workbook.

2. Manage your sleep

Aim for your seven to eight hours of sleep. Do not kid yourself that you can live on anything less; the reduction in your effectiveness will wipe away the hours you 'gained' by not sleeping enough. Stop checking emails two hours before you go to bed, so your brain has calmed down and gets a proper rest. Depending on your challenges with getting a good nights' sleep, check out other resources like Arianna Huffington's book. Consult a doctor if you struggle with the quality of your sleep. Whatever you do, do not think you are so unique that you can perform well with less than seven hours of sleep. No one can.

3. Find hobbies and sports that demand skill, goal setting, and discipline

Combine what we learned in the previous chapter about what drives us and use it to stay healthy. If you run, challenge yourself and set a goal, like a half marathon. If you're at a different level, no worries. Don't be coerced into some cookie-cutting fitness program that defines success for you. Define your own goals and own them. Find intrinsic motivation in your mastering of skills. Find activities that give you skills and challenges that boost your energy levels. It's called re-creation for a reason. Use the exercise in my workbook to list activities that help you balance your neurotransmitters and hormones.

4. Set aside a small budget for wellbeing

Most of the activities I am going to suggest are free but some will require you to get your wallet out. What I hope to have conveyed by now is that these activities are not mere luxuries. Us sales professionals need to take care of our bodies, and if we need to invest some minor amounts of our salaries into staying healthy, so be it. After my accident, I set 2 percent of my monthly budget aside for activities that keep me healthy, both physically and mentally. I know the ROI is unmeasurable, but I no longer struggle sleeping, and I haven't suffered a foggy brain for a long time. As a result, I am more refreshed and clear headed. I make fewer mistakes and can get things right the first time – which has freed up time.

5. Do yoga

Before my accident, I would not have taken this advice very seriously. I used to think that maybe it works for others who don't have busy jobs, but not for sales people like me. Sales people don't have time to waste on a yoga mat. Of course, I came to that judgement without having even tried it. I simply never believed I needed to. Jo changed all that. Three years after my accident, I took a one-month introduction course in a studio just a ten-minute drive from where we live. It wasn't a big commitment, just four Monday evening sessions lasting one hour. Because of my busy work, I wasn't sure if I wanted to commit to doing this every week. I thought I'd do the introduction course and then continue at home using one of the many yoga apps or YouTube channels. But after that month, I wanted more. I hadn't become more flexible in that short period, but was refreshed after each session. I came up with answers to questions I couldn't resolve before the session. I felt more relaxed and started to sleep better, too.

When I started researching what could be behind that, I found that yoga decreases cortisol levels – the stress hormone. Us sales professionals can do with a reduction of cortisol, and yoga is a fun and relaxing way to help you do exactly that. Yoga is the perfect cocktail for other reasons; it encompasses autonomy, mastery and purpose. The rewards help develop motivation to persevere. After a year of doing yoga twice a week, I was more flexible than I was before the accident. When I do yoga today, I make a habit of looking around to see how my flexibility stacks up to the other yogis. I'm easily in the top 10 percent. If I can do that with dozens of screws throughout my body, so can you.

6. Increase your serotonin levels

As you might recall, serotonin is our 'happy neurotransmitter'. High serotonin levels create an overall sense of wellbeing, which allows us to feel relaxed and happy. Low levels of serotonin go hand in hand with low self-esteem, disturbed sleeping patterns and high anxiety levels. Lucky for us, we don't have to rely on pills. There are a few 'natural hacks' that can help us increase our serotonin levels.

- Find some sunshine. A 20-minute walk in the natural sunlight has been proven to increase serotonin levels. That conference call about the new discount approval process? Take it outside, and go for a walk. That 1:1 with your manager? Have it while walking around the block.
- Exercise. Speaking of walking, activities like running, swimming and hiking have maximum benefits for raising your serotonin levels. If you feel down, and can't motivate yourself, don't

'just keep going'. Break the pattern by getting some exercise and feel how serotonin increases your overall wellbeing. Yoga has proven to have the same effect. Find a gym or yoga studio close to the office and lock down an hour a week. Then, get back into work with renewed energy levels and more motivation.

■ Get a regular massage. Serotonin gets released during a massage, which is one reason why you tend to walk away feeling energised. It's also proven to lower levels of cortisol and it's this combination that makes you feel so relaxed after a massage. And, like with yoga, you no longer need to leave the house for a massage either. Google 'in-home massage' or run a similar search in the app store and you'll find a mobile masseur or masseuse is a click away. Whenever you go on business trips, see if the hotel offers massage services; typically, they are not the cheapest, but it surely makes the trip less stressful.

7. Increase your dopamine levels

You will recall that dopamine is often described as the pleasure chemical, even though its main function is to not let you *experience* pleasure. Instead, dopamine feeds your drive to pursue things and to stay motivated. When we win a deal, we want more. When we get rejected, our motivation to keep going gets challenged. While neuroscience is a field that demands a lot more nuance than this book can provide, in sales, it is important to avoid low levels of dopamine in your brain. Low dopamine levels make it hard for you to motivate yourself to make a cold call or to get ready for another important presentation. Again, ensuring you get enough sleep is key to keeping your dopamine levels at the right level, but there are a few other things you can do to keep dopamine levels up.

■ Eat well. The nutritional chemicals you let into your body are key to balancing your dopamine levels. Representing the ultimate proof of popular media's oversimplification of this complex field, chef Tom Kerridge, launched a diet book called *Dopamine Diet: My Low-Carb, Stay-happy Way to Lose Weight* (2017). Like most diets, it promises weight loss (Tom lost 70 kilos), but this one's different because it '... is a lot easier to maintain because you're enjoying it ...'. Sure. I already went way outside my area of speciality when I ventured into explaining neuroscience, and I am not going to take more risks by advising you what you should eat. I am not a dietician, but I can give you two tips. If you feel low, struggle to get motivated, and keep procrastinating, one cause could be your poor eating habits. Just be aware of that link, particularly towards the end of the quarter. Secondly, to understand what makes a good diet, just Google it. I believe I adhere to a healthy diet, but that doesn't mean I'm an expert who's able to prescribe what would work for you. I just know that when I'm eating poorly, I am putting my overall motivation at risk. Just like your sleeping habits, your eating habits can impact your ability to keep going. Be aware when you're working too hard or partying too hard and not eating well. Don't fool yourself by thinking your body is somehow built differently from what medical research has proven to be the case. The only thing that's different is that your role is more demanding than the average. Remember, you only have one body.

- Try Meditation. Like with yoga, I have always been a sceptic of this practice, even though I never tried it. Or more correctly, I was a sceptic *because* I never tried it. I never wanted to make the time for it, because I didn't see the point. That all changed once I read that practising meditation can increase dopamine levels. I now regret not having picked up this habit earlier in my sales career. I could have been so much more productive, and so much more enjoyable to be around. Yoga was my soft introduction to meditation; the two practices have been around for thousands of years and are very much linked. Yoga is not just focused on the physical practice, there is an equal emphasis on focusing on the mind. Meditation helps with just that. It's beyond the scope of this book but I suggest you read up on the tons of helpful resources by just Googling it. I signed up for a $125 meditation course at our local community centre (one hour a week for four weeks), but probably could have done without. There are some great apps that can help you get great results with less of an investment of time and money. A friend of mine swears by her daily half-hour meditation on the bus on the way to work, using a guided meditation app (free, with optional in-app purchases). I only do a ten-minute session each Monday, Wednesday, and Friday after work, but I am amazed by how it calms down my brain. I feel clear headed after those ten minutes and can put things in perspective. Appreciating the Power of Now makes me more motivated to keep going.

8. Put on a happy face

When your mum told you to simply put on a happy face when you were having a tough day at school, it probably didn't come across like a sound way to reduce stress. But as we've seen, science has backed her up: If we smile more, we stress less. I'm not suggesting you should walk around with a fake smile; just be aware of your facial expression. If it's tense, and you constantly frown, you're more likely to get yourself stuck in a negative spiral. The people around you will respond to your grouchy expression, too. They might think your angry demeanor means you're pre-occupied and they might avoid approaching you, or offering help. If you had a bad meeting with a customer, don't take all that negative energy into your office. Let the taxi drop you off a few blocks early, and walk the last couple of minutes so you calm down, order your thinking, and establish a more positive mindset.

Perseverance Destroyers

1. Don't have lunch at your desk

Research has shown that going for a walk after a meal ('postprandial walking') helps with food digestion and lowers blood sugar levels.[34] So after lunchtime, make it a habit to get up and go outside. Just a 10 minute walk will do. Have your lunch in a different environment, preferably with others, and you'll come back more energised. The work you were aiming to do during lunch, will now take half the time.

2. Ditch the delivery app

While Uber Eats, Deliveroo, DoorDash or whatever food delivery app prevails in your neck of the woods, and might present itself as a short term convenience, you're making it harder on yourself in the long run. Go the extra mile and venture outside. Your body and brain need that refreshing break, particularly if you've been sitting in front of your laptop (or on the couch watching Netflix) for hours. Don't accept the path of least resistance just because it's there.

3. Don't run on a treadmill

When you do decide to take up sports, get out in the fresh air to do them; appreciate how great it is to be outside. Of course, the city or climate around you might not cater for that, but that doesn't mean you should develop habits that make you stay indoors all year. Leave the phone and earbuds at home and give your brain a chance to calm down. I cringe when I see people running in gyms with their headphones on while the sun is shining outside. They would get double the results, if they went outside and stopped the constant stream of noise.

4. Don't spend unlimited time on social media

A steady stream of research is being published on the negative impact of social media apps like Facebook, Snapchat and Instagram on our mental health. Expect these warnings to become louder, especially as we see younger generations coming into the workforce and having to deal with setbacks in the real world. We are conditioning our brains to seek confirmation in 'likes' and develop a fear of missing out if we're not part of the noise happening on these channels 24x7. Anxiety and depression sit at the receiving end of social media's aim to 'engage'.

To protect yourself from the downside of social media, set time limits. Better yet, delete the apps. I am not active on Instagram, Snapchat or Facebook and while I know I miss out on social updates and possibly even business opportunities, the downside that comes along with the upside is simply not worth it for me. On the social side, I don't miss staying in touch at a superficial level with people I don't really know. I prefer quality over quantity. In 2019, the average person spent two and a half hours a day on social media.[35] For me, that's zero, which means that I have an 'extra' 900 hours a year to do other things. That's nearly 40 days a year that I spend on the very things I share in this book. And whenever I do get tempted and download Instagram, I am shocked by how quickly my brain starts to yearn for updates and reactions on stuff I post. My brain might be extra sensitive to these things now, but when I look at kids around me, I know their young brains are being challenged more than mine. It's outright scary, and I am convinced that in a couple of decades, we will look back in disbelief at this social experiment, in the same way we now look back at smoking in the 1970s. We should be selective about the impulses with which we bombard our precious brains.

5. Don't accept the default notification settings of any digital channel

The constant disruptions from incoming SMS and WhatsApp messages, Slack chats, phone calls, LinkedIn updates, and email alerts really are a big hindrance for your ability to stay motivated. There are two main reasons for this. First, this 'always on' mode intensifies your constant state of alertness, which drains your energy levels. You're conditioning your brain to be alert and, worse, to respond whenever something happens. This means that by the end of the day, just like your precious iPhone, your batteries are close to empty and you'll find it harder to concentrate, to get stuff done, to solve complex challenges, or to think straight. In sales, we need to use our energy wisely, and that means taking control of how we spend it. Secondly, when you stick with the default setting of 'notifications turned on', your productivity drops like a brick.

Every time you look at one of your screens to see who sent you a message, or every time you see an email notification pop up, your brain's energy is used to digest that impulse. Meaning, you'll have less energy to do the task you were originally doing, which was ... *uh, where was I*? That seemingly small toggle in your brain to go from one task to the other is referred to as 'context switching'. It takes a few extra seconds to get fully focused on a task, so when you toggle between tasks, you lose time and energy to context switching. A loss of a few seconds might not have been a problem a mere decade ago when we received a couple of calls a day, but today we're at the mercy of these incoming distractions every single minute. Manage these distractions wisely.

- For email, in Outlook or other mail clients, turn off the default alert for incoming email and then create a 'rule' to be more selective. A really effective rule is to move all emails that do not come from within your organisation (for example, 'from' does not contain '@yourcompanydomain.com') to a separate folder, like 'mails from outside'. You can then decide how you want to be notified for messages landing in that folder, for example, play sound, bounce icon, or pop-up alert, depending on your mail client.
- LinkedIn is free, right? No. Someone else is paying for your brain to be engaged. Around $2 billion of LinkedIn's revenue comes from advertising. In other words, there is a direct link between

its revenue and its ability to distract you. To see what that looks like, go to 'setting & privacy' and click 'communications'. There you'll see that each of the LinkedIn 'channels' (web, email and the App) has dozens of different notifications you can set. This ranges from being notified when someone views your profile, to something happening in your network, to invites, posts and much more. As per the end of 2019, these added up to a total of 136 different notifications. And yes, the default notification setting for each and every one of them is 'on'. You need to be smart about what distractions (of the 136) are worth it. Some can make you more successful in sales, but the majority of them don't. Just spend five minutes on this to decide for yourself and toggle these notifications to 'off'.

■ Slack is another of these attention seeking, productivity killing apps. The factual downside of the app (distraction) is bigger than the promised upside (improved collaboration). In some organisations, Slack or similar tools end up being used as the go-to channel to ask stupid questions, like 'Where can I find a good case study for a bank?' or 'Who knows where the latest NDA is?'. Those things should be published on the intranet, and if they're not, it doesn't mean you should sacrifice your productivity and commission cheque to constantly be responding to someone else's lack of organisational skills. People who respond to such distractions tend to be the ones who don't have enough time in the day to call more prospects. Again, go to notification preferences and be thoughtful of how these impact your productivity.

■ Used in a corporate setting, WhatsApp has similar challenges. While there is the potential upside of increased collaboration, the reality is that the additional distraction makes it a net extractor of concentration and productivity. Consciously manage the alerts on your phone. On the iPhone's notifications menu, for each app, including WhatsApp, you can turn off those annoying banners that pop up when a message arrives, but keep the little round circles on the app's icon to show messages have arrived ('Badges', Apple calls them).

My workbook contains detailed how-to guides to configure tools like email clients and LinkedIn.

6. Stop multitasking

In the same vain, resist the temptation to multitask. Even a completely healthy brain cannot do it. It's the biggest time waster you can let into your day. You can gain a couple of hours a day (!) simply by setting clear time slots for tasks and committing to them. Don't get pulled into other directions, finish what you're doing first. Not convinced? Here's a simple exercise to test if you are this wonderful person with a truly unique capability of multitasking efficiently. Write this sentence with a pen: *I want to work more efficiently.* Then, under each letter, write a number, starting from zero, all the way to the total number of letters in this sentence (26). Time the whole exercise with a stopwatch. Then, do it again, but this time you'll multitask by writing the first letter, then the first number under it, the second letter and the second number, and so forth. You're now asking your brain to do one of the simplest multitasking exercises, by switching its focus between (simple) language skills and (simple) numerical skills. Time it again.

Your stopwatch timing for the second exercise will prove that it's actually not that simple for your brain. It will take considerably longer to do both tasks in parallel, compared to doing them sequentially. I do this exercise in many of my coaching sessions, and I always see the same results. The average brain needs around 30–34 seconds for the first exercise. But for everyone, it takes around 45–50 seconds to do the same exercise in a multitask fashion. That's a 50 percent drop in productivity. Extrapolate that to a full day and it means that activities you can do in eight hours, will take 12 hours if done in a multitask fashion. If you don't have enough time in the day, stop multitasking. My workbook outlines the above exercise in more detail, plus a fun one you can do by yourself or with your team.

Not convinced? Do you think you can create a presentation and respond to emails at the same time, because it's an autopilot task that doesn't take much energy? Ok. Let's do another exercise. Practice your 3-minute elevator pitch while you're not doing anything else. Just lock yourself up in a room and deliver the pitch out loud, in under three minutes. Then, when you're fluent at it, try it again but this time in your car on the way to a client. Start just before you get to a busy intersection and see what happens. See if you are the one unique individual who scientists haven't discovered yet. Chances are you are just like everyone else; two tasks that you were perfectly able to deliver in an autopilot fashion – driving and pitching – become a challenge when combined. However well you practised your pitch, your brain will force you to stop and prioritise bigger challenges at hand - like not hitting that truck that's coming from the right. And you'll see that when that (rather important) distraction has passed, you'll struggle to pick up the other task (your elevator pitch) where you left it. The elevator pitch that was delivered so smoothly before, not only has intermittent silences but you actually end up back peddling and repeating sentences. When a little complexity is added, like navigating that busy intersection, the brain literally shuts down on the other task. It (luckily) prioritises your safety over the smooth delivery of the elevator pitch.

Of course, the brain does not perceive the office environment to have many life-and-death situations. It'll let you do your day-to-day activities in parallel, if you decide to. In the background, however, the brain will struggle and will take more time and energy. If you want your brain to focus, do not distract it with other things. Still not convinced? Get used to working overtime.

7. Don't suppress your tears

The (often macho) sales environment doesn't make it easy to share our raw emotions. Instead, it might seem easier to suppress our emotions and avoid exposing negative feelings. But that doesn't make this coping strategy (because that's what it is, after all), the best course of action. As explained earlier, there are health benefits to crying. I am not saying you should be bawling your eyes out every time a prospect refuses to meet with you, but you should accept that if your stressful emotions are overflowing, your body is telling you to release these chemicals, and crying is a completely natural mechanism designed for that. Doing so in the middle of the office is probably not the most inviting scenario but that doesn't mean you should keep your tears to yourself. More on that in one of the later chapters.

Chapter 5: Learn to let go

'I've got this'

Kitesurfing is an extreme sport. It's an exciting mix of wakeboarding, wind-surfing, paragliding and surfing. The kitesurfer holds onto a large kite connected to lines of around 25 meters long and races over the water using a kiteboard or surfboard. I'm sure you've seen them fly around on a body of water near you whenever the wind picks up. The sport first gained popularity in Hawaii in the late nineties with a Wipika kite designed by the Legaignoux brothers from France. Their design was a large kite that, unlike previous models, maintained its open shape through pre-formed inflatable tubes. Previous kite designs used carbon batons, which made them heavy and difficult to relaunch once they hit the water. This also made the sport safer. It takes a lot of power to pull a grown man forward through the water, and even more to get lift-off. For many, including myself, it's the jumping that makes it such an exciting sport. The more control you have over that power, the safer it is.

I love doing big airs

I started kitesurfing in the Netherlands in 1998, around the time when the first inflatable kite became available. Since then, lighter and stronger materials have improved kite design, and better board designs have allowed the sport to advance massively, pushing it into the mainstream (particularly in the last ten years). Today, there are specialised kite holiday destinations all over the world, kite schools in every city close to the water, and kitesurfing competitions for speciality skills like wave riding, jumping, freestyling, foiling, and more. The global kite equipment market alone is worth over USD 2 billion.

However, one thing hasn't changed. As a kitesurfer, you hook yourself onto your kite using a harness tied around your waist. Rather than constantly fighting the power of the kite with your arms, hooking into your harness allows you to use your body weight and steer the kite with a bar connected to the lines. When you first learn to kite, it's rather unnerving to be hooked up to this huge sail flying high above you. But you soon get the hang of it and learn to control the power of the wind. However, no matter how good you are, it is still a high risk endeavour. Being at the mercy of the elements means you're never fully in control. A big gust of wind or sudden change in wind direction can force an easygoing session into 'code red' territory in seconds. That's why the bar is equipped with a 'quick release' system. This is a safety mechanism that, when pulled or pushed, disconnects you from the kite instantly.

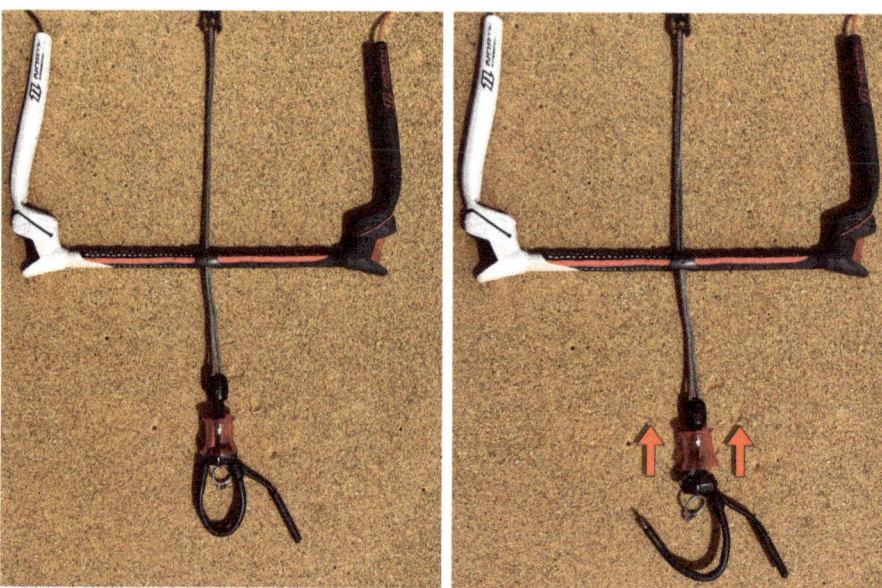

The quick release system

When I became entangled in the other kiter's lines, I didn't pull the quick release. I should have. My kite would have completely detached from me and reduced the resulting danger and damage. I would not have been lifted up in the air, and I would not have landed on the beach face first. There would have been no helicopter ride, no coma, no operations, no 47 screws, no two-year recovery. But I decided to hold on.

I'll never know what was going on in my head when it happened. As I shared earlier, I was pretty tired from all the stress, jet lag and months of poor sleep. Clearly, this challenged my ability to make a split-second decision. My kite buddies, who were standing on the beach and saw it all unfold, told me later that I had a stubborn expression on my face as if to say 'I've got this', even as they were shouting for me to pull the quick release. But 'letting go' is sometimes foreign to a sales professional. 'Holding on' is what we get paid to do. We go after deals and won't take no for an answer. To be successful at sales, we need to stubbornly hold on and not let go. And it's that stubbornness that landed me in a coma.

Following your gut

When I challenge reps about their chances of winning a deal, and whether it's worthwhile to keep holding on, I try to focus on the facts. We'll go over the elements of the qualification formula we've agreed on, the discovery template we'll use, call notes, annual reports, anything that helps assess our chances, and helps us determine the required next steps. The rep's response often is a mix of some of these facts, plus elements of, let's say, *less factual information* – what floats between opinions and fabrications. When I scrutinise this, I am faced with defensive language like 'I assume', 'my feeling is' and 'it's just my intuition'. And this is where things get tricky.

In life, your ability to 'trust your gut' is extremely important. Such intuition arises as a feeling within your body that inexplicably tells you what to do. Rather than relying on conscious reasoning and rational facts, this instinct helps avoid overthinking and allows for efficient decision making. It is the ultimate act of trusting yourself. In sales, 'trusting your gut' makes things easier, too. But it deserves caution. Let's look at a quick example.

James was a newly hired account executive in the commercial sales team of a San Francisco based SaaS company. James had seven years of sales experience under his belt: first as an SDR and then as a commercial rep in another SaaS company in a different industry.

When he first joined the company, he didn't have a clear strategy; however, he made up for this in energy. He wanted to make a mark. Whenever James hit an obstacle, he believed he could overcome it *simply* by leveraging his sheer levels of energy. Whenever a meeting didn't go as he hoped, or whenever he lost a deal, he *simply* told himself that the next one would go better. He was just following his gut and knew he'd get there, he told me.

James impressed me and those around him. He had an internal energy source that allowed him to keep going, with a chin-up attitude that showed everyone that eventually, he'd get there. He lost five big deals in a row, and finally won the sixth. It wasn't a big one because he had to 'discount it to the max'. But he closed a deal, proved to his boss that he could sell, and was keen to win more opportunities. In the following quarter, James hit some obstacles. He lost key deals and late-stage opportunities somehow disappeared into thin air.

The solution consultants began to vent their frustration. They wanted to be assigned to opportunities from other reps, so they had a bigger chance to make their target. Unfazed, James dug deep and found more energy to keep going. That one deal he had previously won led him to believe that his intuition had been correct, and that he could do it. He just had to keep going. But his impressive energy levels couldn't save him. Before the year was over, James was completely exhausted and he resigned in frustration. He told me that the product he was supposed to sell was just too expensive, and the user interface was too clunky. The market wasn't ready either, he believed. Whatever it was that prevented his success, it definitely wasn't him. He left to work for a competitor 'with better data integrations'. Although his LinkedIn profile says he's still there, I heard he lasted just six months with that competitor.

I come across a lot of people like James. They follow their gut, set their course, and go for it. When things go ok for them, their energy levels pay off. But when they get stuck, those energy levels aren't enough to save them. Worse, the rest of the team starts questioning its actions and starts dragging its feet. They don't buy into that gut feel of the rep, and as a result, the rep not only needs to convince his prospect, but also the very team that is supposed to help him win the deal. When the rep gets challenged with fair arguments, he gets worked up and becomes even more determined.

We do this because once an opportunity is qualified and shows up in our pipeline report, we tend to find it hard to let go and flick it to 'lost'. Once we've defended it internally, we get emotionally tied to the opportunity and lose the ability to objectively assess whether to spend yet another hour on it. We don't cut our losses easily, and for some masochistic reason, we would rather have the customer put us out of our misery than make the call ourselves. We keep opportunities open for too long and only move them to 'closed-lost' or 'closed-no decision' when the customer tells us or, worse, hasn't called us back in a month. But until that happens, we waste time chasing opportunities based on a weak gut feeling that maybe it has legs.

It's not just the rep's time that is wasted. Other expensive resources like solution consultants and sales managers will continue to ask for updates. When the opportunity gets pushed out to the next quarter, even more people start scrutinising it and wasting their time. The flow-on effects on the sales team's time availability are huge. It's common nowadays to say that we should 'fail fast': if we try something and it doesn't work, adjust course and try again. While that might work in agile product development departments, failing fast is not a concept that works in sales. With so much stacked against us, we can't just give up after we hit a stumbling block; we can't quickly change our sales approach, pitch, sales methodology, product or pricing. Prospects would become very nervous from all that flailing, and it is our persistence that prevents us from failing fast. We hold on even when we shouldn't.

We need to protect ourselves against this ugly downside of our persistence. We need to be careful around what opportunities we decide to go after. The lack of discipline around deciding what to go after, and what to walk away from, is at the source of why many sales people fail and eventually give up. Unfortunately, it is also an area where our sales processes do not support us. In fact, most sales management processes are unintentionally designed to make 'letting go' a very hard thing to do.

What's wrong with the B2B sales process

For B2B sales teams, the sales process invariably looks like this. The first stage is 'prospecting': finding a prospect that potentially has a need for your product or service. This is followed by 'qualification', with validation steps around BANT (budget, authority, needs, timing) or something similar. When that's cleared, the whole sales train comes into motion with numerous activities focused on linking your solution to the prospect's needs: discovery, demonstration, proposal, negotiation etc.

In reality, the buying process (all that happens on the prospect's side) begins much earlier than the sales process (this happens on your side). At the prospect's side (where the buying process happens), a company typically goes through phases before they start looking for a solution: something changes, which causes or aggravates pain or friction, which gives rise to needs. This, in turn, triggers the search for a solution. For instance, the change that sets the whole buying process in motion could be the prospect's competitors creating price pressure or a new government regulation or margin erosion or an incumbent vendor not performing. Or – the Big Change – the prospect's customer (often the consumer) is changing. They want things faster, easier, in a self-serve fashion, or cheaper (because that's the expectation set by companies like Netflix, Amazon, Uber, or other companies that don't play in the prospect's industry).

This change creates pain because the prospect's current processes and infrastructure were created before this change occurred. The prospect then realises something needs to be done (or not); they define their needs, and start looking for a solution to meet those needs.

In those phases, where change leads to pain and needs, some crucial decisions are made on the prospect's side. And not all of them are made explicitly – some just 'happen'. The internal owner of the problem is assigned; the priority over other business problems is determined; and an initial business case is established to determine whether to move forward. The needs are defined; a rough view of the solution is formed; expectations around timelines are set; and resources and budget are earmarked. Once that's established, the search for a solution starts.

The main stage in the sales process, which covers those first three important phases of the buying process, is the 'prospecting' stage. Of course, the reality does not always follow that linear path, but key factors that determine the potential fit of your solution are shaped in these very early stages. In other words, fundamental decisions that impact your ability to win the deal are made in the prospecting stage – before the evaluation starts. The reality is that once an opportunity clears that BANT qualification hurdle, your ability to influence is greatly reduced. The train has left the station, and if you weren't steering it, there might be no point jumping on board.

This is where the sales process design nearly always is wrong. *Sales effort and emphasis actually increases as the ability to influence reduces.* Sales management tends to only get involved once opportunities are well progressed – post qualification. Solution consulting and professional services assign domain experts once it gets to 'discovery' or 'proposal' stage. Management start scrutinising things once an opportunity is in 'decision' stage – when the reps or sales manager's ability to influence the outcome is minimal. CEOs are introduced at the tail end, when the processes that have been set in motion typically don't allow prospects to change tack, even if they'd wanted to. Yet, that super important prospecting stage – where the ability to influence is at its highest – hardly gets any scrutiny.

It's typically delegated to the least experienced members of the sales teams: the Sales Development Reps (SDRs, also called Business Development Reps, or BDRs). These are young, hungry, up-and-coming sales talent who often have the single biggest influence on how the rest of the sales team will be spending it's time. Their unintentional power is disproportional to the sales experience they bring to the table. It's a bit like hiring a teenager as the doorman at a nightclub. The selection process around 'who gets in' is not exactly going to be stringent. Even when it's the rep who's responsible for qualification, there typically is no scrutiny from management or even a process to have multiple sets of eyes carefully decide whether time should be spent on a specific opportunity. In fact, in most organisations, 'qualification' isn't really the gatekeeping stage that the name implies. It's merely a subjective decision by an individual who often is desperate to get more pipeline.

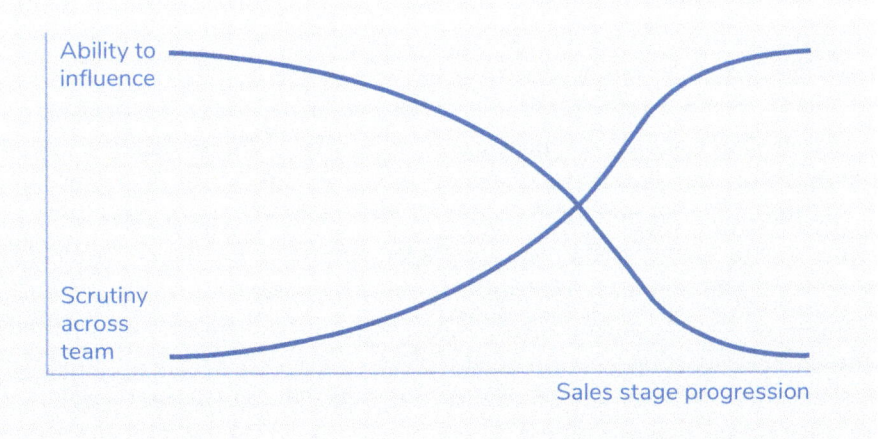

The sales process defect

There's no mechanism to help protect the individual against desperation or naïve hope that leads them to hold on for too long. And the person making the all-important decision to go after an opportunity hardly ever realises the impact that their decision will have on the time spent. It is this defect in the sales process that can seriously impact a sales team's productivity.

In my sales coaching business, I come across sales teams whose number of 'lost to competitor' opportunities is less than half of their total 'lost' deals. The rest fell into that bucket of 'wasted time', categorised by the sales stage 'no decision', 'clean up', 'gone quiet' or similar. So much time was spent on opportunities that weren't really opportunities. *Letting go* is the single hardest skill to develop, particularly for less experienced sales professionals. But it is the skill that will make the single biggest impact on how you spend your time. Give me a sales rep who exceeds target and I'll give you a sales rep who's selective about what to spend energy on. Give me a sales rep who enthusiastically runs after everything that moves, and I'll give you an exhausted professional who won't stick around for long.

How to protect yourself from positive delusions

Trusting your gut only works if you have sufficient experience selling 'that' solution in 'that' market. If, like James, you are new to an organisation and haven't sold its product before, you can't rely on your gut yet. It takes time. It takes a few dozen sales cycles to learn what makes a good prospect, and what makes a good opportunity. Depending on the average length of your sales cycle, gaining this experience could take a year or longer. If you come from a competitor or sold a solution in the same ecosystem, it'll be quicker. Still, if you're new, be very careful of *trusting your gut* in that initial period. That voice in your head that's telling you to go after something might be positive and optimistic, but it could lead you to a state of positive delusion. This is when you convince yourself that you have a good chance at winning the deal, regardless of whether facts support such a view. Such conviction could stem from you wanting to prove yourself to your manager, and win your first deal quickly to establish credibility with the team. However good such positivity is, be cautious, for all the reasons outlined above. Such caution can only be instilled if you acknowledge that your gut hasn't fully formed yet in that first period. This requires an honest self-assessment devoid of ego. The Gut Curve model below can help create your awareness.

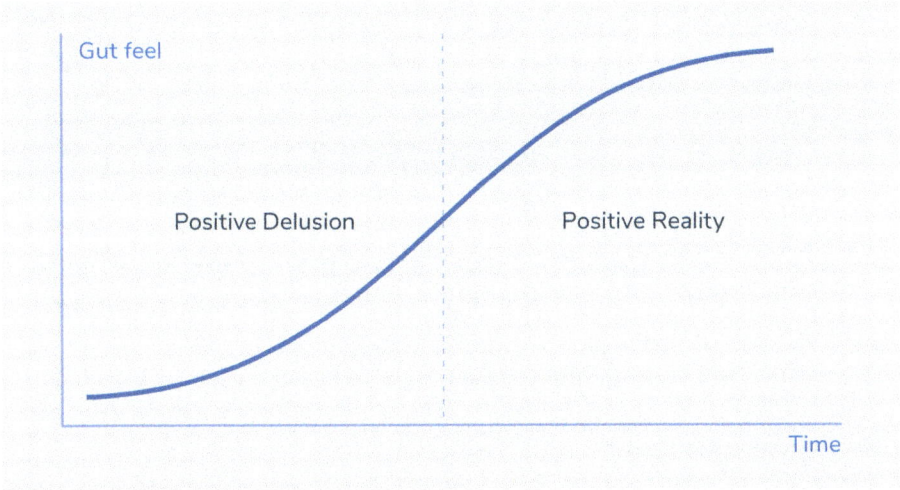

The gut curve: are you trusting your gut too soon?

When you're new, your gut feel might land you in a state of Positive Delusion. Once you have a few wins (and lots of losses) under your belt, it strengthens to help create a state based on Positive Reality. You still won't know (100 percent) if you'll win a deal – this is sales after all – but you'll find that relying on your gut will pay off more and more.

To accelerate getting to that point, there's only one solution. You'll need to rely on others – a second set of eyes, particularly from cross functional teams like solution consultants. As described above, your sales process might not make this easy. The next section provides several practical suggestions on how to cope with that.

Perseverance Promotors

1. Create a qualification review

By review, I mean some assessment that involves more than a single person working off some subjective and ambiguous set of criteria ('Authority? Yes, my contact person has that!'). It's in everyone's interest to keep the rep honest and agree on what to go after. The aim of this process is not just to reject all average looking new opportunities until a perfect one comes along; rather, it's to provide feedback to the rep and SDR about what makes a great opportunity and what doesn't. Most of all, it is to share the responsibility of deciding what comes in at the top of the funnel. As you can see in the below figure, other reviews will be needed farther down the funnel.

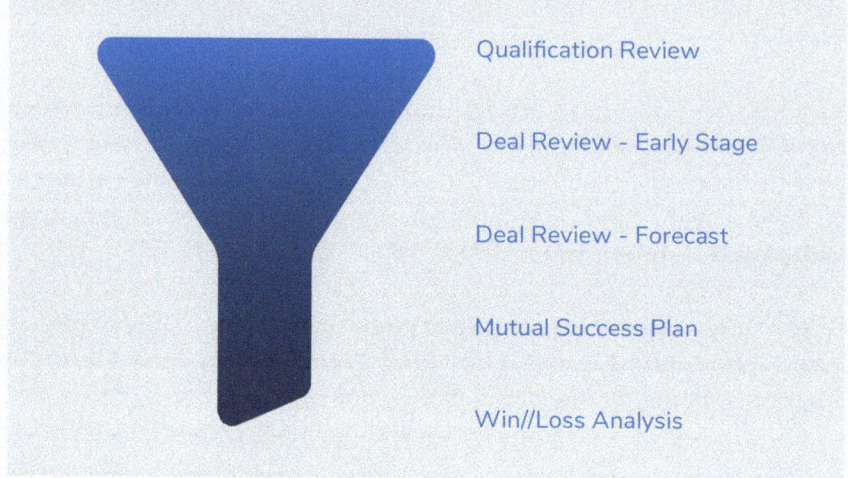

Don't just have review meetings at the bottom of the funnel

2. Set up a deal review meeting

Reps will normally get ample scrutiny on deals that are in forecast stages, like 'proposal' and 'negotiation'. To shift more attention towards the earlier stages where a real impact can be made, get SCs, sales managers or sales coaches to constructively review early stage opportunities (past qualification). This is not a forecast meeting where the rep is grilled; it's a meeting where suggestions are shared about how to increase the chances of influencing and winning a deal in those early stages. With one of my clients, we set aside one hour a week to review three pre-proposal deals from three reps. Resulting actions nearly always involve the

SCs, sales managers and even the managing director who's super keen to get involved early-on, instead of playing his usual reactive dive-and-save role in a later stage. Find a completed example from an Early Stage Deal Review in my workbook.

3. Think like a CEO

Above suggestions require a broader organisational change. If it's too hard to implement such changes in your environment, there are still a few things you can do at an individual level. All of these require you to think like a CEO. As a sales rep, you're the CEO of your territory. You decide what happens in your patch. You'll need to be clear and align the activities from your SDRs and marketing so that they create the right top-of- funnel activity. If you don't give this guidance to the people who are there to help build your pipeline, you'll end up wasting everyone's time. Make sure you have regular catch-up meetings with the other departments and decipher if there are any misalignments that need your attention. For instance, do the SDRs have the right qualification questions? Don't blame sales enablement if they don't, but instead roll up your sleeves and help the SDRs create better quality pipelines that lead to less time wasting for you. Likewise, don't blame marketing for shitty leads if you haven't actually told them what a good lead looks like. Get involved. If you're too busy for that, step back. Are you so busy because you're perfectly on track to get to your annual target or because you're focused on the wrong leads that don't go anywhere? If it's the latter, break the cycle; sit down with marketing and fix the top of the funnel.

4. Define your ICP and segment your market into ABC

Determine what an ideal customer would look like and create an Ideal Customer Profile (ICP) of the companies you want to go after. Go deeper than the standard 'Fortune 500 finance company', or 'manufacturing' or 'services companies in APAC'. These definitions are not sufficiently thought through and will lead to wasted time later on. Instead, go deeper into what makes a good prospect, and agree on what makes a bad prospect. The concept of ICP is best implemented organisation-wide, but if you can't rally the troops, there's nothing holding you back from defining one for your own territory or sales region. Here are some practical tips on how to do this:

- Segment your territories on *propensity to buy* by implementing the ABC Model. 'A' accounts are those that are most likely to buy, 'B' are less likely and 'C' are those you want to avoid (even if they joined five of your webinars). Develop a parlance where marketing, SDRs, sales reps and sales management show an understanding that the companies they go after should fit in either the A bucket, maybe the B bucket, but definitely not the C bucket.

- This ABC distinction should be done on three areas of characteristics: firmographics, technographics and demographics. Your current segmentation most likely already covers some of the firmographics. These are the things you can easily determine from the outside: the number of employees of the prospect, its industry vertical, revenue, business model (and hence, likely processes), and geographical reach. But as I said, you need to go deeper.

- In SaaS, the technographics often say more about likelihood to buy; they reflects the current technology footprint of an account. Buying SaaS often requires a level of maturity, which is revealed by other technology solutions the prospect already uses. At its simplest, Prospect A, who uses your cheaper competitor is more likely to be ready to 'upgrade' to yours than Prospect B who has never bought SaaS and still uses manual processes and spreadsheets – even if Prospect B is of the right size and in the right vertical. Determine what these technographics look like for your A, B and C accounts. Then, use tools like Ghostery, Builtwith or Datanyze to see what technologies are in place at accounts in your territory; get the enterprise edition so you can integrate it with your CRM and do your segmentation there, rather than in spreadsheets.

- As for demographics, look at the people-side to determine the propensity to buy. *Companies tend to develop (or recruit for) specific skillsets before they buy the technology. Not the other way around.* Look for key skills and role titles that are telltale signs for a readiness for your solution. Who is more likely to buy from you? Person A who used your tool before and just started a new role in a different company that's growing rapidly? Or Person B who's been in the role for ten years with a company that has hardly invested in new technologies, and hence, skills? Again, decide what these skills and roles look like for your A, B, and C accounts. Then, see what's out there. Tools like Zoominfo and Discoverorg offer some value, but they don't always have good data for companies and contacts outside the US. LinkedIn is your biggest friend here, particularly the jobs section, where you can create alerts that let you know when certain roles pop up. Go after companies that are hiring for relevant skills and roles as they will likely, soon, be in the market for a technology like your solution.

- Have a workshop with marketing, the SDRs, the CSMs and the AEs to determine what makes an A account, and what makes a B or a C. This exercise will create several aha moments that will lead to more focus in your marketing and sales activities, and free up time. Focus will create clarity. It makes things less ambiguous, and it leads to a more action oriented culture.

- Create a field in your CRM that allows you to earmark accounts as either A, B, C or '-' (not assessed yet). Then, sit down with marketing to make sure it focuses its marketing campaigns only on A and B accounts, so that leads coming in align with your ICP. Make sure you tell your outbound SDRs to only focus on A and B accounts, and be clear how to qualify accounts that don't meet the ICP. Ensure reps and SDRs catch up at least once a week to agree on their plan of attack on these focused accounts.

- I know this sounds like a lot of work, but remember, not focusing your top-of-funnel activities will create a huge trailing impact on time for everyone. Some of the tools mentioned will make this effort easier, and predictive analytics solutions like Leadspace, Mintogo, Insideview and 6sense can automate much of it. However, they don't always have quality data sets outside of the US. And since propensity to buy characteristics in APAC or EMEA are not necessarily the same as those in the US, be careful on relying too much on such technologies. There might be merit in spending some time doing things manually for your territory for now.

- The effort of thinking through this ABC segmentation will create more focus in sales. It is not meant to be an algorithm that's 100 percent correct, but it will provide a more granular appreciation for what makes a prospect more likely to buy from you. It will also create a culture where it's acceptable to step back and question whether a certain opportunity is worth going after.

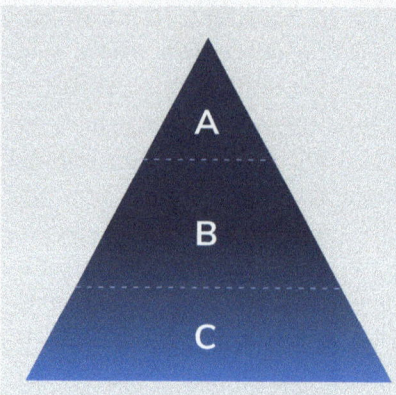

IDEAL PROSPECT
Most likely to buy; they are mature, have pains and understand the value and how we can solve their problems.

LESS IDEAL PROSPECT
Not ready – their pains and maturity levels have not developed much yet. They won't appreciate our differentiators and likely buy something simpler.

BAD PROSPECT
They don't have the pains we normally solve and are unlikely to develop them. Ignore and find a way to say no in a friendly way.

The ABC model helps create focus on the right accounts

5. Create a go-to-market sales role

One of my clients avoided the trap of SDRs and AEs chasing the wrong leads by implementing a structural fix. Rather than having the ABC model executed at a local level (by AEs), they created a global go-to-market (GTM) sales role. The purpose of the GTM person is to:

- Define the ICP (together with product, marketing and sales leaders).
- Do market research across all territories on the characteristics that make the ICP.
- Flag each account in the territories in the CRM with A, B or C.
- Communicate to the field what to focus on and how.

This allows the SDRs and AEs to focus more on sales execution with the right accounts. A role like this does require a proper global view of the ICP. An ICP at headquarters in the US or Europe does not necessarily make an ICP in Latin America or APAC, for instance. Most of all, CRM data in all regions will need to allow this global segmentation exercise. There's nothing worse than defining one vanilla-flavoured ICP across the globe, only to find out the reps in various markets struggle to get traction with them. Make sure to create an in-region feedback mechanism to support the global GTM role.

6. Apply the Eisenhower matrix

Confusing urgency with importance is one of the biggest deceptions we fall into. There is a compulsion to prioritise all things that somehow get labelled 'urgent' over other work. Particularly in high-pressure sales environments with cultures that fail to assess the real decider for priorities: importance. For instance, in a commercial sales team, you might automatically accept that closing deals in the last few weeks of the quarter is the key activity. While that task may be the most urgent, it doesn't necessarily make it the most important. If you haven't made your quarterly target twice in a row because your pipeline was too low, you could be setting yourself up for another bad quarter if you don't break that cycle by also doing lead (demand) generation. It would be more *important* to lay the groundwork for the *next* quarter. A blind RFP is another example of an urgent activity that automatically tends to get more time and attention. Everybody works like crazy to respond within the deadline, but realistically, this is unlikely to be an important activity as chances of winning blind RFPs are super low (4% at one of my clients). It would be better to disqualify and spend time on finding good opportunities. The common attitude around such conflicting priorities is to decide that *both* should be prioritised. But that doesn't work – you'll just keep on chasing your tail. The Eisenhower Matrix could help avoid that.

Before Dwight Eisenhower became the 34th President of the United States, he served as Supreme Commander of the Allied Expeditionary Forces in World War II. In those roles, he had to make tough decisions on an ongoing basis. In a speech in 1954, he referred to two kinds of problems he struggled with: urgent ones that were not important and important ones that were not urgent. Time management disciplines have since referred to this challenge as the Eisenhower Matrix. If you think like a CEO, this is one tool you want to adopt in your sales practices.

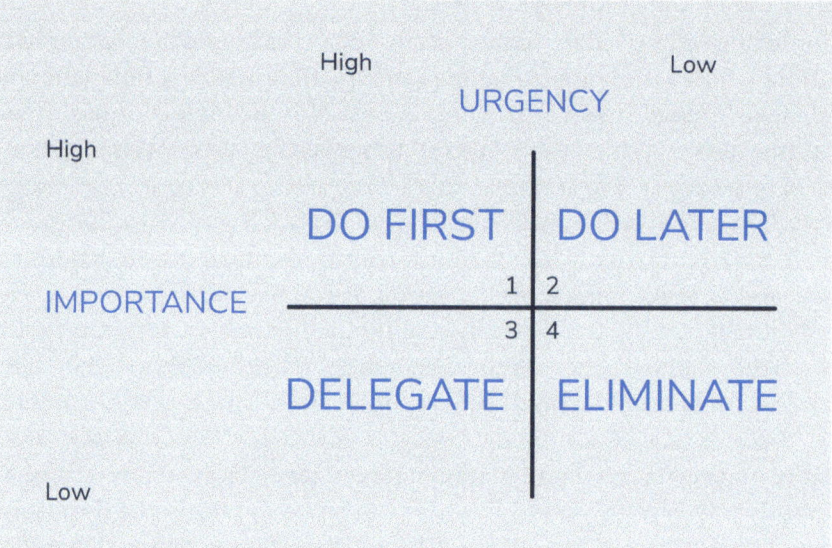

High   Low

URGENCY

High

DO FIRST | DO LATER

1 | 2

IMPORTANCE

3 | 4

DELEGATE | ELIMINATE

Low

The Eisenhower Matrix helps set the right priorities

The Eisenhower Matrix is a two-by-two matrix with 'importance' on the vertical axel, and 'urgency' on the horizontal – a total of four quadrants.

A typical 'chasing your tail' situation occurs when we focus on activities that are deemed urgent, even though they might not be that important – quadrant 3 activities. And then, when we get to the end of the quarter, we find ourselves in quadrant 1 with 'highly urgent' activities that are also 'highly important' but we simply don't have the bandwidth to keep all balls in the air. And even if we would, it might be too late to turn the ship around. That's the tyranny of urgency: it creates an automatic assumption that something that is urgent gets priority regardless of whether it's important. Sometimes, you need to accept a short-term pain to create a long-term gain.

At the start of each week, write down your key activities for that period. Then, plot them into the four quadrants. Your aim is do important things before they become urgent, and delegate urgent things that aren't important.

Do the activities in quadrant 1 first. Examples could be a preparation for a prospect meeting the next day, or obtaining internal discount approvals for a proposal that's due this week. Examples of activities in quadrant 2 (which are also important, but not urgent) are the creation of a sales plan for the quarter, lead gen activities, and preparation for a big RFP response in a couple of weeks. Set clear deadlines for these activities before they become urgent. We tend to spend the most time on things that aren't that important but somehow seem urgent (quadrant 3). See if you can get help from others so you can spend more time on the activities you planned in quadrant 2. Could you hand over a fast moving deal to another rep? Could you ask the SC to help create a first outline for the demo? Some things, like finalising your online training or submitting your expense report, can only be done by you. Still, this rational representation of your priorities takes the emotion out of it and will help you realise you need to take control, before you're in knee deep. I also suggest you print out an empty version of the Eisenhower Matrix and hang it near your desk so you can keep it top of mind. When, at any given time during your busy week, a task is thrown at you, quickly glance at the matrix and do a priority check to see in which quadrant that activity sits. Tasks that clearly are neither urgent nor important, should be eliminated.

7. Create a weekly planner

As we've seen, the brain needs structure. It is more efficient if it can focus on similar, repetitive tasks, than when it keeps on having to switch from, say, cold calling to responding to emails, to updating the CRM. You can free up numerous hours in your week simply by structuring your day around specific activities based on a well thought-through plan. Most sales professionals I coach dig their heels in when I broach this topic. They believe sales is too hectic a profession for which to create a structure. 'You never know when a prospects calls, or when you suddenly have to create a big presentation or proposal: you can't plan for that'. My response is simple: yes, to a large extent, we are at the whim of our customers. But that's only more reason why we need to plan. We can't just sit around reacting to what gets thrown at us. Those who do, will never make target because they have no control of where they're going. We can, and should, create a solid foundation of activities that *we want* to perform, regardless of what happens around us, so that we make progress and have enough time available to jump into the unexpected things coming our way. *Planning does not lead to inflexibility. Instead, good planning enables flexibility.*

If you want to create time, create a weekly planner *before* you start your week. List key activities you intend to complete by the end of the week and/or day. For instance, as an AE, you might set aside the first half-hour of your day to determine your goals and activities for the day. Then you might skim your emails and action the most important ones. Next block an hour to research ten prospects and prepare for your reach-outs. You'll spend 90 minutes cold calling and emailing those prospects. The next two hours, before lunch, you block for customer meetings. After lunch, you spend an hour going through your emails and updating your CRM. Then you have an hour for internal meetings (sales meetings, forecast meetings, SDR, 1:1s etc.). The next hour is focused on cold calling again, followed by customer meetings. Then you end the day with posting something on LinkedIn and reviewing relevant social media updates. The last activity you undertake is to create a quick plan for the next working day, so you limit the time it'll take to get back into the swing of things.

A weekly planner will support your time management challenges in three ways. First, you'll create an honest set of goals for that period to which you can hold yourself accountable. It makes expectation setting with yourself and others more realistic. This helps you avoid wasting time by providing updates on things you weren't really going to finish anyway. Second, it will help you develop discipline to focus on activities so that you can finish them before you jump to the next one. As you read in the previous chapter, this saves valuable time on context-switching; the overhead process of letting go of a task, getting started up on a new one, and then getting back to the original task only to realise you lost your train of thought. And third, it creates a clear signal to your colleagues when you are available for their distractions and when you're not. The reality is that your colleagues represent the biggest level of distraction – not your customers. That constant stream of emails and Slack messages drains your time. A plan helps you set and communicate boundaries that will quickly limit the number of distractions simply because people are aware they shouldn't bother you during certain hours. For example, you can tell them that you blocked your Tuesday, Wednesday and Thursday from 10 am till noon for customer meetings and cold calling. Tell them you won't be responding to internal emails, unless it's urgent. In such a case, a phone call is the only means to get through to you. You'll see that just communicating that simple framework will drastically reduce the number of incoming messages. People tend to send more messages to people who are open to being distracted – it's as simple as that. If you don't respond, they'll go somewhere else.

The examples used here are examples only. You will need to decide what works for you. Use my workbook to review detailed AE and SDR examples, and use the template to create your own.

8. Do the Energy Units Exercise

Everyone is different. We get our energy from different things. Our metabolisms are different, too. This means that how *my* motivation eventuates will be different to *yours*. We need to be aware of how we consume our energy, and whether that aligns with how we build our energy. The Energy Units Exercise helps us to do just that. It consists of three simple steps. First, list how you perceive your energy levels to be across the day, and across the week. Do you feel fully charged up at 9 am in the office, or are you a late starter who only gets going in the afternoon? For one week, simply keep track and list how you feel every hour. A level 1 means you're feeling tired, 2 means you're ok, 3 means you're feeling all charged up.

Then, list all the tasks you'd normally do during a typical week in sales. From cold calling to planning for the call, to having meetings, to updating the CRM: list them all. After you've done that, indicate how much energy such an activity tends to consume. Again, we're all different. I don't like cold calling, but I really enjoy first client meetings. You might be the opposite. Next to the activity, list either +2 to depict that that activity is fun. +1 if you don't mind but don't derive a lot of energy from it. -1 for things you don't like but are ok at doing, and finally, -2 for activities that create anxiety simply by thinking about them.

Then you step back and bring the two lists together to determine key insights around how you should be working. For me, my energy levels in the afternoon are generally lower. This means I should not be cold calling during this time. I am particularly low on energy on Friday afternoon, so I reserve that for updating the CRM or doing expenses – easy tasks for me. It would be bad planning to do such things on a Monday morning when I'm buzzing with energy and would rather take on tasks that demand much from me.

With those insights, you can create a weekly planner. I used to do that in a spreadsheet but now have built enough habits to automatically decide when I do what kind of activities. The bottom line is that everyone is different. Don't just follow the work patterns of the people around you. As a manager, don't assume people have the same energy units and consumption as you – you might be a morning person, but forcing that onto your team can drastically reduce productivity and motivation levels.

You will find the template and a filled-in example of the Energy Units Exercise in my workbook.

Perseverance Destroyers

1. Don't accept meetings without an agenda
Say no to meetings that don't have an agenda on the invite. For internal meetings, create an effective meeting culture by insisting that each invite needs to have a one-sentence objective and a set of agenda points. It's not hard. For instance:

Sales meeting: let's decide on the key activities for next quarter's demand generation.

Agenda:

- Go through numbers
- Agree on key priorities
- Discuss demand gen options
- Make a decision

For a meeting that doesn't have this, reply to the organiser by asking for the purpose and agenda. You'll see that, unfortunately, meeting organisers often don't have a clear idea. You can't have their inability to plan their day result in you wasting your time. An effective meeting culture can be created quite easily; people tend to agree that meetings are often a waste of time and are open to someone calling that out by constructively providing a framework that will free up time for everyone.

2. Don't make all meetings 60 minutes

There is this unexplainable coincidence that 90 percent of meetings somehow take exactly 60 minutes. Regardless of the complexity and audience involved, we all seem to accept the silly notion that when we book a time slot and meeting room for 60 minutes, we can't leave early. When we've established an agreeable outcome 40 minutes in, we tend to glance at the time and slow down just to fill the full hour. Fight that impulse and fight it hard. See if the meeting can be scheduled for a 15- 30- or 45-minute timeslot or start the meeting by saying you're busy and would like to see if the meeting can finish up early. Again, people won't crucify you for it, but if you don't provide that reasonable signal upfront, the default convention kicks in. People, however busy, will happily lower productivity levels just because that seems to be the norm. Develop discipline to change that norm and be surprised how many keen followers pop up.

3. Don't forget to take notes

In all meetings, and particularly those with customers, take notes. Avoid summarising their ideas in your own sales speak, and write down the particular words they use. This will help you tailor your messaging to the customer's language, which will make them feel you've listened and understood them.

4. Don't keep your notes to yourself

For pivotal meetings, I advise that you share your notes with the customer and ask for quick feedback 'to ensure I fully understand what we discussed'. You'll see that, often, a customer will respond by disclosing new information, which due to time constraints didn't get the attention during your meeting. It's also another opportunity to repeat your key messaging because it's likely that they were not taking notes.

5. Don't 'just have a swing at it'

Some reps, when challenged, admit that their chances of winning a deal are low. 'I'm just having a swing at it,' they'll confess. 'It's only just one quick presentation.' Don't. Even when we decide to go after an opportunity 'just to have a swing' at it, we underestimate how much time we're committing as a result of that simple decision. After the presentation, the (bad) prospect will want to see a demo or another follow up meeting, and we can't help ourselves. Before we know it, we'll drag other resources into time-wasting meetings that we all know will lead to nothing. Us sales people don't just have a go, whatever we tell ourselves. We go after something and then *won't let go.*

The exception is when you're new to a sales role and need to practise your pitch. Having a swing could help develop that gut feel. But, do two things: first, pick an account that's segmented as a C account, so you can make mistakes without doing damage. Learn, and get better so when you meet an A or B account, you're ready. Second, don't forecast these deals. Don't even create an opportunity if you're not 100 percent sure. Resist the temptation to want to impress the team. If you're just having a swing, while you know you don't really have a chance, you are creating a long-term distraction for yourself and everyone else.

6. Don't assume all requests from customers are urgent
Use the Eisenhower Matrix task when customers send requests your way. A simple question like 'can you send me over some pricing?' should be followed with a 'sure, and when will you need this by?' I started doing this way too late in my sales career because I assumed that everything coming from the customer was a No.1 priority. In reality, the customer is likely to answer something along the lines of 'oh, we have our first budget meeting next week, so maybe by the end of this week. I won't have time to look at it any earlier'. Never assume *everything* is urgent; it will avoid tail-chasing. Asking time-related questions also sets the scene for you to put forward follow-up questions about what would happen next.

7. Don't binge watch
I have always made a habit of asking colleagues on Monday morning what they did over the weekend. Those who say they watched TV or binge-watched a series are always the least enthusiastic and energetic to start the week. They seem to struggle more when things don't go well and are counting down to the weekend by Wednesday. Colleagues who spent their weekends outdoors or in some other way have *actively* enjoyed themselves are more refreshed and seem to struggle less with the demands at work.

Use the same Energy Units Exercise to determine what gives you energy in your free time, and find recreational alternatives that help you build perseverance.

Chapter 6: Find perspective

The two squares

Earlier, I talked about the air vents in the ceiling above my hospital bed. Initially, they were far apart, but overtime – as my double vision reduced – they moved closer. However, progress stalled – they remained two separate squares, which stubbornly wouldn't fuse into one. Dr Shane, the facial reconstruction surgeon who you'll meet in the next chapter, explained to Elvira that the position of my right eye had changed due to the new eye socket. The initial facial reconstruction had been severely complicated by the swelling in my face. Now that the swelling was dissipating, it turned out that the new eye socket had been placed a tad too high. Yet another operation was needed to loosen some screws, lower the eye socket, and tie it all back up. There wouldn't be a guarantee, but there was a chance the operation would reduce double vision. In the weeks following the operation, every morning when the nurse came in and turned on the light, I looked up in the hope that the two squares became one. They didn't. At least not initially.

Around New Year's Eve, the squares slowly started to overlap. Hearing that news, Dr Shane said it was a good sign – he had done everything physically possible and the eyes were *as much aligned* as he could possibly get them. 'Now, it's up to your brain,' Dr Shane said. 'Your brain needs to realise what's wrong and hopefully can change the way it processes the data coming in from your eyes'. If not, he'd told me I'd have to use an eye patch for the rest of my life; it would be easier to have no depth of vision, than to live with double vision. That projection really stressed me out. What would it mean to only have one eye for the rest of my life? How would it limit me? Would a lack of depth of vision stop me from having a normal life again? Would it look weird to have an eye patch? Would the headaches stop?

Luckily, all that stress proved unnecessary. My brain did well. Every morning, I'd see the squares getting closer to one another. Then, on 19 January, I looked up and saw one single square in the ceiling. Eight weeks after the accident, my eyes were working properly again.

In the days before, doctors had started giving indications that I might soon go home. The anticipation helped keep me going but the horrendous sleep cycles depleted my energy to such a low level that I wasn't always in a positive mindset to appreciate the progress. I struggled during those last days. Finally, after 57 days and nights in hospital, I was discharged. On 21 January 2014, under the watchful eye of my wife, and on crutches, I wobbled back into our home. I was over the moon to have Elvira with me around the clock, to sleep in my own bed again, to not hear the constant noise from doctors and patients, and to eat proper food (no offence, *Chef de Cuisine* of Royal North Shore Hospital).

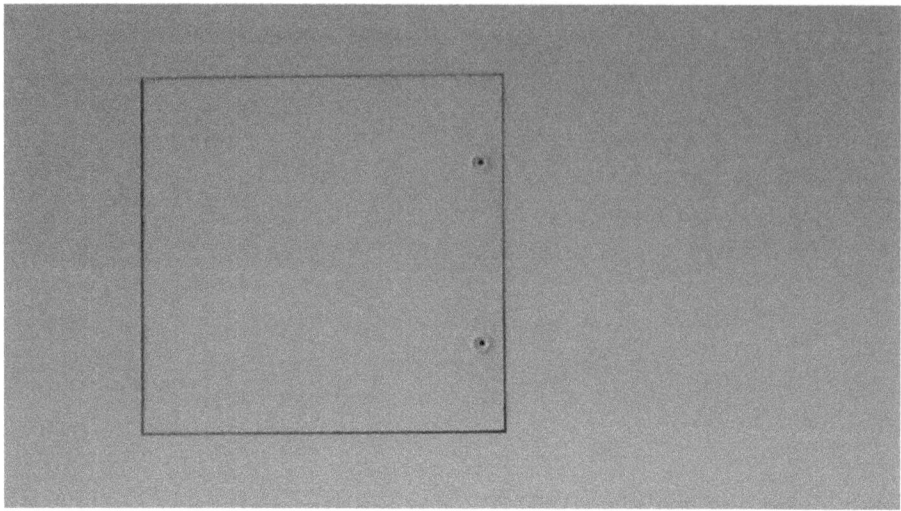

A picture of the ceiling of the ICU room I was in, showing the (one) air vent

For Elvira, the initial weeks after my accident had been a harrowing emotional roller-coaster. For me, it was different. I hadn't experienced those months in a rational way to really understand my predicament. Being in the safety of our own home brought me to terms with the hallucination episodes – albeit slowly. It all felt like a bad dream. Being home, and within the care from Elvira and family and friends, gave me a sense of protection that calmed me and allowed me mentally to 'close off this nasty chapter'. In that comforting state, I didn't realise that *my* emotional roller-coaster ride was only about to start. Just as I was settling in to the familiar surroundings of our home, it readied itself for a big corkscrew dive.

Meet Max, my dental surgeon

It started in March 2014, five months after the accident. I had just managed to walk on my own. I wasn't exactly steady on my feet yet but found extra bouts of energy and motivation in my newfound mobility. As long as there were enough doors and chairs close by, I could do short distances without those annoying aluminium sticks. That progress helped me gather the confidence to tackle the next step – my teeth. I didn't know exactly what the damage was as it wasn't something the hospital cared about. I struggled to open my mouth wide after it had been wired shut for so long, and in all honesty hadn't gathered the guts to have a detailed look with a mirror. I had parked it as a minor challenge that would be easier than, say, learning to walk again.

I never liked dentists, let alone dental surgeons, but at that stage thought I could handle it. *After all that time in the hospital and the many operations, a bit of work on my teeth would be a walk in the park, right?* Elvira had booked an appointment with Associate Professor Max, a dental surgeon in Sydney referred to us by the facial reconstruction team. Max had studied for a Bachelor Degree (with Honours) in Dentistry, a residency in oral surgery, and a Dental Technician Diploma followed by a four-year full-time PhD program in the field of dental ceramics. He then completed a three-year Clinical Doctorate in Prosthodontics. His diplomas and awards proudly greeted us from the walls of his sterile waiting room when we stumbled in on a hot late summer afternoon. We must have been quite a sight when he first saw us: Elvira carried a folder containing scans, surgeon's reports, insurance papers and referral letters. I had a bandage around one leg, my face was a mess, a few front teeth were missing, and my right arm was still in a sling. I kept my left hand close to the wall as Max guided us into his room.

Elvira told the story of my accident and recovery. I had just started speech therapy with Katy and still struggled with pronouncing 'p' and 'b'. Some of the muscles in my lips had regained strength, but the scars on the inside of my mouth made it hard to talk properly. Leaning back into the dentist chair, Max assessed the damage. Within seconds, the roller-coaster went into free fall and pulled me into an emotional trough. All the confidence I built in the weeks after coming out of the hospital disappeared when Max asked his assistant to take notes while he assessed the damage.

An implant was needed for tooth 42 (in my lower jaw). *Yep, I'd expected that.* But tooth 24 had a nasty fracture and needed to be pulled. *More implants. Ok, that makes sense.* Tooth 27 required a complex procedure called crown lengthening. He would cut the gum from the jawbone so the bone could be filed back. *What? Why?* It would allow the remaining bits of the tooth to be more exposed so that composite would bond better to form a whole tooth again. *Oh.* The section next to that looked ok, but he was worried about my lack of sensation. Maybe the nerves were damaged or maybe a root canal therapy was needed. He stopped. I was hoping to hear that buzzing sound of the chair going back up, but Max continued.

Tooth 31, a molar in the back, needed to be removed. *What? I didn't even know that one was broken.* He could probably rebuild teeth 4, 5, and 7 with synthetic composite. Tooth 12 definitely needed a root canal treatment before he could even determine what to do with it. He looked at his assistant who struggled to keep up, and then continued. Same for tooth 13, which also needed a post and core. Then again, that would depend on how much room was left. 'Note it as a potential extraction', Max dictated with a monotone voice. Tooth 14 needed a crown, but maybe he could bridge it with the other two. Then it was quiet again. Dazed by all the dental lingo and realisation that a) people apparently have around 30 teeth and b) I didn't anymore, I feared for the worst. Finally, the chair began to gently vibrate as it slowly moved me into a seated position.

'That's a fair bit of damage Frank. It's impressive to see how the reconstruction surgeons pieced the temporomandibular joint back together. Very impressive.' However, it would still likely complicate things, he continued. 'That's where the jaw connects with the skull, and there isn't enough range to get access to the teeth in the back.' I simply couldn't open my mouth far enough and needed more physio before he could even have a better look. Max rolled his chair over to the assistant's monitor and went over the notes while Elvira stood next to me holding my hand. After a couple of minutes he turned around. 'A lot of teeth need to be repaired, Frank. A lot. Fourteen in total. This is going to take a while. I'm estimating 15 sessions over the coming two years. Maybe more. Some teeth that look salvageable now will only reveal their true state after the nerves grow back.'

I sat in that chair trying to hold back my tears while Elvira quietly asked Max questions to which she wouldn't remember the answers.

We both left Max's practice with a dizzying realisation that we were nowhere near the end of the letdowns. My recovery was only entering its next phase. A few scary weeks followed, in which I struggled to see joy or notice the progress my body was making. I felt bad for Elvira, who continually came up with ways to cheer me up. She found a new place for coffee every time we had to go to the hospital for yet another checkup. She dislikes cooking but tried extra hard to prepare nutritious liquid and soft meals for my battered mouth. She organised a few days away down the coast, in between physiotherapy appointments, dental sessions, speech therapy and checkups with Dr Susan. She tried so hard to cheer me up. I felt guilty, and this only made my emotional state more precarious. One day, Elvira said, 'Remember the two squares a couple of months ago? We were all stressed out wondering if you would be walking around with an eye patch for the rest of your life. And look how lucky you've been. I'm sure you're going to be lucky again with your teeth'. My mind fluttered between seeing her point of not wanting to forget what happened and 'what could have been', and rejecting the notion that I should feel better 'because it could have been worse'. Yes, I could have lost the eye. I could have been in a wheelchair. I could have been dead. But somehow, that didn't make my current situation more bearable. What if Max couldn't save these teeth? What if I'd end up in pain for the rest of my life? Whatever Elvira tried, my mind kept pulling me back into very pessimistic territory.

One day, when we were heading out to meet up with friends, I told Elvira that I couldn't eat the cake she baked for them. I did so in a very clumsy and self-centered way based on my problems, my limitations and my sorry state. She burst out crying just as I headed to the front door. She stood there in the hallway so helplessly in her beautiful summer dress, with a big pink cake with silver pearls, and tears streaming down her lovely cheeks. 'I know it's hard', she sobbed. 'But I can't change that. But it's hard for me, too. I've gone through hell and I want nothing more than to see you happy again. I want the old Frank back'. It hit me like a ton of bricks. It hurt so much to see her struggle. She had told me a couple of times about the nights she came home to a cold and empty bed, in those first months. I had tried to understand but was just too preoccupied with my own suffering to really grasp what she had gone through. She had kept herself so strong, so focused and so positive, that I had taken for granted how lucky I was to have her by my side. We went back inside and plonked down on the couch. After all these months, all that stress and exhaustion, all that pain and uncertainty suddenly came out. We cried together while holding each other as tight as we could.

It was that evening that I decided I wanted to stay positive for Elvira, while dealing with my setbacks. I began reading up on mental mindset, positive psychology and other research around how people cope with disappointments. I learned that my negativity was a common trait. Everyone has dark nagging doubts that creep in and slowly deplete their energy levels. In fact, evolution has wired us that way.

Why the brain prioritises negativity

Imagine this scenario: thousands of years ago, when food was scarce and people were completely dependent on the elements, lived Otto and Peter. Otto was an optimist. He saw the positive in everything and while he understood there were struggles and setbacks on his path, he assumed all would be ok. For Otto, the positives were always front of mind; he couldn't spend a lot of time ruminating about all the stuff that 'could' go wrong. Peter was more of a pessimist. He worried about not having enough firewood for the coming winter. He stressed about not having enough food and vividly remembered coming back empty-handed from their last hunting trip. While Otto kept telling him to cheer up, Peter worried about his chance of survival. He'd become so paranoid about a tiger he'd seen lurking around their camp that he lay awake thinking about building a barricade of tree trunks at their cave's entrance.

Now, when Otto and Peter encountered a setback, who would have been better prepared to deal with it? Who would have created a stronger shelter to fend off that tiger? Who would have collected enough food before winter? Who would have survived those conditions so that he had a chance to pass on his genes? Otto or Peter? Clearly, Peter's negative disposition prepared him well for these possible setbacks, and gave him a much higher chance to survive. Peter's offspring would have a similar inclination of prioritising negative over positive signals, increasing chances of their genes getting passed on.

The story of Otto and Peter is not that foreign to us today. We raise our children to be careful. We constantly alert their young brains to be aware of danger. We tell them not to climb on furniture or get too close to the stove or play with fire. When we get older, the warnings that 'life's tough' and 'you better work hard to prepare for tough times', is omnipresent. It's not only the cornerstone of religious messaging (burning in hell isn't exactly a positive reinforcement) but the cautionary message is repeated in folklore and stories in Western culture. Just think about *The Three Little Pigs*. The first pig prioritised playing over constructing his hut from straw. The second pig was a bit more serious and chose to go with sticks. The third pig was rather paranoid and build his hut from bricks. While the other pigs were having fun the 'big bad wolf' devoured the first two pigs but couldn't get to the third. The morale of such stories is clear: you can't go through life hoping everything is just going to be fine. It pays to be paranoid.

Now, back to the brain. After thousands of years of evolution, our brain is built with a greater sensitivity to unpleasant signals. In psychology, this is referred to as the brain's negativity bias. This notion explains that things of a negative nature have more impact on one's psychological state than something of a positive nature – even when it's of the same intensity. We are wired to put more value on the negative. A simple but worrying proof of this is the negative messaging in the media. News organisations' business models thrive on clicks and they've found that negative headlines draw more attention than positive ones. Politicians are well aware of this fact, too.

It is the reason why your brain is super alert when one of your teeth starts to play up. Even a small chip makes your tongue incessantly check what's wrong and send alarms to your brain. But after your dentist fixes it all up, your brain moves on to the next challenge like nothing happened. You went through all that negativity without getting any reward or other recognition of value. You even end up forgetting you had the setback in the first place! It's the main reason why I asked Max to remain my dentist for simple half-yearly check-ups. I find it comforting to sit in that chair thinking back to how bad it used to be. It makes me appreciate my current state and that creates perspective. The Perseverance Promotors and Destroyers listed later in this chapter will provide tips to help you feel that way, without seeing a dentist.

Another concept aligned with the bias of the brain is a concept known as 'loss aversion.' This aversion refers to people's tendency to prefer avoiding losses over acquiring equivalent gains. There are many research experiments that prove this point.

Have you heard of the one with the coin toss? Researchers asked people to join in an experiment with a random coin toss. If they guessed the outcome correctly, they won $5. However, if they'd guess incorrectly, they had to pay $5. They could also decide to pass which most people did. When researchers steadily increased the reward, they found that most people would participate when offered $10 for a correct answer, if the risk was they could lose $5 for an incorrect answer. People like the idea of winning $5, but the (factually equal) price to pay for losing isn't perceived to be sufficiently equal. In other words, we tend to feel a loss twice as severely as we experience a gain. We're wired to put more focus on the negative.

Negativity can be good if you have perspective

This also explains why, in sales, messaging that purely focuses on the positive (say, if you buy our solution you will create more efficiencies), tends to create interest but not necessarily an action. Negative messages (if you don't buy our solution and stick with the status quo, you will lose money) often make the brain prioritise a problem and act. I am not saying fear-based selling is good. It is much better (and more fulfilling) to focus on the positive reasons for acting. However, when a prospect is convinced your solution is the right one but starts procrastinating, negative messaging can help create urgency. Fear is a powerful motivator that gets people to act.[36]

Your sales pitch should focus on the negative before the solution (the positive) is presented. You first need to get buy-in to act, and fear does that better than stories about how awesome your solution is. Not creating such buy-in is the biggest reason for 'closed–no decision' losses. It's also why I started this book with the challenges we face in sales. I needed you to buy into the problem so you would continue reading.

For sales professionals, negative thoughts can be a good thing, too. For me, the fear of failing in sales is what often pulled me through dark periods. Like for Peter, the pessimistic caveman, it kept me focused; I wanted to avoid the bad outcome my brain was warning me about. But it was draining. I often got stuck in a negative mindset and wasted unnecessary energy for me and Elvira. Particularly in my younger years, I often missed the ability to balance the negative with the positive. When something bad happened, I'd lose perspective.

It's not like we can make fear, stress, or disappointments disappear. In fact, as we read in Chapter 4, we shouldn't want that – a certain level of stress can be good. But we need to be able to find perspective – to see the good *and* the bad – even when we're right in the middle of it. For me, that session with Max felt like the start of my recovery. There were two years of ups and downs that followed: I could see again, I could hear again, I could feel most of my face and eat steak again. But not everything turned out ok; my hand never healed so I will never be able to bend my wrist. I will need physiotherapy on my legs for the rest of my life to avoid pain. Oh, and Max sent me his invoice.

Finding perspective

In the hospital, I learned a trick that helped get me through the sessions with Max without too much stress. In the two months after I came out of the coma, I was on painkillers. Initially, they were administered intravenously: a continuous drip through an injection into the vein. Later on, I would take them orally: small cups of liquid and pills every couple of hours. The type of pain killers used depended on the severity of the pain. For mild pain, paracetamol, ibuprofen and other non-opioids tend to work well. For severe pain, like in my first months of recovery, stronger alternatives are called for: Oxycodone, Panadeine, Morphine and Endone. I was on the latter for a couple of weeks. These are opioids, a more modern term that only vaguely manages to distance itself from its origins, opium. They act directly on the central nervous system to decrease the feeling of pain.

Such strong painkillers can make you drowsy, tired, and confused. To top it off, opioids can cause hallucinations. Opioids, in particular, present an extra risk of addiction because they don't just reduce pain levels, they trigger a release of dopamine. As we saw earlier, dopamine is the hormone that makes you want to pursue things that lead to a rewarding outcome. Opioids are present in heroine and cause the addictive effect this illegal drug has. Too long a reliance on drugs like morphine does the same; it can create an addiction with some nasty consequences.

That's why nurses follow a carefully balanced regime that provides just enough relief but not too much to cause an addiction or other side effects. It's based on the Pain Assessment Tool.

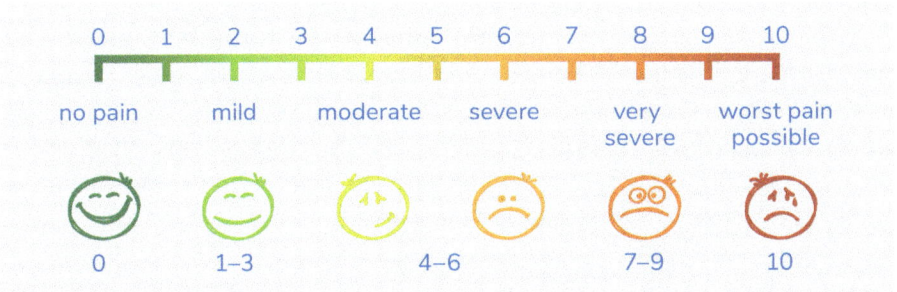

The Pain Assessment Tool

The nurse would ask me to point to the level of pain I was experiencing. Painkillers would then be administered depending on my answer. If the painkillers stopped working, I'd press the button to call the nurse and the whole process was repeated. Nurses were very clear on the risk of overdoing it; there never was a hurry to provide painkillers. I noticed that there was a formal process that required a second nurse to be present. Questions were asked clearly and carefully before a decision was made. Even during the first month, when I was dazed and confused, I understood that painkillers like morphine weren't administered lightly. It made me hold back on pressing the button. When the pain became unbearable, I'd hit it and hope the nurse would show up quickly. But here's the thing: when I hit that button, in my mind I was experiencing the worst pain possible, a clear ten. But when the nurses showed up with the Pain Assessment Tool and asked me to carefully think about my pain levels, it didn't feel that bad anymore. It wasn't the worst pain possible. It was severe, maybe very severe, but not the worst.

That simple process to step back and really think whether this is the worst possible situation, or whether it's not that bad, proved to be very powerful. Whenever I had another excruciating session with Max, I thought about the Pain Assessment Tool and not one single time, did I conclude that my situation was the worst possible. *This simple process of 'rationally scaling' the severity of the situation you're in, reduces the severity levels.*

It's a simple trick we can use in the world of sales, as you'll see later.

Super compensation

It's common in sales – particularly in companies with US headquarters – to motivate the troops with sports analogies. Sales leaders and trainers love referring to some athlete or coach who miraculously turns the game around and wins the game. They're heroes, and we seek to learn from, and get inspired by, their actions. I'm all for that. That is, as long as we are also aware of a key difference between the world of athletes and the world of sales professionals. We can't copy their approaches blindly into sales without addressing an immense difference – the practice of recovery.

Sport psychologist Jim Loehr, has been working with professional athletes for decades. He helped develop practices that drove people like Martina Navratilova, Pete Sampras and Monica Sales to peak performance. He then turned to the corporate world and concluded that some fundamental aspects of our behaviours don't allow for peak performance. 'Energy, not time, is our most precious resource,' he wrote in his book *The Power of Full Engagement* (2005). In the world of athletics, energy levels are carefully managed through a principle called Sports Periodisation. The aim of this systematic training regime is to reach the best possible performance in the most important competitions of the year. Athletes train in line with progressive cycles that build towards peak performance right when the need to perform is highest, like a season game, or an annual race or sports event. Whatever the time period, there are three phases that help an athlete get the best results within a competition cycle.

There's the *preparation phase*, which tends to cover 60–70 percent of the total cycle. This is the training phase that has specific and general preparations. Examples of specific preparations are perfecting a swimming stroke or timing the steps towards a hurdle jump. Generic preparation examples are swimming 200 meters or running on a treadmill or race track. The aim is to build the best technique and fitness levels to peak in the *competitive phase*. This is when the athlete's competence is tested. It involves further fine-tuning, like trying out new gear or pre-race meals, or adjusting race tactics. This phase ends with the actual competition. The third phase is the *transition phase*, which aims to let the body fully recover. This phase puts a lot of emphasis on psychological rest and relaxation. There's no competition, and often no training in this phase. The sole purpose is to provide a physical and mental vacation before the next cycle starts. There are also cycles within these cycles: a micro-cycle can be as short as a week. The macrocycle typically outlines the annual plan that works towards peaking for the main competition of the year.

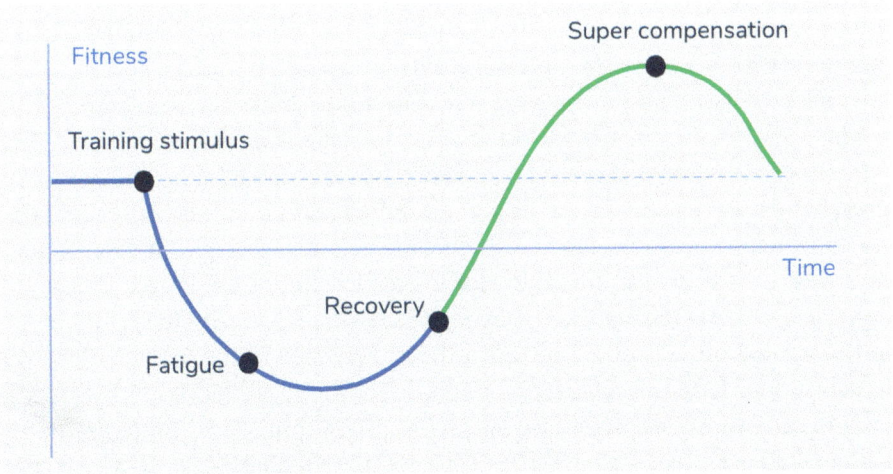

The importance of recovery

The transition phase, in which the athlete recovers, is vital to strong performance. Depending on the sport and athlete, this period can span several weeks or months. It's key to the athlete's success because the recovery phase is what will set the athlete up for *improved performance during the next cycle*. It allows the athlete to peak. In the world of athletes, this concept is called Super Compensation.

Without this recovery, performance will be hampered, and fitness levels and results for the next competition will be poorer.

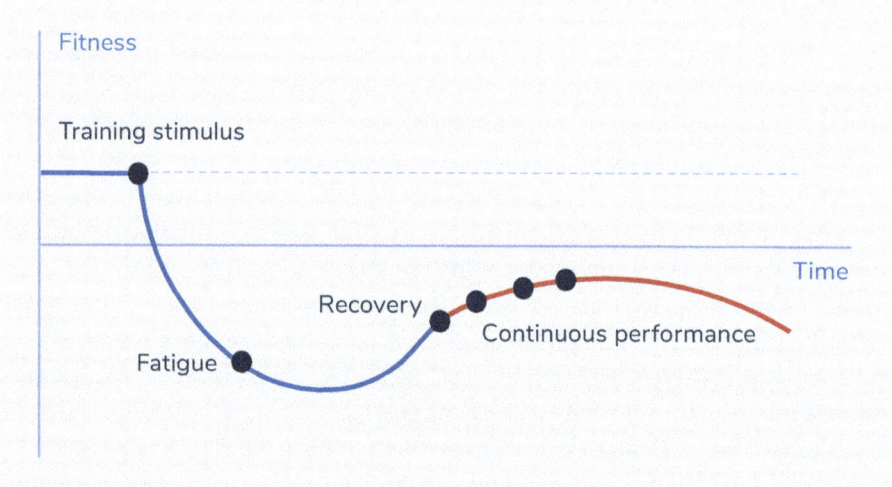

Lack of recovery hampers performance

The above illustrations show why comparing ourselves to professional athletes is problematic. Us sales professionals try to peak 24/7 for a whole year. We don't take weeks off after a big pitch. We don't take time to recover from a good or bad week. We don't take breaks between meetings – we just keep going. This is detrimental to our success. As Loehr says, 'we learned that the real enemy of high performance is not stress, which, paradoxical as it may seem, is actually the stimulus for growth. Rather, the problem is the absence of disciplined, intermittent recovery'.[37] In sales, this recovery should, of course, not be of a physical nature. Rather, the recovery of the *corporate* athlete should focus on the mental and emotional energy levels. We need to recover from energy depletion and help ourselves to regenerate mentally. This doesn't mean you need to take weeks off after every pitch or RFP submission. There are other ways to step away and recharge. The next section includes several tips on how to do just that.

Perseverance Promotors

1. Use the Pain Assessment Tool

Rather than letting your anxiety send you down the path of negativity, challenge yourself with a different way of thinking. Ask yourself two questions:

a. On a scale of 0–10, how well is <my week, this deal, my lead gen progress> going? (0 is the best, and 10 the worst.) This question shouldn't take much brainpower, even if you are at a particularly low point.

b. Why didn't I pick a higher number? Why is it not the *worst* possible?

Even though I've been applying this exercise for a couple of years, it still catches me off guard. It's like those two nurses are giving me a shake and forcing me to look at the full picture. Acknowledging that you're not stuck in the *worst* possible situation takes away a lot of your stress. To create this conscious awareness, print out the tool and hang it near your desk or above the toilet. You'll find a printable copy in my workbook.

2. Do the Anxiety Assessment

If your current situation is ok, but you're stressing out about what is ahead of you, ask yourself three simple questions: 'What's the worst that could happen? What's the *best* that could happen? What's *most likely* to happen?' Spend three minutes answering each question in a few sentences. Write it all down to make sure you complete your thoughts. Knowing I can easily get drawn into negativity unnoticed, I have printed out a one-pager, which you can find in my workbook, and have hung it above my desk. It shows three emojis: a cloud with a lightning bolt, a sun partially covered by a cloud, and a sun circled with beams. It reminds me to always be ready to step back and ask myself these questions and not get stuck into a dark spiral. I consciously have printed it rather than burying it in a folder on my laptop. I want that exercise to be top of mind the moment I sit down.

3. Count your blessings at home

Elvira and I decided to not let go, and even put some effort into holding onto that gratefulness we initially felt when I survived the accident. We decided to count our blessings, and you can do it too. At the end of the day, just before you turn off your bedside lamp, write down three things you appreciated that day. Positive things. Just three. Every day. It could be something simple like *the sun came out while I was waiting for the bus or that guy really made me laugh*, or realisations like *I am glad my tooth ache is over, or I am healthy*.

Sometimes, after a tough day in the office, I need to dig deep to find something positive, but in reality there are dozens of positive events that happen to us every day. It's easy to let the negative ones overshadow the positive. But they're there. Before you go to sleep, prioritise paying attention to those positive things. If you don't, when you wake up, your brain will naturally draw you to what it's been wired to focus on: problems and fear. If you make your brain focus on positive things before you put it in rest mode, over time, your brain will be able to find that perspective.

Studies show that people who express gratitude have a higher sense of wellbeing.[38] Although that isn't going to happen overnight, you can rewire your brain so stress levels come down. I didn't notice the impact of this exercise until months later, when Elvira said I am laughing more and sleeping better. I am more able to put problems into perspective now, and this simple exercise is the main reason. We've actually expanded this exercise to a special one on Sunday: I write three things Elvira did that I appreciated, and she writes three for me. Then we read them to each other. This helps us appreciate our relationship and it has brought us closer.

You'll find a template of this exercise in my workbook.

4.   Count your blessings at work

In sales, it's easy to only focus on the stuff that isn't going well, or the huge list of things that still needs to be fixed. Again, like in your personal life, find some time to acknowledge the things that are going well.

- Start each sales meeting with a quick *thank you* to someone who did a good job: an acknowledgement that more leads have come into the funnel, a new case study has been finalised or a new deal has been won.

- Throughout the week, find three things that prove you and your team are making progress, even if the mountains of work ahead of you seem to dwarf it. Send short emails to acknowledge such progress. Focusing on the positive creates perspective that helps build the energy needed to deal with the things that aren't necessarily going well.
- End each week by writing a quick email to yourself. Spell out three things you were happy with that week. *My presentation delivery is getting better. I am working on two key opportunities that I didn't have in my pipeline a month ago. Team work with the SCs has become a lot of fun.* It's a great way to end the week, but also a positive first email for you to read when you start your next week.

I'm aware that these practices can be perceived as pointless feel-good exercises. They're feel-good, but they're not pointless. They're also not quick wins. Over time, a constant balancing of the positives while acknowledging all the negatives will develop a stronger sense of perspective among team members.

5. Appreciate the small things throughout the day

Not being able to see for two months, not breathing through my nose or mouth for all those weeks, not hearing clearly, and not having a sense of touch in my face and hand have had a profound impact on me. There's not a day that goes by where I am not reminded of 'how it was'. This has created a change in my brain – I find joy in the small things now.

Luckily, you don't need to have experienced trauma to learn how to rewire your brain. Shirzad Chamine, Stanford lecturer and author of *New York Times* best-selling book *Positive Intelligence* (2012) has developed an app that helps you build 'your positivity muscle'. The program is focused on training your brain throughout the day, to help build the right neurological pathways to increase your mental fitness. Many of the two-minute exercises during the six-week program focus on creating an awareness of your senses, like listening, hearing, seeing and touching.[39] I highly recommend making that investment in your brain.

6. The Three Gifts Technique

In his book on positive intelligence, Chamine also suggest a simple trick to take the negativity out of a bad event. He calls it the Three Gifts Technique: Come up with three scenarios where your supposedly bad situation could turn into a gift and opportunity. Say you just lost a deal. Rather than getting all worked up and angry, ask yourself what three gifts could come out of this loss. Here's what one of my coachees recently came up with after losing a deal:

a. This could be the moment where AEs and SCs agree how to better prepare for a demo.

b. The partner that we went with has now seen our wares, and we could build on that momentum to find more opportunities with them.

c. This could make our product management organisation prioritise improving our User Interface (UI).

The aim is not to downplay the loss. Rather, the aim is to not get stuck in negative emotions, but enable you to find perspective that helps you switch to a more positive solution mode. For instance, I consciously decided I didn't want my accident to lead to 'no value'. Sharing what I've learned in this book, was a deliberate decision to turn that bad event into a gift. Without it, my accident would have been a waste of time.

7. Create a loss analysis

The power of win and loss analysis is discussed several times throughout this book; it's gold for many reasons. For one, when you write a loss report, incorporate a section on the above-mentioned three gifts. Did you learn that your presentation techniques need improvement? Will you insist on doing dry-runs for the next presentation? If you think a poorly coordinated demo led to the loss, what will you do to be better positioned next time? A loss will make you gain knowledge or insight, and if you are consciously striving to embrace those learnings, you'll come out stronger. *A loss is only a loss if you don't do anything with it.* Even if you can't find a single positive from that experience, could you use it as a trigger to improve another aspect of your life to at least make that loss worth it? Could you decide to eat more healthily or spend more time on sports, and tie that resolve to the loss to make it worthwhile?

8. Write it down

If you're uncomfortable sharing your emotions with friends or colleagues, write them down. Seeing your doubts in black and white often makes you step back to reflect on your perspective. Combined with the Anxiety Assessment, this can be a very powerful exercise. Just writing the sentence 'I am worried that ... will happen' is a great way to take the emotion out of things.

9. Find a coach

A good coach can help you create perspective when things go bad. They will ask questions that help you better understand your doubts and fears. Often, being asked to articulate your fear is enough to put it all in perspective or even find a solution. A coach can also keep you honest and hold you accountable to execute the things you say you're going to change. Even if your company doesn't want to foot the bill for a coach, consider investing in one yourself. Ask around and find a good one. I've been working with a coach myself and the return on investment is a no-brainer. I easily get ten times as much in incremental value as I pay my coach. If I'd had one in my early years as a sales rep, I'd have accomplished more with less energy. Get one.

Perseverance Destroyers

1. Don't keep your fears to yourself

Involve your manager and peers, and share your anxiety, your doubts or whatever negativity is leading your thinking. You'll find that everyone has such thoughts, including your manager and that other sales guy who always seems to be so positive. Not everyone will be responsive to such conversations, but more often than not, you'll find that they face similar mental challenges. Peter was their forefather too. Opening up this way will make you realise it's quite normal to be negative, especially in sales. Moreover, I've found that allowing vulnerability in the workplace increases team work. We're not just descendants of Peter, nor are we robotic sales machines – we're people.

2. Don't make 'deals won' your only measure of success

When thanking people, or otherwise acknowledging success, don't just focus on the deals won. You also want to motivate those reps who didn't close any deals – yet. Particularly in enterprise sales, deal cycles are long, so to keep everyone motivated, ensure there's a broader definition of success in your weekly sales call. Chapter 9 has a few practical ideas on how to do this without creating false praise.

3. Don't forget the team

Don't make the sales guy or girl who closed the deal the hero of all the work that marketing, the SDRs, and the SCs also did to make that happen. Make sure you share appreciation with people who weren't (directly) involved in that deal. This should be a consistent effort in sales meetings, but also (especially) in win reports that are shared with the broader company. It's not a chance for the sales person to beat their chest. It's a chance to acknowledge everyone who played a part.

4. Don't forget to recover

Elvira and I lock down our vacation times at the start of the year, and make sure we evenly spread them throughout the quarters. At a micro level, I am conscious about finding a few moments during the day to mentally recover from everything that is asked of me. Halfway through the morning, I head downstairs to grab a coffee from the friendly barista in the foyer. I could get free coffee from the office, but I love this micro break, for which I consciously block ten minutes in my calendar. At the end of every day, I walk 15 minutes to the bus station, with my phone on airplane mode and some funky music on my earphones. I could take the train, and do it in five minutes, but I love this time off. It helps me mentally recharge.

5. Don't make life too hard for your partner at home

If you have a partner at home, be nice to him or her. Don't keep your frustrations and doubts bottled up in the office and then let it all flow out when you come home. Being married to a sales professional can be an emotional roller-coaster in itself. Even it if feels good to vent, it's not fair on them. Try to find a good friend who's willing to listen and spare your partner. And even then, do some load balancing to avoid a single person getting the full brunt of your tribulations.

6. Don't limit yourself to your own tribe

It's easy to limit your group of friends to people with similar careers. But sales people often are extrinsically motivated, requiring you to put extra effort in exploring your intrinsic motivation by yourself. Instead, find and nurture friendships with people who are not in sales. One of my good friends is a teacher, and it is refreshing to hear what drives him. His world does not consist of commission cheques or promotions when he does well. He was a teacher at 25, and will be a teacher when he's 50; he needs to find his own rewards on that journey. I love catching up with him and have come to appreciate his fresh point of view and motivations, which are way more intrinsic than those of the average sales professional.

As a sales manager, you should aim to form a culture of different perspectives, too. Diversity in age is one way to serve that purpose. Another friend of mine was looking to hire a CSM team manager to deal with the key account group, and decided to go with a person who stood out because of her age. She was a 62-year- old senior manager who could have retired, but wanted to do something more meaningful. My friend initially felt he took a risk due to a possible culture clash, but soon realised the fresh perspective from the new hire was exactly what the team needed. 'It has completely changed the dynamics in my team, in a good way.' he told me. 'Her age-based seniority gives her the authority to take the heat out of discussions; she can easily call BS on people without offending them, and is better at planning than anyone I've ever hired.'

It might not necessarily be difficult to find talent in the older age brackets of the population. In Australia, people over the age of 65 represent the single fastest growing age group securing work.[40]

Chapter 7: Plan as best you can

Whoever said 'failing to plan means planning to fail' got it right. As you will see in this chapter, I could not have recovered from my accident without a plan. But before I share how I planned my recovery, and how we can apply that in sales, I'd like you to meet Dr Shane. I've talked about him before, but never really introduced him properly. He was the facial reconstruction surgeon who rebuilt my face. Dr Shane is big on planning.

Meet Shane, my facial reconstruction surgeon

The helicopter that lifted me off Long Reef Beach brought me straight to the emergency department of Royal North Shore Hospital. There, initial MRI scans revealed several broken ribs and a pelvic fracture. It was clear there was a lot more damage but these findings would receive all the attention over the next few days. It's often not the fractures themselves that determine the chances of survival but the complications that can arise. A broken rib could mean a damaged liver or spleen. A pelvic fracture can rupture the bladder, which in turn creates internal complications. And the sharp ends of any broken bone can create internal wounds leading to internal bleedings, which are hard to stop. In my case, most vital organs seemed to have been spared. However, there was a considerable amount of internal bleeding around the pelvic area. Elvira, who had been rushed to the hospital by one of my kite buddies, was told that the first 24 hours would determine my chances of survival.

Scans from the second day showed the internal bleeding had stopped, so attention shifted to the bigger picture. More scans were done on my face and brain. Dr Shane was on duty that day and would take charge of the facial reconstruction efforts. Dr Shane obtained his medical degree after a six-year undergraduate program. He did some years of surgical training at a hospital and then decided to specialise in plastic and reconstructive surgery – a five-year training program. This was more than enough training to reorganise my face with 42 screws, 11 titanium plates and a new eye socket. A year later, I visited Dr Shane to understand exactly what he had done and how he went about doing his work. The scans intrigued me but were too 'unreal'. I wanted to hear from the guy who did the work.

Dr Shane walked me through the process. First, he had to establish what was wrong. He performed scans from different angles on the face to understand the damage. X-rays showed how the face had been broken into seven separate pieces, a 'Le Fort 3' fracture, he called it. The lower jaw snapped in half and dislocated. The upper jaw, which holds the upper teeth, had completely separated from the nose and cheekbones. The cheekbones had broken away from the side of the skull. The scans also revealed the biggest complication: the right eye socket 'had been crushed like a hard-boiled egg'. CT scans were taken to investigate the soft issue, particularly around the eye and the nerves. Dr Shane initially expected that even if the optical nerve (which connects the eye to the brain) wasn't overly damaged by the mess of sharp 'eggshell pieces', the operations he would be performing could do further damage. 'I needed to move the eye aside to get access to put in a new eye socket, and it's this stretching that typically creates long term complications.'

Then, he got the trauma team to coordinate with the other teams. More scans, including MRIs, were done to understand the impact of the haemorrhage in the brain. It wasn't Dr Shane's field or responsibility; he would take guidance from the neurology team as he planned his procedures. He also needed the Ear, Nose and Throat team (ENT) to determine how to keep me breathing. The swelling in my face blocked my airways, so they performed a tracheostomy. They cut a hole in the windpipe just under my Adam's apple, jammed in a tube and hooked me up to an oxygen machine. I'd be breathing through that tube for more than a month. Another team was responsible for my hand. Another one for my pelvis. All in all, seven teams were involved.

The first challenge Dr Shane encountered was resources. He needed several of those teams together in one room to start planning for the facial reconstruction. Agendas had to be freed up, and operations on other patients had to be rescheduled. And that wasn't easy. *The planning meeting itself took a whole day.* All teams involved had to review the scans and assess how to put it all back together, and in what order. 'We first had to decide how we would open it all up. In your case, we agreed we could make incisions around the eyes and from within the mouth. The usual procedure to reconstruct a face is from the top down – we work from the forehead down.' They attach the cheekbones to the forehead near the eyes, the nose to the cheekbones, and then the jaw to the nose – in that order. But Dr Shane worried about complications with the eye, which would only be revealed once he opened up my face. 'Scans only reveal so much. We always encounter surprises and we take guidance from the neurological team to ensure we don't damage nerves'. Therefore, he also created a *plan B* – a more unusual reconstruction from the bottom up, which he ended up executing. First, he installed plates to join the broken lower jaw together. Then he'd place screws in the top jaw and connect it to the lower jaw with wires. He would link the upper jaw with plates to the cheekbones. The big challenge was how to replace the eye socket – the spot where the face connects to the forehead.

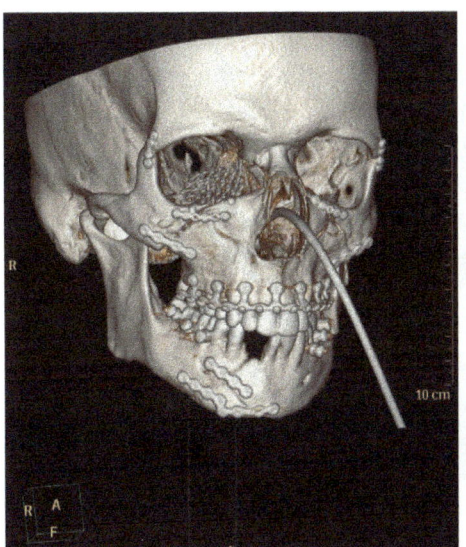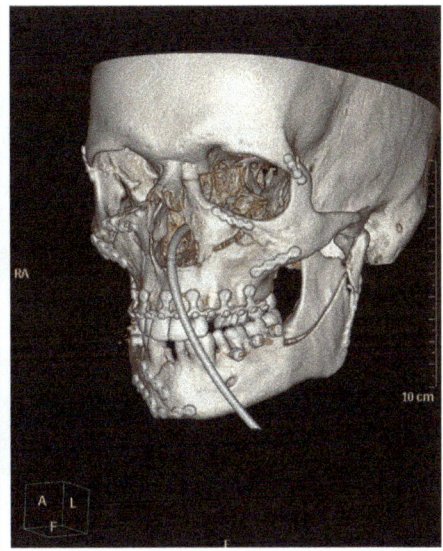

CT scans of my face after the operations. The white line is the feeding tube.

Dr Shane showed me the detailed 3D X-rays overlaid with drawings of each plate and screw he was going to put in. 'The teams of specialists discussed the best placement for each screw from a strength, muscle and nerve perspective. We didn't want a single unnecessary screw or plate in there; each little screw bears the risk of infection or complications later.' He also explained how he worked with a specialist who would be working on the new eye socket, in parallel, while Dr Shane and his team were operating. 'Once we could see what we could really play with, she created a mould from plastic, which I fitted in place of the original eye socket while not trying to damage the eye.' There were some back and forth adjustments until it finally fit. The specialist then started to create a titanium eye socket from the mould.

Dr Shane remained working on all the other stuff, and by the time he was ready to join the two parts of the face, he was handed the titanium eye socket. He put it in place, screwed it tight and then joined the two pieces of my face together. In the scan, you'll see all the rectangular plates, as well as the titanium eye socket – the mesh in the top left corner. All in all, 11 people were involved over a 12-hour operation. Some roles, like the nurses responsible for monitoring my vital signs, were rotated every couple of hours. Other people were on standby to take over during lunch.

Then I asked him about all the forms Elvira was asked to sign before every operation. These forms provided a long list of all possible complications, risks, and things that could go wrong during and after the operation. I wanted to talk about those risks, and how Dr Shane would plan for them. 'So much can go wrong in such a complex operation; we can't leave things to chance. We needed to plan,' he said. 'That's why we needed a *plan B*. We need back-ups to ensure we can deal with all the surprises that come our way. Because we'll only have *everyone* in the room once. We only want to open you up once; we can't just come back a day later and open all those wounds again. We have one shot at it, really.'

Hearing Dr Shane talk made me think back to those big sales presentations at the end of a long sales cycle. You only have *all* the decision makers in the room once. You have one shot at it, really. Yet, I often see sales reps go into these crucial meetings insufficiently prepared. They leave things to chance. How, I wondered, could we be better at planning in sales?

Back to zero

You worked super hard to hit your target, but this year, the sheer number of unexpected ups and downs made it near-impossible. Your key sponsor at that mega deal you've been working on resigned from his job, pushing your deal into next year, at best. For opportunities that you did manage to close, prospects threw you so many last-minute curve balls, that your whole legal team unfriended you on Facebook. They even ignored your outreaches on LinkedIn. Your best solution consultant resigned and joined a competitor, and although the new guy has potential, that wasn't exactly what you needed in the last quarter. To top it off, management introduced new pricing and discount approval processes that make you wonder what they mean when they tell you to be more customer-centric.

Still, somehow, at the end of the roller-coaster ride that we call Q4, you made it. You hit target. Like Tom Hanks' incomprehensible dodging of bullets, grenades, shrapnel and rockets amid the complete chaos on Omaha Beach, you made it and you're still in one piece. Phew! Then, in the first week of the new financial year, it slowly sinks in. That shitty inner-voice you've been suppressing during your well-deserved, but all-too short, break, gets louder. When the invite for SKO lands in your inbox, there's no way around it: you have to face it. You. Are. Back. To. Zero. Yep, your YTD bookings are exactly $0. Your new target looks 'pretty big and improbable' and you're not sure where to start. Welcome to the new financial year.

My 'big and improbable' goal

That first big meeting I had with Max, my dentist, put me in a dark place that, in a way, resembled the first week of the new financial year. I had fought so hard through all the ups and downs, just to get to zero. This was the start of a complex recovery journey; I had been told that numerous operations still lay ahead, as well as several months of hospital check-ups, and at least a year of physiotherapy. But that session with Max, where he outlined the two-year plan for the repair of my teeth – that was something else. I felt like I was standing in a deep hole and had to come to terms with the fact that I had a long journey ahead of me. I made it home, but didn't feel like celebrating. A bit like SKO.

I wanted to get to the end. I wanted to *Get My Old Life Back*. I just wanted what I had before the accident. That felt, well ... 'pretty big and improbable'. But that all changed once I decided to create a plan. My plan to *Get My Old Life Back*. Intuitively, I applied a model I had been using throughout my sales career: SMART planning.

SMART explained

I learned about the concept of SMART goals early on in my career. My first ever sales boss had a project management background. He wasn't your typical sales boss, but I was too young and naive to have an issue with his lack of sales experience. His seniority made me very receptive to anything he could teach me. And luckily, that turned out to be a good thing. He was the first person to explain how to go about breaking down, big, seemingly unmanageable tasks – like reaching my first ever sales quota – through SMART goal setting.

The acronym originates from the 1960s, when numerous theories around organisational performance and goal setting took shape. The letters stand for Specific, Measurable, Attainable, Relevant and Timely, and the purpose of it is to help you create verifiable trajectories towards a certain objective. SMART goal setting not only brings structure and traceability to your goals, it helps create transparency and acts as a 'reality check' to keep you honest. Let's go into each of them in more detail. I'll explain them in the context of my own personal goal, and after that, I will bring it back to sales so you can apply this approach in your role.

Specific

Specific means you need to *specifically* define what you want to achieve.

Get My Old Life Back is not exactly a tangible goal that can be measured; it had to be more specific. So, I defined it into specific things I should be able to do, both physically and mentally. I decided it had to entail walking, swimming, getting back to my old body weight, driving my car, weight lifting, and lots more. Elvira helped to create a spreadsheet. We typed my goals one by one in the rows of column A. Column A represented the very specific targets that, combined, represented having my old life back. They built up chronologically, starting with walking. The last line item was 'working full time'. It would represent me being completely healthy again, physically and mentally, and leading a life without the relentless stream of hospital visits – just like before the accident.

Breaking down my goal this way made the path ahead clearer. I could see the underlying activities I wanted to work towards if I wanted to feel like my old self again. But something was wrong with that specific definition. The last line item bothered me. While I was in hospital, the company I worked for was taken over by a much larger one. I would never have applied for a job with this company; I never saw myself as a 'big corporate' guy. I was worried that my autonomy would be limited in such an environment. Most of all, I feared my learning curve would flatten in such a big company; it would definitely not be anything like the startup experience I had enjoyed so much before. There would be too much process, which would likely hinder my growth and development as a sales professional. Also, it was clear that a lot of my colleagues weren't up for the transition; many had already resigned before I even left the hospital. Was I really going to work on this for a year or longer if that was the finish line? Was that really what was going to keep me motivated to persevere when I faced setbacks? I needed something more aspirational. I needed something more aligned with my drivers, my True North.

Kitesurfing had always been my everything. It had been part of my life for over 15 years and I'd never imagined a life without it. Obviously, it didn't seem like a viable option anymore. Soon after that session with Max, I had taken pictures of my kite gear and put it all up for sale on eBay. I had no intention to use that gear ever again. I did hope I was going to find some other hobby, but had no idea what that would be. I simply didn't know what my physical capabilities would be after I healed. However, I soon found myself stuck in a loop that prevented me from making any headway. I became much more careful and doubtful about my abilities as I was looking for proof of progress without defining it. And because I couldn't find it, I didn't know what to aim for. I was trapped in a spiral that quickly reduced my confidence levels.

Elvira watched me struggle and waste energy like a rudderless ship. She realised that Frank without confidence wouldn't be the Frank she married. It was Elvira who brought up the topic of kitesurfing, half a year after the accident. 'I don't like the idea of you kitesurfing again, but I like the idea of you sitting at home like a defeated old man even less,' she said after a particularly dark day. 'Why don't you give yourself the objective to kite again, just so you can show yourself that you can do it?'

My initial reaction was a clear 'no'. I wouldn't do that to her, and moreover, didn't even feel like I was ever going to be capable of it. But that was exactly her point. Kitesurfing would represent a tangible activity towards my goal. Most of all, it wasn't just a 'nice to have so I can enjoy life again', it represented a very relevant True North aspect of my life, which would help me get my confidence back. I needed this specific goal to reach my overall goal. I had to get back on the horse. Not doing so would represent defeat, with all too many negative consequences for my mental state.

As I learned throughout my recovery, more than any other goal I had set myself, kitesurfing embodied *Get My Old Life Back*. It represented not being defeated but, most of all, it was measurable. If I could kitesurf again, it meant 'I would be me' again.

I added a last line item in the spreadsheet. It simply read 'kitesurfing'.

Measurable
Simply saying you want to kitesurf doesn't make it a plan though. How do I know if I have reached that goal of kitesurfing again? While it might sound pretty specific, it needs a quantifiable element to make it indisputably true. Is it just a one-minute run in super light winds and flat water, or is it a two-hour session in 20 knots of wind in the surf at Long Reef where I had the accident? I decided for the latter. Having such a clear goal would make reaching it undeniably true.

I did the same for all the other goals. Each and every one had a quantifiable element to it, so I was crystal clear on my aim. Soon, that spreadsheet became too big to handle on my laptop (too much scrolling back and forth), so Elvira printed it on two A3 sheets and hung them up on our bedroom wall. It gave me one comprehensive overview of all my goals, from walking, to driving, to being able to swim, to fixing my teeth, to finding a new job and so much more. Interestingly, just defining my goals at that level, and seeing them so clearly in front of me, made them seem easier to reach.

The *Get My Old Life Back* goal felt too dramatic, too 'big' to really own and believe in, but deconstructing this goal into measurable parts made it specific and easier to reach. The specifics of measurability also carry another purpose: we can keep track of how we're progressing and determine if it needs adjustments. As you'll read in Chapter 8, being able to measure progress is an important factor in helping you develop perseverance. Progress itself becomes the motivation, even if the end goal hasn't been reached yet.

Attainable

The A stands for Attainable, but Achievable is often used as well. Whatever my goal, I had to believe it was possible for me to reach. I knew it wouldn't be easy to *Get My Old Life back*, but I was highly motivated to accomplish it. Of course, that didn't mean I was certain I would reach my goal. Doctors said my pelvis would 'most likely' be strong again, but my wrist 'definitely' wouldn't. When I brought up the topic of kitesurfing with Dr Susan, her face had this particular look. It was a look that sat between *incredulousness and are you crazy?* I got that from friends and family, too. But, like the doctors, they didn't kite. I'd been accustomed to that look from before the accident and had decided that people who don't understand the joy it gives me, simply can't assess whether it's achievable, or even worth the effort.

Clearly, this is not as black and white as the more objective elements of SMART goals. Whether you think something is achievable comes down to your own beliefs. I believed it would be possible to kitesurf again because I had done it before. From a rational point of view, I had the time and the resources. The Australian medical system readily provides access to the best doctors and surgeons, and my medical insurance covered me for extras like speech therapy and physiotherapy. Most of all, I had support from other people, including my wife, friends and family. They were not only there to help out with practicalities like driving to the doctor, they also provided mental support during the darker periods. All of that made me believe my goals were attainable.

That didn't mean I believed I could do *anything*. Elon Musk believes landing a rocket on Mars is achievable and while I believe he can do that, it's a bridge to far *for me* to accomplish. When you decide on attainable goals, don't be unrealistic, but don't be too timid either. Don't automatically discount things that seem hard. Don't convince yourself that you can't/won't/mustn't/aren't able to do things. Popular psychology refers to such negative presumptions as self-limiting beliefs. These are assumptions you have about yourself (or the world around you) that hold you back.

Limiting beliefs can be your biggest enemy, not just in sales but in how you live your life. There are millions of people who don't maximise their potential simply *because they aren't trying*. They convince themselves that there's no point. As I would learn during the long trajectory of physiotherapy, it's one of the most frustrating human traits that physiotherapists have to deal with; they know what the body is capable of and often have a realistic view of what a patient can achieve. But often it's the patient who doesn't believe it, and as a result, it's the patient who effectively lowers the bar. They end up accepting a lesser quality of life with more pain or limited movement, simply because they have told themselves it's no use, or they stopped trying and prioiritised TV binge-watching over their physio exercises. Limiting beliefs are detrimental to your ability to develop perseverance. You need to have the right mindset to keep yourself honest and to create a fair chance of achieving success. As you'll see, one of the great things about working out your SMART goals is they will help you with that mindset and avoid limiting beliefs.

Relevant

The R stands for Relevant, but is often classified as Realistic. The camp that uses Realistic isn't exactly wrong when they say you need to assess the resources you have to determine if your goal is feasible at all. However, I think those aspects of your goals should be covered under the Attainable (or Achievable) heading; there's just too much overlap between Realistic and Attainable. Whatever you use, make sure you incorporate Relevance when you determine your SMART goals. Singling this out as an aspect to review simply ensures that you consider the motivation behind a goal.

Overall, the autonomy I would regain in *Getting My Old Life Back* made this goal obviously relevant. The kitesurfing goal represented the ultimate motivation that incorporated my drivers for autonomy and mastery. When Elvira said she wanted me to be the *Frank* she married, and not a defeated old man, my goal had purpose – it wasn't just about me. Elvira's quality of life was also at stake. Once that sunk in, I became more motivated to persevere. That's before I even started trying. I simply knew that what I was striving for would be worth the blood, sweat, and tears I would encounter.

Timely

As I've already described, putting an actual date to a goal makes it a lot more specific. Saying that I want to kitesurf again without specifying a date, made it ambiguous; therefore, not so SMART. Deadlines do not only provide account-ability, they motivate, too. If you want to reach your target in 12 months, what will you commit to doing this week? If you want to become a CEO in ten years' time, what will you aim to accomplish in the next year? The easiest way to tackle these questions is to start with the end and work backwards.

I set myself a goal to kitesurf for two hours on Long Reef Beach in 20 knots of wind on the 1st of January 2015. Long Reef is where the accident happened, so it was indisputably the purest way, physically and mentally, to test if I'd be my old self again. Working backwards from that date, I deducted the following. If I wanted to be strong enough to be in the waves at Long Reef by the 1st of January, I had to be able to handle 15+ knots wind in the safe confines of Fisherman's Beach (which is flat water), on the 1st of December. Working further back from that, my first session in the water, just for a couple of minutes, had to be on the 1st of November, with light winds around 12–15 knots. Fisherman's Beach would be ok for that. The idea was to launch the kite, get wet, body drag away from shore and get back to the beach without actually kitesurfing. I formulated that goal with a mental test in mind: would I feel safe enough to go into the very environment that nearly killed me? Finally, the 1st of October would be the day I would launch a kite and fly it on the beach to see if I'd have enough strength in my arms and hands.

Here's the interesting thing that happened after I broke down that goal so methodically. Just looking at the cells on my spreadsheet made it feel very *plausible*. Rather than having this pretty big and improbable goal hanging there like a dark cloud, it suddenly didn't feel that difficult anymore. I could easily picture that first step. I could see myself standing on the beach with a kite on the 1st of October. This allowed me to feel optimistic about following through on the three steps that would follow. Breaking it down like that, with specific dates, made it all seem within my reach, which created a can-do mindset, even though I could hardly walk without crutches when I plotted this plan.

In short, good planning helps you build perseverance in three ways. First, it creates a course of action that takes you to your goal. A finished plan 'guides' you towards your intended outcome. The second value lies in the exercise itself – making the plan. Thinking through what you want to accomplish and how to get there is half the battle. It creates clarity. Clarity creates motivation that will help you persevere. Finally, it will give you shorter term objectives. Rather than having a 'big and improbable' goal, breaking it down will help you establish more immediate results. The stuff you can start on, *today*.

Perseverance Promotors

1. Create a Sales Productivity Model
If you've just received your target and think it's 'big and improbable', break it down using the following example:

Patrick has a target of $1m. From past deals, he knows that the average deal size is roughly $100k. That means he needs to win ten deals. His CRM tells him the company has been winning one-in-three qualified deals. So Patrick needs 30 of them. He can also see that 75 percent of opportunities that came from the SDRs were qualified. So he needs 40 stage 1 (pre-qualified) opportunities. SDR data shows that to find a stage 1, he needs to set up three first meetings. In other words, 120 first meetings are required to get to Patrick's target. SDR data further shows that he needs seven outreaches to get to one first meeting. Patrick sits down with the SDRs to agree on how they're going to spread their activity to get to 840 outreaches for his territory. They'll decide on an industry-led push: every month, they'll focus on either finance, retail, or tech to get to the required activity. Every week, they sit down to discuss progress and fine-tune their approach and messaging.

Numbers will never be perfect, but that's not the aim. Activity drives opportunity and breaking it down like this creates the awareness that will form the basis of *action and accountability*. You'll find a template of a Sales Productivity Model in my workbook.

2. Log everything in your CRM
Defining your goals in detail through the SMART framework helps develop perseverance but it doesn't *guarantee* an outcome. In fact, we're

going to be wrong. We think we'll win one in three deals, but at the end of the year, one in four turned out to be more accurate. We thought we needed to make 20 calls to find one opportunity, but 12 turned out to be the magic number. You need to believe that the numbers and dates are at least close to correct for SMART planning to be helpful. And the only way you'll get that confidence is by measuring what's actually happening. Don't merely use you CRM as an expensive forecasting tool or address book. Use it to log every single activity you perform so you can refine your SMART plan every quarter. This includes all emails, calls, and other quantifiable activities you broke down in your plan. You want to get clear confirmation whether the activity you planned for, at the lowest level, leads to outcomes at a higher level. The more data you have to back up your productivity model, the more confident you'll be.

3. Refine

A key element of SMART goals is represented in the A (Attainable). You need to believe that what you're aiming for is actually possible. By breaking down your 'big and improbable' goal into specific activities, it could very well be that you really can't see yourself, or your sales team, executing on (all) these activities. As you start looking at the data in your CRM, you might wonder if you can actually reach your ultimate goal – your target. Here are a few ideas on how to tackle this challenge.

You have a $1m target and your average deal size is $20k. That means you need to close 50 deals – more than a deal a week. But sales cycles are 3–6 months, and even if you win 33 percent of deals, you'll have too many balls in the air to get to a successful outcome by year end. You might conclude your target is too high, but your manager won't readily change this. However, if you show them your SMART thinking and the numbers on which you have based your conclusion, you can have a much more constructive conversation. Is there a way to shorten the deal cycle? Could we involve SCs earlier in the process and get to demo stage quicker? Or, if you think you'll close two deals a month at best, the only way in which you would make your target is if you increase the average deal size. Can you come up with a plan to only target accounts that are more likely to pay $40k a year? A lot of SaaS products are usage based, so you'd have to segment your territory into those accounts that are likely to be heavy users, and have bigger budgets. Refer to the ABC segmentation framework I discussed in Chapter 4.

If there is no way you can get the average deal size up, the only way to make your target is to get more leads. Can you get more support from the SDRs or marketing? It'll be in your manager's (and your whole team's) interest to work towards goals that are attainable; it will avoid surprises early on. Working out and articulating your sales planning along the SMART framework tends to open the eyes of the broader sales organisation. No one wants to blindly work on something that technically can't lead to success. Discussions resulting from this could focus on increasing the number of leads, but also on increasing win rates. Do we need more training to get our win rate above 30 percent? Should we be more selective about what we let in at the top of the funnel and change our qualification process, as described in Chapter 4?

Sales organisations with a predominantly inbound model often have limited control of what leads come in. Marketing does its thing, and sales is too busy responding to the inbounds to free up time to create an alternative pipeline (for example, outbound based). If you see your average deal size going down every year, it might be time to take control and be more selective about which and what accounts you want to be selling to. An insight like this could help redefine the collaboration between marketing and sales, or even shift activities towards an outbound model. Again, using the SMART framework will help you proactively trigger these insights and conversations, rather than being disappointed at the end of a year that never was going to be successful.

4. Plan your call or meeting

It's hard calling into your prospect to get their attention, particularly when you've never met them. Such calls are important steps that will determine how your deal progresses and whether it'll lead to success. Yet, SDRs and sales reps typically don't plan these pivotal moments. They simply pick up the phone, or show up for a 'catch-up' to see where it takes them. Instead, spend 2 minutes before your call or meeting to work out the following:

1. **Goal.** What specifically is it that you want out of this call (or meeting)? By the end of the call, will you have agreed to meet face to face? Will you have buy-in for another call? Will you have uncovered specifics for technical discovery?
2. **What questions will I ask?** Write down the questions you will be

asking to get to that outcome. Think them through in advance, so you don't have to improvise – you'll come across more structured and confident and it will keep you calm when the plan doesn't go as you had hoped.

3. **What might the prospect ask you?** Think through the likely questions or objections that will be thrown at you. Then write down your answers so you don't have to do this on the fly.

4. **The close.** How will you conclude the call? Often, the last minutes of a call or meeting are rushed and lead to ambiguous agreement about next steps. Prepare for it and tie it back to the goal to ensure you're booking progress.

Also, make sure you have prepared a script in case the call goes to voicemail. Don't be caught out. Use it as another opportunity to communicate your key messages for that stage of the cycle. Always leave the ball in your court. Don't ask the customer to call you back, instead, end the voicemail by saying you'll call again soon. If you're calling someone's mobile, don't leave a voicemail as people find retrieving voicemails cumbersome nowadays. Send a text message instead, and again, leave the ball in your court.

You will find an easy to use pre-call/meeting template in my workbook.

5. Plan your RFP response

The accumulation of weeks (or in enterprise sales, months) of meetings, often ends in a request for a proposal, an RFP. In enterprise sales, these tend to be formal processes aimed at giving all vendors a fair chance and avoid unethical activities at the customer's side. It's not uncommon for submissions to cover numerous sections from the company background, to the solution, the integration, the implementation, the financials, the legal framework, and compliance to industry and environmental standards. Submissions often require weeks of effort and easily end up exceeding 50 pages – sometimes more than double that. With smaller, less formal, prospects, or in commercial sales cycles, proposals could be just a handful of pages covering fewer topics. Proposals take effort, unless you're selling high velocity, small deal size, solutions (ARR < \$20k). They need to be tailored to the prospect's brief and require input from SCs, professional services, legal, and sales ops. Unless your organisation has dedicated bid managers, the role of the AE shifts here to a project manager. The AE needs to take the lead and plan towards a high-quality proposal that is submitted on time.

I sometimes come across AEs who blame the losing of a deal on the poor quality of the proposal from the SC. My advice to them is simple. Step up. It's your deal. It's in your interest to submit a high-quality proposal, so it's you who needs to coordinate it. To limit the overheads of this project management work, create a simple template project plan. For small proposals, it could be a simple Google Sheet. For million dollar bids, I suggest you use project management tools like Microsoft Project. Divvy up who will be responsible for which section and be clear on the dependencies. For instance, pricing can only begin when the scope section has been completed. Discount approval can only be chased after that.

You know these processes take time, so start with the end and work back from the submission date. Create deadlines for each item and get buy-in from the contributors to avoid last minute rushing. All too often, it's this rushing that leads to cutting corners and poor-quality proposals. It's a shame to see weeks or months of great sales work fall apart due to poor project management and planning. In sales, if you fail to plan, you plan to lose. You'll find a filled in example of a project plan for an enterprise RFP submission in my workbook.

6. Plan your presentation

Sales might not come close to the life-threatening situations Dr Shane usually deals with in his line of work, but that doesn't mean we shouldn't be as meticulous. Sales presentations often play a determining factor in the outcome of an evaluation process. After all these meetings and proposals, it comes down to a presentation where you show how your solution helps solve the business problems of your prospect. Yet again, sales reps often plan poorly for these important sessions; instead, they show up and hope for the best. Particularly if multiple people are involved on either side, it's important to carefully plan what you intend to do and avoid surprises.

- Again, start with the end. What will you have accomplished when everybody walks out of that room? I once had a manager who joined me in an important meeting with a key prospect. I planned it well with the SC, but omitted to walk my manager through the plan. He surprised me by claiming the last minutes of the meeting and asking the client for their business even though they had already explained to me, in detail, what their evaluation process was. He also surprised the prospect who didn't like his advances and wasn't too keen on meeting him again. I lost the deal but only I was to blame for this unfortunate outcome.

- Develop your presentation in chapters, for instance:
  a. Introduction. Everybody in the room is to introduce themselves.
  b. Summary of the problem. A summary of the key objectives and pain points.
  c. Our solution. Architecture, integrations, demo.
  d. Proofpoints. Case studies and customer stories.
  e. Close. Q&A, and agreement for next steps.
- Determine how much time each 'chapter' should take. Be particularly clear on how much time you want to set aside for the close. All too often, those important final moments are used as the buffer for delays in the preceding hour, which is a huge missed opportunity to get buy-in on what happens next.
- Work back and agree who will present what and how many minutes each slide gets.
- Agree who will answer questions. Create categories (technical, support, pricing, client success, competition, implementation etc.) and assign owners to avoid eager colleagues inadvertently stealing the show. They may say things they shouldn't or simply spend too much time on one topic (which then eats into your close time).

My workbook has an example of a presentation plan that can be used as a template.

7. Create a Mutual Success Plan

We've touched on this topic in Chapter 3. Create a plan that helps guide you *and the customer* to a success without surprises. Avoid calling it a 'close plan' and start with the end – the point where the customer starts seeing value. Work backwards from there and see if timelines are realistic. If your team struggles with forecasting and keeps pushing the deal out, a 'mutual success plan' for all deals will drive a huge amount of improvement. It will also provide transparency on poorly qualified deals that would have ended as 'no decisions'. See my workbook for an example that I shared with the customer.

8. Do role plays

Dr Shane spent over a dozen years in a classroom before he decided to go into medicine. Do you think his first operation would have been on a real patient? Of course not. In his field of speciality, surgeons build their experience by performing operations on synthetic dummies and cadavers before they are allowed to treat actual patients. Anatomical models and 3D simulators are used during the training and planning procedures. They 'sit in' on operations performed by experienced surgeons to observe what happens in the real world and build familiarity. When it was time to do the real thing, Dr Shane would have been well prepared, in terms of skills as well as mindset.

In sales, we should do the same. Practise your pitch on a colleague first. Find a peer for that cold call, ditch the awkwardness and feel free to make mistakes without paying the price. If you don't have team mates you can practise on, ask a friend, or record your own pitch and evaluate it yourself afterwards. Whatever you do, don't let your first shot be the real thing.

9. Do dry runs

For important presentations, do internal dry runs. It is outright irresponsible to have a multi-person sales team work on a deal for six months to then let it all depend on an unrehearsed one- to two-hour presentation. It's the riskiest move sales people make and the one that's easiest to avoid. Simply get the team together and rehearse the pitch and the demo. Use the presentation agenda to create awareness within the team that 'going off course' will create timing issues later on. Agree on signals you'll give to get other presenters to accelerate. Agree on who answers what type of questions to avoid 'eager talkers' getting all the air time. Finally, decide who takes notes and who studies the body language of the audience members of your prospect.

10. Be patient

All that planning has a valuable by-product: it'll create patience. If I hadn't planned my recovery and merely 'aimed' to go kitesurfing again, I would have lost a lot more mental energy getting there. Not having the guidance of a plan creates anxiety, simply because you're not sure what's ahead of you. In sales, there's often this notion that everything needs to happen fast. We don't like to see meetings postponed, sales cycles taking longer than we expected, or deals getting pushed out. Often, the resulting anxiety is self-inflicted because the sales activities weren't properly planned for in the first place. And because customers really don't like to be pushed, an anxious sales professional can create distrust, or in other ways hamper the relationship. Creating a plan, and trusting it, will lead to a more patient and pleasant approach that will bring in more business.

Perseverance Destroyers

1. Don't merely report on lagging indicators

Lagging indicators show results coming out of sales activity, like deals won or deals closing this quarter. *Leading* indicators report the input required to get to an outcome, like the number of first meetings. Too often, sales teams only measure the lagging indicators, and then, if things don't go to plan, get confused about what needs to happen to turn things around. Avoid a culture with a focus purely on lagging indicators. Have your CRM dashboard include reports on leading indicators like number of calls made, number of new leads found and number of first meetings. Better yet, create leaderboards on these activities. Rather than only celebrating the lagging indicators (for example, those individuals who have won deals), celebrate progress accomplished on leading indicators. Activity creates opportunity, so ensure there's awareness and appreciation around the importance of these activities.

2. Don't keep your plans to yourself

Of course, you'll be sharing your plans with your other team members but also sit down with *your prospect* to go through your presentation agenda 'to ensure we're making maximum use of everyone's time on the day of the presentation'. Customers tend to not appreciate how much time is needed to go into the detail they expect, and it is your responsibility to avoid a train crash. For instance, if they want you to discuss five topics in the demo alone, but also want to understand the integration, case studies, pricing and support, then your draft agenda might show that there is very little time to cover the requested five demo topics. Let your prospect then decide what's more important. You're also going to get extra nuggets of discovery when you do this pre-presentation session with your prospect.

I once did such a walk-through and was advised that one slide on data integration would be scrutinised by the IT manager who would be in the room (he had a habit of hijacking such meetings). I asked my SC to call the IT manager and walk him through that specific slide over Zoom to avoid surprises on the big day. It worked. The client ended up going with us because 'You were the only vendor with whom our IT manager seemed confident. When it came to your integration slide, he was happily nodding. He grilled the other vendors so badly, and they stumbled. For us, IT's confidence in the solution was key, so we all wanted to go with you'.

3. Don't think it's all going to be fine

This might sound counter intuitive; conventional wisdom has it that positive thinking is supposed to excite us and motivate us to act. However, the psychology of positive thinking can work against us if we don't break things down. That's the conclusion Gabriele Oettingen reached after twenty year of researching human behaviour in relation to goal setting. In her book, *Rethinking Positive Thinking* (2015), she outlines that blind optimism, a trait often believed to be valuable in sales, does not motivate people. Instead, it creates a level of 'relaxating complacency': a state of mind that prevents taking action. 'Positive fantasising,' as Garbielle calls it, might have some short-term merits, but in the long run, it is detrimental to success. One exercise she explains is a technique called 'mental contrasting'. She asked a group of third grade students to picture a candy prize they'd receive after finishing an assignment. She asked another group to do the same, but also think about behaviours that could *prevent them f*rom winning. That latter group outperformed the group who were mainly daydreaming about all the good that would come their way.

Be like Peter the Pessimist, rather than Otto the Optimist, and pre-empt bad situations before they occur. Here are a few practical examples:
- Assume your key sponsor will resign. However good your deal is looking, make sure you don't go single threaded – have a *plan B*. People change jobs every three years or so, so if your pipeline has

12 opportunities, you will see at least one of your contacts leave this quarter.

- Never assume a client meeting starts on time. How often have you been waiting at reception for a one-hour meeting with a prospect, who shows up ten minutes late? Or even when they were punctual, how often did you lose valuable minutes because someone else wasn't in a hurry to leave the meeting room you booked? This time delay can mean you miss out on delivering those important final slides and can rattle you enough to stumble through the rest. In sales, you have to assume all of this will happen. If you really think a 60-minute presentation will give you more than 50 minutes to present, you'll set yourself up for failure.

- Don't assume the internet will work. Don't lose valuable minutes trying to log on to the corporate network; always bring your own hotspot.

- Download your presentation to a USB before you head to the client. If you use a Mac, AV connectors can be a hassle and you might have to go with *plan B* and use the presentation facilities in the room. Create a PDF version, as the Keynote to PowerPoint conversion can be messy. Just click 'export to PDF' and tick the box 'print each stage of builds'.

- Always anticipate who in the audience will ask questions that could derail your presentation, and determine, up front, how to deal with this.

- Whatever you planned for, assume things won't be going completely to plan. Use the Pre-Presentation checklist from my workbook to save time and walk in with confidence.

- On a personal level, anticipate bad times and save money. Use some of your commission to create a financial buffer to weather the bad times that tend to follow the good times.

- Better still, make sure you have health insurance and income insurance. Income insurance is the ultimate way to pre-empt surprises from a financial point of view. Elvira and I had income insurance, so we didn't have to struggle with an extra set of obstacles. This allowed me to focus on reaching goals that otherwise would have been severely challenged. Preventing the setback is easier than overcoming it.

- Finally, get a 'power of attorney'. It's a simple piece of paper in which you appoint someone else to act on your behalf in situations when you're not capable.

4. Don't assume the projector works

Buy a portable spare projector. They cost less than $200. This is a small price to pay and will insure your team against AV problems. I carried around a projector for many years and used it in probably 10 percent of my presentations.

I once ran a 12-month sales cycle with an airline in Australia. Our final three-hour presentation was in a room with a projector that had a pink hue and every time I touched my laptop, the screen would scramble. Luckily, my audience didn't have to deal with that distraction as my own little projector shined like a star.

5. Don't let the presentation room mess up your chances

For really important presentations, make it a habit to go to the prospect's office the day before. Explain to the receptionist that you have a big presentation and you want to make sure your laptop works with the projector. The point is not just the projector, you want to get a feel for the room and pre-empt any logistical issues. All too often, WIFI is poor, seats are limited, or the table setup is wrong. You want to know all this so you can act before it's too late. Create the circumstances that allow you to focus your energy on delivery when it's showtime.

When I checked the presentation room for the above-mentioned airline presentation the day before, I not only found that old pink-hue projector, I also discovered the room was jammed full with tables and didn't have enough chairs. The receptionist was happy for me to clear it all out (others had complained about it but hadn't done anything about it). That presentation was a highlight of my sales career; it was the best presentation I'd ever witnessed a sales team deliver, and we did so in a very relaxed way. We won the deal. A couple of months later, my key sponsor, who was in the room during that final presentation, told me how our obvious preparedness provided the confidence his team had been looking for in a vendor. When I asked him for details, he told me that our main competitor presented after us, in the afternoon slot. They had not brought a spare projector and had to use what was in the room. The pink hue wasn't the only problem; the projector's fan turned on ten minutes into the presentation and zoomed loudly for the next three hours. That, in turn, heated up the room to such an extent that they had to open the doors. The canteen was at the end of the hallway, so foot traffic was high, and even more noise came in from outside. 'It wasn't a complete debacle', he said, 'but we spent three hours looking at this pink screen and got tired pretty quickly. The IT manager was sweating, my boss could not hear everything the vendor presented, and we all struggled to stay focused.'

6. Don't forget to fine-tune

Sales organisations often create territory or account plans once a year, only to put them in a drawer and not review them during the year. The goal of planning is to break down *and* measure your activities throughout the year, so they can be adjusted. Create activity reports in your CRM that show the activities you know will be leading indicators for success. Fine tune your activities as results and insights come in. As a sales manager, spend time reviewing the execution of the number of emails or first meetings committed by a rep, during the regular 1:1. As a rep, meet with your SDR and review their activity on a weekly basis; see how you can help. I often hear reps say, at the end of the year, that they didn't make their target because they didn't get enough leads. That leading indicator needs to be discussed on a weekly basis. If it's only used as an explanation when things are too late to be adjusted, it's just a lame excuse.

7. Don't leave reference calls to chance

Make sure your reference call leads to success. The most common mistake is that the wrong people are lined up to make the call and they are unable to answer your prospect's questions. Your prospect ends up unsatisfied and will ask for another referee – if you're lucky. Set expectations with your prospect and the referee, so they know what to prepare for. Also, use the orchestration of the reference call as an opportunity to enforce your key messaging.

See my workbook for examples on how to line reference calls up in an effective way without being too 'controlling' to the parties involved.

8.   Don't have a to-do list on your computer

What? Did you read that correctly? Yes. You probably have a to-do list in Evernote, a draft email, a Word doc, or as a note on your phone. Do keep track of everything you need to do, but don't put it into digital form. Buy a *notebook* and *write* down your to-do list. If you really want to stick with digital, use different colours for the tasks you've already completed. Don't delete them. Why? Chapter 8 will explain the importance of this seemingly small change that can make a huge impact on your ability to persevere.

Chapter 8: Appraise your progress

The SMART planning I intuitively applied after I came out of hospital played a huge role in my recovery. It helped me define clear goals, which gave me peace of mind and set a well-defined path that guided me towards those goals, however 'big and improbable' they seemed. A couple of months into my rehabilitation, I uncovered another powerful tactic which helped me strengthen my ability to persevere. And that happened after I reached the roundabout.

The roundabout

The roundabout wasn't a thing in my life until it popped up on that spreadsheet Elvira hung on our bedroom wall. As I said, the last line item at the bottom of that printout was *kitesurfing*. It had a lot of empty cells on the right and one cross in the column that represented the deadline of 1 January 2015. I had listed sub-goals of flying a kite on the beach above that line and intended to only embark on those sub-goals *after* I tackled other walking-related goals listed in the rows above.

My specific goals for *walking* started with *touching the bedroom wall* and ended with *hiking the Govetts Leap Lookout track*. Located in the Blue Mountains close to Sydney, it is one of Australia's most spectacular walks. It's a narrow track that starts near the top of a waterfall. After a couple of a hundred metres, it drops into the beautiful Grose Valley. The trail is cut from a huge open-faced wall that plummets 200 metres (600 feet) into the valley below. For most of the two hours it takes to get to the bottom of the waterfall, there's no handrail. Instead, there are spectacular views that challenge you to stay focused on putting one foot in front of the other – carefully – while finding a solid hold to keep your balance. Once you reach the bottom, there's a natural pool big enough for two people to swim in. When you look up, you'll see millions of water droplets gently falling and rainbows flaring up whenever they reach the sunbeams that make it into the valley. It's a great way to regain your energy for the slippery walk back to the top of the waterfall. It's spectacular. It has always been a favourite hike for Elvira and I, and in my mind, it represented the final test of strength for my legs before I would tackle kitesurfing again.

On my printed-out spreadsheet, I committed to the Govetts Leap Lookout trek by the 1st of September 2014. Being able to do that walk would be a confirmation that my pelvis (and my muscles around it) would be strong enough to go kitesurfing. Working back from that goal, I aimed to do shorter and less demanding hikes during the months of June, July and August. And in the months before that, I would focus on flat walks near the beach like Dee Why Beach to Manly Beach, which is a 60-minute walk. In turn, I had broken that down and gave myself a target of walking 10 metres (300 feet) from our apartment to Dee Why Beach by the 1st of April.

Dee Why Beach has always held a special place in my heart, and being able to reach it by foot was one of those sub-goals I was super motivated to reach. To do so, I first had to make it to the halfway point between our apartment and the beach: the roundabout. I had been walking and driving past that roundabout for many years, but never made a big deal out of it. It's a roundabout. Pretty nondescript, like any roundabout. Two not-so-busy residential roads from our neighbourhood come together in a circle less than ten metres in diameter. There's a cafe and a bus stop on one side and a block of apartments on the other side. Whenever the bus for Sydney shows up, it doesn't even commit to the turn and ends up driving straight over the top. I knew this because before my accident, on most days, I would be on the 7:06 am bus. You'd have to find a seat quickly before it hit the roundabout. I planned to conquer the roundabout the week before.

The first time I managed to walk without crutches was on the 18th of February. It was only a short distance to the bedroom wall but represented a major accomplishment after three months of mostly lying flat. Then I started venturing around our apartment. I managed small distances initially, with Elvia monitoring my every step. I soon built enough muscle strength to think about leaving the building. The front of our apartment block has seven daunting steps with a hand rail on the right hand side only. My right hand was still in a sling. It took me a few weeks to gain the confidence to tackle that obstacle, by carefully walking backwards so I could use the left hand. It was easier than I thought. From the front of the building to the main street is another 10 metres, and it would be another 40 metres to get to the roundabout. By then, the roundabout had become more like basecamp to me. It was going to be a big undertaking, and it was *halfway* to the beach. On the 24th of March, we ventured out and started our approach of the roundabout. The stairs were easy. So was reaching the street. But the overall experience of being out on the street was pretty intimidating. I hadn't walked outside for nearly four months. The indoor environment of the hospital and of our own apartment had given me a sense of security that suddenly evaporated. Cars and motorbikes were trying to outrace each other, some jogger zoomed past, and the kids from across the street were running after their dog. All that commotion around me suddenly made me wonder if I'd have enough energy to get back or whether my legs would start to hurt. Doubt started to creep in, that same doubt that had taken up so much of my energy as I was trying to exceed target in the years before. Could I do this?

With Elvira by my side, I calmed myself down and looked up to see the round-about at the end of our street and to my right. I had studied it on Google earth when I planned the trip, and realised it didn't seem as big as I thought. My estimate of 40 metres seemed about right though. 'Let's do it,' I told Elvira and we slowly started walking towards it. Nothing else mattered. The roundabout got bigger and bigger, and suddenly, we were there.

The roundabout halfway to the beach

I looked to the right and saw people waiting at the bus stop. People who were going about their daily lives. I wondered if I should do another 20 metres and sit myself down at the bus stop, but I felt my legs becoming unsteady. For what seemed to last an hour, I just stood there and soaked up the fresh air. I could tell Elvira was keeping a close eye on me but I knew that she was as jubilant as me. We headed back towards the safety of our building. We made it to the front door and bumped into one of our neighbours – he couldn't believe his eyes.

We took the opportunity to chat and rest, and then continued up the stairs to our apartment.

When we got inside, we settled on the couch and soaked up the significance of the accomplishment. I had made it all the way to the roundabout. And back! It was a massive step towards my bigger goal. That evening, we opened a bottle of champagne and ticked off my accomplishment in the spreadsheet. I made it, on the date I had targeted. I came back without pain and a massively increased level of confidence.

Beyond the roundabout

On the 26th of March, five days before my deadline, I made it to Dee Why Beach – 120 days since I last had been there. After all the hospital rooms, surgical theatres, and physiotherapy centres; all the blood, sweat and tears, I took off my shoes and walked into the Pacific Ocean until the water was hip high, with Elvira holding my hand. Swimming was not an option, the wound on my hand was still healing after some of the pins had been taken out the week before. Moreover, I still couldn't fully close my mouth. But standing there and feeling the water on my skin, at a perfect temperature after a summer I had completely missed, was enough. Standing there, I didn't spend much more time looking back at those 120 days. I simply looked further north, towards Long Reef Beach – where my next goal awaited. I wanted to walk from Dee Why Beach to Long Reef Beach.

Of course, the goal of reaching Long Reef embodied a mental challenge; it was where the accident happened. For all those years before, Long Reef had given me so much joy and health; I wanted it to still have that connotation for me. Of all places in the world, Long Reef could *not* be the one for which I would have negative emotions. So I made a mistake. I changed my original date for that goal (the 15th of April), to the 1st of April. I was ahead of schedule, without pain, and felt confident enough to start aiming higher than the goals I had set within the safe confinements of my spreadsheet. When I had met with my physiotherapist, Jo, she advised me to slow down. I was on the right track and steadily making progress, but I had to be careful not to go too quickly, she warned. The leg muscles are the strongest in your body; they bear your entire weight. All those months of inactivity had completely dissipated my muscle power and regaining it needed a careful and steady fitness regime. Overdoing it may increase the strength of one muscle group, but a weaker muscle group could lead to imbalance, she said. I didn't listen, and paid the price.

When I made it to Long Reef on the 1st of April, my legs were hurting. Muscles around the pelvis – the glutes maximus – simply weren't ready to deal with the strain. Other muscles tried to take over as the glutes struggled on that walk to Long Reef, and by the time I got back home several of them were inflamed. They couldn't deal with the demand yet, and protested with a clear signal that my willpower had to back off until they were ready. Unfortunately, that took two months. There were a couple of weeks of relieving those muscles so the inflammation could disappear, and another period of carefully building up their strength. I was in crutches again and needed six extra weeks of physio. Once again, I found myself on a mission to reach the roundabout without crutches.

I adjusted my goal sheet and kept going. I managed to make it to Long Reef again on the 24th of May, and make it back home without pain. A couple of days later, I made it all the way to Long Reef headland – a steady 500-metre climb to a point overlooking the spectacular beaches to the north and south. The 90-minute walk to Manly followed soon after in early June. In the weeks after, I progressed pretty fast. We did bigger hikes in Ku-ring-gai Chase National Park, north of Sydney, and made it to the lighthouse at Palm Beach. We conquered Govetts Leap Lookout on the 18th of August, two weeks ahead of schedule. I was on a roll.

That doesn't mean I was protected from setbacks. I had plenty. Two that rattled my confidence. By that time, I had become familiar with the range of pain throughout my body. My relationship with pain had changed by then – I learned it had two aspects. There was the *known pain*, the actual pain from teeth playing up, muscles getting inflamed and bones and joints healing. And there's the *unknown pain*, the set of emotions that make you scared and worried about how much more pain is coming. You can shift your thresholds for known pain quite easily. If you know something will only hurt for two seconds, you'll just deal with it. If you know your hip has this nagging feeling as if you hit the corner of the table, and it's not getting any worse, you'll learn to accept it. I had 17 sessions with Max, my dental surgeon, over a period of more than two years. This has given me an understanding about the range of pain I'd encounter during and after the surgery. I wouldn't be fazed if he'd pull another teeth or put in another crown. I know I can handle it.

It's when you're not sure what will happen that the pain becomes unbearable. Much of the pelvic rehab had made that so challenging; it wasn't as clear a range. One night in October, I woke up with a screaming pain between my right pelvis and ribs. Soon, my shoulder started to ache too. I tried to move around to lessen the pain, but soon it reached levels I hadn't experienced in a while. A visit to the doctor the next day produced a diagnosis of gall stones. Looking at my recent history, the doctor in charge wasn't surprised. Long periods in intensive care often lead to gall stones. Bile (or 'gall') is produced by the liver and is used to break down fatty food in the digestive system. Extra gall is stored in the gall bladder so the intestines can call upon it after a par-ticularly fatty meal. Not much is used when you get fed liquid food through feeding tubes. The unused gall in the gall bladder becomes sludge and even-tually hardens into gall stones. By the time the small intestine signals it needs extra bile, those stones are stuck in the ducts that connect to it. And that hurts. Within days, I found myself back in Royal North Shore Hospital to have the gall bladder removed. Same hospital, same forms, same beds, same white coats. But at least I walked in. One of the nurses recognised me. I wasn't sure whether to read wariness into her disbelief about my kiting plans, and just as our reunion turned awkward, Elvira came to pick me up. Within days I was ok again.

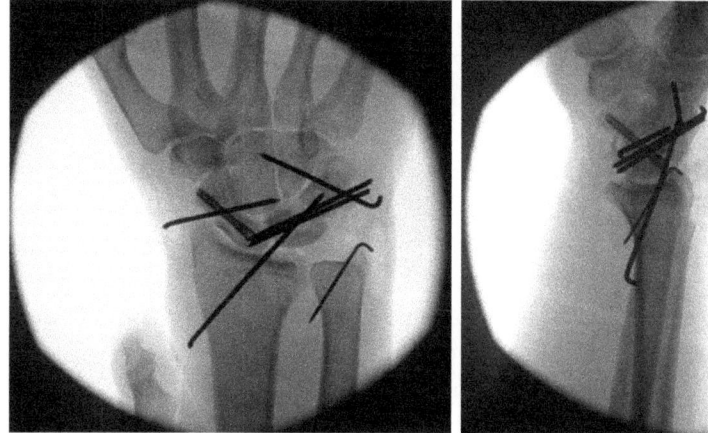

The wrist just after the operation. The pins would come out, but the big screw in the middle stays.

Another big setback took months to play out. Several bones in my wrist were broken so badly they couldn't heal properly and started 'fusing'. This is the process where bones grow together at a joint, preventing movement. Such fusing happens when cartilage is damaged on the point where two bones con-nect. Cartilage is a smooth, firm tissue that wraps around the end of bones. It enables the bones to gently glide over each other in a joint. It doesn't regrow, and no artificial replacement has been invented yet. Without cartilage, bones will rub over each other like a poorly lubricated engine piston, which can cause severe pain. To avoid pain, you limit movement. In bad cases, that limitation makes the bones grow together – to fuse. And that's what happened with me. Pain reduced, but so did the functioning of the wrist. Within a year after my accident, it became clear that I wouldn't be able to bend the right wrist at all – ever.

Although the physical challenges got all my attention, the mental challenges crept up on me and made it harder. Before I'd try kitesurfing again, I wanted to try surfing. I'd surfed for many years, and in many ways, expected it to be an easy introduction to returning to the water. However, that seemingly easy step became a huge stumbling block that tried to draw me back into a dark hole. When you surf, you lie flat on your board. You wait for a wave to come and paddle like crazy to match the speed of the wave. I had set myself numerous goals around just that exercise over a period of three months. Once you have paddle power, it's all about the pop-up: you go from lying flat to standing up as fast as you can. I hadn't thought a big deal of that, but I had never assumed my wrist would fuse.

To stand up on a surfboard, you put the palms of your hands on the board to get the wrists at a 90-degree angle. My right wrist didn't allow for that. It stuck out flat, at zero degrees. I gave myself a new objective: to do one handed push-ups, using the left wrist instead. I made some progress on land, but once I tried it in the water, I found the board to be unstable. My kite buddies created wrist braces and developed ideas for special holds on the board. All of them made practical sense, but my mind was objecting. I'd become scared that I would slip, or something would go wrong and I'd end up with more injuries. I had to find a way to use both hands. I practised putting weight on the fingertips of the right hand, by leaning into a wall. I increased the angle a little bit every day and tried to find the range of pain the wrist could handle. Eventually, I managed to lie flat on the floor in the living room and quickly pop up with the left wrist bent, and the right fingers outstretched. It took five months longer than I had foreseen, to develop enough strength and confidence to catch my first wave.

It made me doubt my goal to go kitesurfing again. Surfing had felt like such a logical step on the path towards my end goal, I had convinced myself it was going to happen in that order. First surfing, then kitesurfing. Jo, my physiotherapist, wondered if that was the right way to look at it. 'Don't you just hold your hand stretched, without bending the wrist, when you hold on to the kitebar?' she questioned. I visualised flying a kite and realised she was right. You don't need to bend the wrist at all – if everything goes well, that is. If I lost my kiteboard or fell in some way, a straight wrist with fingers outstretched could lead to nasty injuries. Again, my mindset became the challenge. I decided to stick with the original plan and started flying a kite on the beach. No board, no falling. It turned out to be much easier than I thought. All tension goes to the kite harness and the pelvis easily handled that. Neither wrist needed any bending, even with sudden corrections on the bar. Maybe the limitation was mostly in the brain; the lack of confidence that a deviation from my plan had brought about.

Every time I faced a setback or started doubting, I remembered the roundabout. Reaching that roundabout had been a huge goal for me. Then, over time, as I raised the bar and focused on the next hurdle, it didn't feel as big a deal. I had become all hung up and stressed about a new goal and had forgotten how big a goal the roundabout had once been. I decided to change my mindset and never take the roundabout for granted again. I never wanted to forget how big an accomplishment it was and how reaching that roundabout should give me confidence in the next challenge I face.

Kitesurfing again

Today, six years later, each time I walk past the roundabout, I feel a level of gratefulness that puts all other challenges into perspective. The roundabout gives me motivation and a desire to persevere. It taught me that when something seems to be a 'pretty big and improbable' goal, one day it will represent a non-issue. It should simply be a circular intersection that fluidly moves traffic through my suburb. But it isn't. Because I made reaching that roundabout such an important and explicit goal, it represents not just the goal, but something much more powerful: it represents progress. It is a very conscious reminder that today, I am doing better than I was in 2014.

It was the roundabout that gave me the confidence to keep aiming for my ultimate goal: kitesurfing. On the 9th of November, well before my original deadline, I walked out of our home with my kite on my back, and my board in my hand. I turned right, walked past the roundabout, said thanks, and kept going. I got to the beach and walked all the way to Long Reef. There, I pumped up my kite, launched it, and, with a big smile, stepped into the warm water to enjoy one of my best sessions ever.

Progress in sales: more than winning that deal

Steve W. Martin did research on the personality traits of top sales professionals. He found that 84% of top sales people 'fixated on achieving goals and continuously measure their performance in comparison to their goals'.[41] But many of us in sales don't spend much time or reflection to monitor our progress; we focus on all that is still ahead of us. We focus on the calls we haven't made yet or the deals we haven't won yet. This can be daunting – even demotivating. Having learned first-hand how much motivation I drew from being conscious about the progress I had *already* made, I started researching this topic. Teresa Amabile devotes a whole book to it: *The Progress Principle: Using Small Wins to Ignite Joy, Engagement, and Creativity at Work* (2011). Together with Steven Kramer, she conducted a multi-year study on what makes people happy, motivated, creative and productive at work. Going through 12,000 diary entries of 283 people in several companies, they found a theme they dubbed the Progress Principle: 'Of all the positive events that influence inner work life, the single most powerful is *progress in meaningful work*; of all the negative events, the single most powerful is the opposite of progress – setbacks in the workplace'.

The researchers made me realise that my work situation had not been very different from a typical work environment: people at work, including sales managers, do not focus on progress. They focus on what still needs to happen. Just look at the agenda of a typical sales meeting. The first two minutes are spent on acknowledging that a deal was won, and the next 58 minutes are spent on all the stuff that still needs to happen. It's important, but not necessarily helpful to keep us going. It's when people feel they've accomplished something that they are the most motivated. Amabile says that 'even when progress happens in small steps, a person's sense of steady forward movement toward an important goal can make all the difference between a great day and a terrible one. This pattern became increasingly obvious as the diaries came in from all the teams in our study. People's inner work lives seemed to lift or drag depending on whether or not their projects moved forward, even by small increments. Small wins often had a surprisingly strong positive effect, and small losses a surprisingly strong negative one.'

In sales, focusing purely on winning deals can be detrimental to motivation and productivity. If we want to develop our perseverance in sales, we also need to look at progress: the acknowledgement of forward momentum. The most logical way to find such acknowledgement is through feedback. Your manager, or colleague, should give you constructive suggestions around what worked and what can be improved for your next call or presentation. Unfortunately, the reality is that sales cultures often struggle with sound feedback mechanisms. Not much time is set aside to analyse past performance, all focus is on what's ahead. One reason for that could be that sales leaders on average only spend 20 percent of their time with their team and, therefore, struggle to understand what's happening at the coal face.[42] *Even if they'd wanted to, they wouldn't always know what feedback to give, beyond the 'you need more pipeline.'*

And when you find a quiet moment with a peer, chances are their feedback is not that helpful. Sales professionals tend to steer away from negative topics and end up with superficial and positive statements, like 'Yeah, well done, great demo'. It's not easy to instill a culture of constructive and open feedback in any department. As a result, Amabile says 'getting feedback from the work itself is preferable' over getting feedback from others. We simply can't rely on helpful confirmation from someone else to build our motivation to persevere.

My roundabout proved that principle. It was an independent, measurable confirmation that proved that I had made progress. The indisputable nature of it gave me energy to keep going; it strengthened my desire to reach my next goal.

In sales, we need to find similar independent and measurable confirmations. We need to find our own roundabouts.

Perseverance Promotors

1. Celebrate the big wins

After a long and grueling quarter, it's important you let your hair down. Celebrate the progress you made, even if you didn't make target. Acknowledge the good work you've done to get there. I never really liked the alcohol-fueled end of quarter parties in the office, so would block a couple of hours to celebrate things my way: by going kitesurfing. I am sure you can find a motivating way to reward yourself of the progress you booked.

2. Celebrate the small wins

Celebrating wins is key to building perseverance. All that pent-up stress needs a release. The cortisol that you have created to stay super focused needs to be broken down (Chapter 4). And as you might remember, dopamine plays a big role in doing just that. It regulates your drive to pursue things. High dopamine levels create a willingness to seek more of whatever generated that state in the first place. If you let your hair down after a big win, you are programming your system to look out for a reward. This is a good thing. You unconsciously program yourself to want more of it, which makes it easier to accept the disappointments that try to overshadow the win.

However, since a win in sales is more the exception than the rule, we need to be thoughtful about *what we* celebrate. If we want to program ourselves to keep going, we need to recognise the small steps that got us to winning that deal. It's the *progress towards* the deal, not just that final step of 'contract signature'. If I would had defined success as 'kitesurfing again', I would have had to wait a year for that celebratory relief. I would have needed to find the motivation to keep going at that 'pretty big and improbable' goal while being hit left right and centre with all the set-backs. Breaking down my goals allowed me to celebrate the smaller wins, like opening up a bottle of champagne when I reached the roundabout. In sales, you should do the same. Based on your sales productivity model from Chapter 6, agree on what sub-goals you will celebrate. This could be a simple acknowledgement of how many calls you made this week. Don't just count the successful ones, count the ones that led to rejection or other outcomes you did not desire. Counting the 'yes and the no' will help you recognise your progress, which will become the motivation in itself.

3. Use a check box to show progress

As Chapter 7 outlined, have your to-do list on a piece of paper. Don't keep track of it electronically as you'll lose sight of the progress you made once you delete a line item. Categorise it on paper so you can *see* the progress you have made at the end of each week. A good way to keep track of the progress you make towards an action item is to draw a small box in front of it. An empty box means you haven't started it. A box filled in diagonally shows some progress, while a box completely coloured in represents the satisfying completion of a task.

Use check boxes that help indicate progress

If you really aren't a 'paper person' and prefer digital solutions like Evernote, OneNote, or Google Keep, use different font colours. Everything you still have to start will be black, the tasks you're working on in dark grey, and those that you've already ticked off you change to light grey. Start the new week by copying everything that's not light grey over into a new note. Create a habit to go over your list each day and you'll realise that even when you've had a hard day with poor results, this simple exercise of ticking boxes will help you feel motivated to keep going at it the next day.

When communicating plans or to-do lists with customers, do the same. Don't just delete activities that already have been tackled. Grey them out or use strikethrough to create awareness of the progress you (both) are making. It will motivate the customer to keep going, too.

4. Call out progress makers

Another problem with only celebrating 'contract signature' stages as wins, is that it automatically focuses all attention on the sales rep – the one who owned the last step of the win. Attention gets pulled away from all the other team members who were involved in the steps that progressed the deal towards its outcome, like marketing, SDRs, SCs, and services. Do give credit where credit is due, and don't limit that to just the deals that reach the 'won' stage. Instead, in your sales meetings, call out the SDR who exceeded their number of calls last week. Give marketing their chance to shine and bask in the glory of an event that went well. Talk about that new qualified opportunity the CSM found. All of these people deliver progress, regardless of whether the combined outcomes led to a contract signature.

5. Do win/loss reviews

Unfortunately, win/loss reviews aren't as common as they should be in sales; all focus is *forward looking*. Sometimes, sales managers insist on such a review for a loss, so everyone can agree on what 'went wrong' and lessons can be learned to improve the chances next time around. If you do loss reviews, don't just focus on why you didn't get the deal, agree also on what areas of the sales process worked well. Even though you didn't win the deal, did the SDR do a great job in discovery or did the SC run a great demo? Acknowledging them will help them find the motivation and energy to go after the next opportunity.

Although they are typically referred to as win/loss reviews or win/loss analyses, it's even less common to actually do reviews on the *wins*. Not much time is spent on acknowledging what helped win the deal. Instead, team members move on with an unverified and implicit personal belief about why the deal was won. It always surprises me that when deals are won, team members often have different views as to *why*. Again, this limits the ability to learn as a team and win more deals in the future.

See my workbook for a win/loss review template.

6. Express appreciation

Sam, a manager I coached, made a habit of always sending a one-line email to individuals in the different teams to acknowledge their progress that day. He told me he deliberately sets aside 15 minutes at the end of his work day to share his appreciation on points of progress, for instance:

- Thanks Sophie, for that great account plan you presented to us today.
- Loved the quality of the RFP we submitted this week, Jim.
- I really liked you sharing that white paper with the SDR team John, thank you.

- Your work on improving the battle cards for our market is super valuable, Helen.
- Andrew, just a quick thanks for your team's timely forecast submission.

He tells me he originally did it to 'motivate the troops' but then realised it gave his end of day a positive ending, which helped him with his own motivation.

7. Create souvenirs

I have a tangible souvenir to acknowledge my progress. I walk past the roundabout every day, and it always puts a spring in my step. There are smaller things, from before my accident, which helped me appreciate the progress I'd made.

After a particularly stressful period a long time ago, Elvira and I went on holiday to the Maldives. It turned out to be the stress release we both needed and it helped us on our course to exploring our move to Australia. The resort let us keep the key chain from the room in which we stayed. That key chain is now tied to the lamp on our bed stand. Every night, it's the last thing we see before we go to sleep, and it serves as a reminder that we can withstand bad times and come out stronger.

Can you find your own roundabout? Can you find a physical object that can serve as a reminder of your progress? I once had a manager who had framed a copy of the first ever contract he signed as a rep on his wall. It served as a constant reminder to stay upbeat whenever he faced a challenge. One team I coached has implemented an 'employee of the week' practice with trophies. It's playful but with a very clear purpose to acknowledge the importance of everyone's role.

8. Maintain a bank of proof document

If you work in a culture where sharing appreciation, acknowledging progress, and trophies don't sound like easily implementable wins, start with acknowledging it *to yourself*. When I started my own sales business, my coach noticed I lost confidence in my abilities. Even though I had years of sales experience, starting my own business was very different. Or so I thought. In reality, I could easily articulate my ideas and values to my prospects, but still doubted if my business had a chance. My coach suggested I create a simple spreadsheet, called the 'bank of proof'. In it, I listed all my accomplishments (many of which I so easily presented to my prospects). 'Whenever you start doubting, just go to your 'bank of proof' and show *yourself* what you have already accomplished,' he said. It really helped me get through the first year of running my own business.

9. Stop, start, change, continue

During each QBR, let every single individual contribute by completing a simple slide with four quadrants. Provide at least five bullets for each of the four areas. For the next quarter, what will you stop doing? What will you start doing? What will you change? And what will you continue doing? To make sure this actually comes alive and gets followed through, print it and hang it above your desk so you are reminded of your plans every single day. See my workbook for a simple template I use in QBRs.

Perseverance Destroyers

1. Don't do 'hero' win reviews

Neill was an enterprise sales rep I used to work with. Whenever Neill would lose a deal, he'd tell everyone it was because of our pricing, the competitor dropping their pants, our poor data integration capabilities, or some other external factor that was clearly out of his control. However, whenever he won a deal, his win report would list his relationship building skills, the SC's demo skills, the 'late nights with legal' and other activities he coordinated that lead to a great win. In other words, the internal factors. I am sure you have met a Neill in your sales career. Someone with the 'If I win, it's because of me, if I lose, it's because of them' mentality. While win reports, that you email around to the broader organisation, are a great place for shoulder-patting (even self-shoulder patting), they shouldn't be the only review. Spend time to also do the win (or loss) review in a more honest fashion. Even if you're nervous about openly sharing these with the outside world, do spend a few minutes to determine what you could have done better. Don't let your ego prevent you from learning.

2. Don't provide dishonest feedback to keep people motivated

When things are down in sales, we tend to motivate the troops by saying it will all work out. 'Ah well, onwards and upwards'. Yes, do stay positive, but don't fall in the trap of only providing positive feedback to peers and direct reports if there is room for improvement. If a presentation didn't go well, say so and come up with suggestions for improvement for the next one. Don't beat around the bush – you're wasting everyone's time and prevent them from becoming better.

Use the Post-Presentation Review from my workbook as a straightforward guide to collect feedback and agree on actions after a presentation.

3. Don't have CRM dashboards only focused on wins

There is no more in-your-face reflection of progress than your CRM. Dashboards in Salesforce, Dynamics, or HubSpot will show happy green dials when things are going well and graphs in alarming red when we're behind. For most sales teams, the main dashboard starts with the number of deals won, followed by graphs depicting opportunities forecast to close this quarter, and the next quarters. The underlying activities required to get towards those end goals, like the number of calls made, or new stage 1 opportunities added this month, don't get the same attention. But it is exactly these activities that represent the leading indicators, rather than lagging indicators, of progress. Make sure your dashboard also shows the progress the team is making at this level by moving these indicators above the fold.

4. Don't ring that bell only when a deal lands

Yes, you should make a big fuzz whenever a deal is won, and ring that bell. It creates great energy when successes are achieved and acknowledged on the floor. But when the definition of success is narrowed down only to 'deal won', it can be counterproductive as well. When the sales team hits a rough patch, it becomes awfully quiet and people start to question if the ship is going to sink. I've worked in sales teams where such a slow phase negatively influenced team motivation. People lose their confidence as the big successes remain waiting even when there is enough progress that deserves recognition and even celebration. To then change the rules and ring the bell to celebrate the smaller wins, would feel like cheating. Instead, create a practice up front to agree on what makes a win for each of the teams. For the AEs, 'deal won' is a clear one, but another public acknowledgment could be 'new opportunity' for the SDRs, or even 'made our weekly call target'. These are all elements of progress that when openly recognised and celebrated, will drive more motivation in the team. If the bell is holy and only to be used for the Ultimate Goal – find an alternative way to publicly articulate this progress, because there would be a lot of it. Simple emails or call-outs during meetings are all it takes.

Ring that bell for every win

5. Don't kid yourself

Moving a deal from one stage to the next in your CRM feels good. It's a great way to acknowledge progress to others, and yourself. Similar to the reaching of a new playing level in a computer game, this accomplishment will release dopamine in your brain, and it's that dopamine that will get you to crave for more, and to make you want a repeat of such accomplishment. However, be careful of these cravings creating an unconscious desire to cheat. While putting an opportunity into the next stage might feel good, progress needs to be real to avoid disappointment later. If you feel you sometimes lack the discipline for an objective assessment, create check points that involve other people. Conduct early-stage deal reviews to keep each other honest and provide constructive feedback. I typically advise my clients to implement a checkpoint at demo stage, for instance. The SC manager will assess the early stage discovery information and needs to agree that the opportunity has progressed far enough to assign an SC. If the manager is not satisfied the criteria have been met, the rep cannot move the opportunity to the next stage, or get an SC.

6. Don't become a lone wolf

My roundabout story might give you the impression that it was all about me booking progress independently. As you'll see in the last chapter, the reality is that there was a hugely important team of people that helped me get to that roundabout, and towards my broader goal of *Getting My Old Life Back*. In sales, regardless of the size of your organization, it's all about team work. A deal never is won by a single individual. Likewise, progress is never the product of one individual. Do acknowledge the steps that others have contributed to. The next chapter provides some models and ideas on that.

Chapter 9: Fend and befriend

At the start of this book, I promised to help you, the sales professional, master skills that build perseverance in sales. I focused on the importance of finding your True North to get to the Why of your motivation. I outlined the importance of taking care of your brain, learning to let go, and how to find perspective. I also provided models and suggestions to better plan for your work, and to let the acknowledgement of progress become a motivator in itself.

You may remember that my last consultation with Dr Susan kicked off my journey to discover how I could help sales professionals develop the motivation to persevere. Throughout my story, you've met some of the other people who fixed me up and helped me on my journey. Healthcare professionals like Jo, Katy, Max, and Shane. There's another group of people who played a huge part in helping me to *Get My Old Life Back*, and I could not have done it without them: my wife Elvira, my family and my (close and even not so close) friends. When reflecting on what was behind my own struggle to persevere, I read many books that clearly showed a common factor that tied everything together – *people*. In sales, we're all held accountable for our own *individual* targets. In the heat of the moment, this sometimes makes it hard to appreciate those very people we rely on to help us get there.

Setbacks and social support

In literature, a group of people who can help you deal with setbacks and stress is called the Social Support Network. Since the 1970s, social support has been a focus of many fields of research, including psychology, medicine, sociology, education, rehabilitation and social work. Such research concludes that support from the network around you can help moderate or buffer the impact of psychosocial stress on physical and mental health. Our perceived availability of support directly impacts our level of psychological distress.[43] The *lack of social support* is, in fact, the biggest *predictor* of Post-Traumatic Stress Disorder (PTSD). However, you don't need to suffer serious trauma to experience the benefits of the protective factors of social support. Social support plays a big role in any stressful event, including education, family functioning, interpersonal conflicts and occupational stress.

One's *physical health* can also be impacted by the (perceived) level of support from the people around them. Those with low social support are at a higher level of risk of death from diseases like cancer and cardiovascular disease.[44] In addition, people with low social support have higher suicidal tendencies and experience more alcohol and drug related problems.[45]

Here are four functions of social support:

1. Tangible support is the help offered through material means like financial assistance, goods or services.
2. Informational support is the provisioning of advice, guidance or useful information.
3. Emotional support is the offering of affection and empathy to show that one cares about the other. It provides encouragement, intimacy and a level of esteem that shows a person is valued.
4. Companionship support gives someone a sense of social belonging. It signals that *you're one of us*, which generates trust.

Each of these functions played a huge role in my ability to persevere.

The buddy system

In the world of kitesurfing, there are very specific rules and guidelines around safety. Some are of a technical nature, like using a life vest on open waters, when to use a leash, or how to set up the quick release system. Others are more geared towards the safety of others; we agree which beaches are off limits, where to launch, where not to jump, and how much distance to keep from other people in the water. The most important rule for beginners, as well as experienced kiters, is to always go out with a kite buddy. A kite buddy is another kiter who helps you launch and joins you on the water. With a kite buddy, you'll agree up front where you go, and commit to keeping an eye out for each other during the session. We use hand signals to communicate while on the water so we can keep a safe distance. If something goes wrong, it's your kite buddy who's responsible to help you out, or, if it really goes wrong, to go ashore and get help. Kite buddies not only make kitesurfing a lot safer, they make it more fun, too. It's so much more fun to be out there with a kite buddy who's having fun, too. The kite community at local beaches tend to be very tight – people know each other by name. That's because the sport involves a fair bit of waiting on the beach. Wind forecasts aren't always accurate, so we often find ourselves on the beach, all pumped up, waiting for enough wind.

Kite buddies develop close relationships. Being out there fighting the elements and having fun together creates bonds. When things go well, relationships are quickly deepened by a new experience and great memories. When things don't go well, relationships grow even stronger. Most of my kite buddies were on Long Reef Beach when my accident happened. Hans scooped the sand away around my face so I could breathe. When I slowly rolled over, he was the first to be confronted with the mess that was my face. Matt called 911. Billy covered me with a blanket and held my head until help arrived. Jono helped clear the way so the helicopter could land. Dave ran to my home to inform Elvira and raced with her to the hospital. Everyone was there during those first scary days at the hospital, supporting Elvira while dealing with the severity of it all in their own minds. The partners of the kite buddies all jumped in too. They consoled Elvira, helped fill in forms, functioned as taxi and delivery drivers, brought food and much, much more.

Elvira was with me, at the hospital, every day from 7 am till 10 pm for the next two months. In the first crucial days, one of the kite buddies or their partners would take a day off work to pick her up, drive her to the hospital and be with her as she strapped herself into that roller-coaster of ups and downs. They made sure she ate and took care of herself and supported her when she began to struggle. They helped with the insurance paperwork, the police report, and other formalities. They kept the rest of our friends up to date so Elvira could focus on doing the same with our families back in the Netherlands. When my father and brother flew into Sydney, my kite buddies picked them up from the airport. Whenever I was undergoing another big operation, they took Elvira out shopping to distract her from all the things that could go wrong. They took her out for dinner whenever there was something to celebrate. Without the kite buddies and their partners, Elvira would not have coped.

And I really needed Elvira. As I've already shared with you, I initially couldn't see much, and only started talking a month into the hospital stay. But whenever she was present, I was at ease. Hearing the sound of her footsteps in the hallway would accelerate the beeping of my heart monitor. It would slow down the moment her hand touched my forehead. I could sense how worried she was, but took great comfort in having her around, and hearing the other kiters' voices in the room. I knew they'd support her and that helped me not feel bad about focusing on myself.

My friends and family were there when I got out of the hospital. My mum flew in with my sister just as I accomplished my goal to make it to the roundabout. Friends from school back in the Netherlands (some now living in Belgium, the UK, the US, Spain, Hong Kong, and Singapore) cheered me on with cards, calls, emails and SMS messages. Colleagues from work visited me in the hospital. With words of encouragement and warm wishes, all of those people helped in an invaluable way to keep Elvira and I going. We even received tangible support from a group we hadn't considered to be that close: our neighbours.

We had moved into our apartment building just five years earlier. It's a property not far from the beach, consisting of around 20 units, mostly occupied by young professional couples and down-sizers. All friendly people whom we knew by name and would chat with in the hallways, or whenever we bumped into them on the beach. They were neighbours who turned into social supporters the day I left the hospital.

Although I had Elvira by my side 24x7 when I returned home, I couldn't walk much and spent most of the day in bed, sleeping. And I ate. I had lost a lot of muscle mass during those two months lying flat in the hospital; my bodyweight had dropped from 67 kilos to 57 kilos. I needed *a lot of food* as my muscles began rebuilding. But that's where things got tricky. As part of my hospital discharge, the social workers had developed a nutritional program to ensure I'd have enough nutrients to regain my bodyweight. It consisted of the same liquid and pureed meals I was given in hospital: omelettes, mashed potatoes, finely minced meat, pureed macaroni and yoghurt drinks. To deliver such haute cuisine might represent a relatively small challenge for most of you, but for Elvira and myself, it was a concern. We're not good cooks. Not by a long shot. Elvira was stressed just thinking of the additional complexity of liquids, the high calorie count, and the implications of getting it wrong.

Our neighbour, Charlie, picked up on this weakness and, unbeknownst to us, organised for everyone in the apartment building to help us. They relieved Elvira from the cooking and the grocery runs. They would take care of it all. They created a roster that outlined who would cook on what day. They hung the roster in the hallway downstairs so everyone could tick off which day they opted to cook for us. Every day, around 6 pm, there was a knock on our door from one of the neighbours delivering a fully home-cooked and pureed meal. Some neighbours outdid themselves with three course meals, complete with soups, purees and puddings. It became a bit of a competition when neighbours carefully started to ask what meals we rated best so far. This tangible support from a rather unexpected source was of huge value. Knowing that people who have no obligation to step in, still went out of their way to help us, didn't just help us from a practical perspective, it gave us immense emotional support.

My kite buddy, Phil, was with me when I first made it back to Long Reef beach. Another kiter, Harold, put his exercise bike on my balcony so I could work on rebuilding my leg muscles. They all joined me on my first paddle out on the surfboard and would cheer me on for months as I tried to find a way to stand up. They bought me fitness weights and audio books, and shared articles and videos from athletes who went through hardship. The story of pro-surfer Bethany Hamilton made a particular impact on me; she had lost her arm in a shark attack and somehow made her way back to professional surfing. They joined me when I bought a new wetsuit and a kite harness. And they were with me for my first post-accident kitesurfing session. I had asked them to keep an eye out from the beach and be ready to jump in if I got into trouble, but when they saw me enjoying my session on the water, they couldn't wait and soon joined me.

The support of my kite buddies embodied all elements a social support network can bring. The tangible and informational support made things practically easier, but it was the emotional and companionship support that *really* kept me going. It felt good to know there were others constantly looking for ideas to help me. Knowing there are other people who empathise and reprioritise their own day to help you is a huge morale booster. It felt like they shared in the load, which in turn created the extra motivation to keep going. Knowing that Elvira and I were not alone in facing our challenges helped us persevere whenever a new setback popped up.

These events have drastically deepened our relationships with the kite buddies and their partners. There's not a week, six years after my accident, when we are not in contact. We organise dinners and coffee catch-ups on a weekly basis. We surf every weekend and kite whenever the wind comes up. Most of all, we don't just share our joys, we share our pains and help each other when setbacks arise.

Meet Barney, my neighbour

Exactly one year after I came home, Elvira and I threw a party for our neighbours. It was a warm, windless, summer's evening. Some neighbours had been dismissive saying there was no need, but during that evening, I had seen what a special time it was for everyone. Tears flowed when I repeated our appreciation for everything they had done. We had *all* been through a challenging chapter and we all come out stronger.

87-year-old Barney from downstairs shook my hand after my speech. We had developed a special bond, not just because Elvira and I had confidentially told him a few months earlier that he and his lovely wife Barbara had won the cooking challenge with their onion mustard soup. Barney had experienced hard times himself and even after we were okay to take care of our own meals, he kept knocking on our door around dinner time. 'Just checking in,' he'd say, followed by some raunchy joke to cheer me up. On this night, however, he was serious. 'Frank, you keep thanking us, but there's no need for that', he said with his soft voice. 'In Australia, we're all foreigners. Everybody here either comes from overseas, from interstate or from some country town far way,' he continued as he looked over my shoulder to the rest of the party. 'Hardly anyone here has family living next door. Yet, we all get challenges thrown at us in life, and that's why we all get together. When the shit hits the fan, it's your friends and neighbours who will take the role of your family.'

Every year, on the anniversary of my homecoming, we organise drinks on our balcony. The one after Barney had passed away was a particularly moving one. I regularly look at the pictures of Barney and me on our balcony, and I don't want to ever forget his beautiful words. Our group of neighbours has become a tight community. We regularly check in on each other and rotate tasks to help with lost keys, light bulb replacements and other odd jobs.

It's easy to overlook the depth of these relationships. Last year, a new couple moved in to the building, and they experienced our annual gathering on our balcony for the first time. The new couple commented on how friendly and tight a community our building seemed to be. 'Everyone knows each other like friends, and you all seem to help each other out,' they said. My initial reaction was to downplay it, but then another neighbour, Cheryl, spoke out. 'That's because of Frank's accident,' she said. After going into great detail to explain what happened, she concluded, 'If it weren't for that stressful period, we wouldn't have become so close. We really bonded during and after those uncertain days'. For me this is the ultimate articulation of companionship support.

Adversity and mateship

Australians, however, don't call it companionship support, they proudly call it 'mateship'. It's a term with such significance, that it was nearly mentioned in the preamble of the Australian constitution. In 1999, Australia held a referendum to see if the people wanted to break loose from Britain's monarchy to become a republic. The referendum was defeated but it triggered another discussion. John Howard, the then Australian Prime Minister and leader of the Liberal Party, proposed the following preamble to the amended constitution.

Australians are free to be proud of their country and heritage, free to realise themselves as individuals, and free to pursue their hopes and ideals. We value excellence as well as fairness, independence as dearly as mateship.

The referendum was ultimately rejected and the preamble didn't survive – mostly due to its 'blokeish' connotation. That doesn't mean the concept of mateship finds disapproval. On the contrary, mateship lies at the heart of Australian culture and how people relate. It dates back to early colonial times, when new settlers and convicts had to learn to cope with the harsh environment on the other side of the world. Drought, bushfires, flooding rains, and the dangers that crocodiles, snakes, sharks, and spiders brought, meant that people had to keep an eye out for each other. More than anywhere, the chances of survival in these conditions depended on a community's readiness to band together. Adversity calls for mateship.

It's a term devoid of political preference. When Queensland suffered a particularly tough time with the devastating floods in 2011, then Prime Minister, Julia Gillard spoke on Australia Day to point out the power of mateship in hard times. 'This Australia Day, more than anything else, we know mateship lives ... We will hang on to our Aussie mateship and our Aussie fair go, in the worst of times and in the best, because we're Australian.'

One obvious aspect of the power of the notion of mateship lies in the word 'mate', which implies friendship. Mate is often used in amicable form to imply personal familiarity, but it can also point to a meaning of equality. Your mate is just like you, going through the same struggles in life. Depending on the subtle fierceness of its pronunciation, it can also have less of an amicable meaning. Nick Dyrenfurth researched the topic in his book *Mateship: A Very Australian History* (2015). He states "The convicts brought with them from Britain the term mate, and they used it amongst themselves. They even rather provocatively termed their jailors mate and the basic message was 'you're no better than us'". It is this classless equality, which Australia is so known for, that improves the ability for a community to deal with setbacks.

David Hurley, who was Australia's Chief of Defence during the time I went through my rehabilitation, pointed out another aspect of mateship, when he said: 'Australian men have a great capacity to come together as one community, to share the burden of adversity, to support each other in the spirit of friendship and mateship'.[46]

That sharing of the burden creates solidarity and companionship. It helps people find confidence in the fact that they're not facing their challenges alone. Perseverance in the face of challenge is more easily forged when you can look over your shoulder and know you can rely on people around you.

Meet Elvira, my wife

Elvira always says that life changed in many ways after one of my kite buddies knocked on our door that stormy evening, nearly six years ago now. The first months were so overwhelming, scary, and uncertain for her. One moment, life felt good, the next she was not sure if I would survive. Particularly, those first few weeks were like a ride on a roller-coaster with continuous ups and downs. She somehow managed to stay clear-headed as the prognosis flipped from 'really bad' to 'bad' to 'better than expected' to 'extremely lucky'. And after it was clear I would survive, she decided that everything that wasn't 'really bad' was simply closer to 'good'. It's funny how you shift your perspective that way when everything is so dire – it was all relative. 'He'll live, so we'll be fine,' she kept telling herself.

At work, she was used to managing stressful projects. She had managed large marketing teams across APAC and the Middle East and had gone through re-brandings, organisational restructures, and complex marketing automation and system implementations. This 'project' was on a different level though. All of a sudden, her sole purpose in life was to somehow get me and herself out of this situation in the best possible way. Just like that, her career was no longer important. After all those years of being a corporate tiger, suddenly, she didn't care about promotions, budgets, or money. The world became very small, with a very narrow focus on just the two of us.

The moment she walked into the ICU, she somehow went into project management mode, where her full focus was on controlling the things she *could* control. She says she has never been so focused, so engrossed into something. If she couldn't control my chance of healing, it would be *everything else*. She showed up at the hospital every morning at 7 am, fully dressed in her best business suit and high heels.

When I was still in a coma, she'd sit next to my bed and go through all her notes to determine what needed to be done for the day, and the questions she needed to ask. She wrote it all down in her notebook, and braced herself for another nerve-racking day. Before she went to bed, she went through all her notes again, to see what questions were still outstanding, and ticked off all the actions she'd done that day. Just like she'd always done at work. She'd turn to a new page in her notebook, and list all actions for the next day. 'These moments gave me sanity, and put me on a clear track for the next day', she would later tell me. 'Even when that new day would throw bad news at me, I had set a course, and established progress in the things that I could control. Without it, I would have been lost.'

Elvira is not someone who easily raises her hand to ask for help. Living through my accident and rehabilitation has made her realise how good it is to do so, though. We've both been amazed to see how many people were willing to help out, and how we could count on the community around us. Relationships changed. People who we'd known for years became much closer. To this day, our bond with everyone who played a role in those months has deepened. We're warmer to each other, dare to be more vulnerable and we are more likely to offer help, even when it's not asked for. We have more empathy, more awareness of each other's struggles and needs. It might sound weird, but the accident really has improved our lives. Elvira even changed her career goals and now is responsible for the marketing and fundraising of one of Australia's largest charities.

The department of people

By the time I went back to work full time, I had 'been out' for a whole year. A year in which I was absorbed in a world of care – a warm blanket. When I returned to the office, I had lost that 'warm blanket' feeling. The SaaS company I had worked for, had been absorbed into a huge global IT firm and many of the people I had worked closely with in the years before my accident had moved on. Those who remained showed empathy, understanding and concern, and were supportive of my slow re-introduction into full-time work, but it was different. Something was missing.

When one of my friends sent me the link to Brené Brown's TED Talk on vulnerability, I instantly knew why it felt so different at work.[47] In her book, *Daring Greatly: How the Courage to be Vulnerable Transforms the Way We Live, Love, Parent, and Lead (2012)*, she writes 'Vulnerability is not weakness, and the uncertainty, risk, and emotional exposure we face every day are not optional. Our only choice is a question of engagement. Our willingness to own and engage with our vulnerability determines the depth of our courage and the clarity of our purpose; the level to which we protect ourselves from being vulnerable is a measure of our fear and disconnection'.

The difference at work was how people interacted with each other. In my 12 months at home, I had become used to people offering help and being sensitive to signals that indicated struggle. Whenever I doubted my abilities, there was someone to help out – practically or mentally. Knowing that made me stronger. It kept me from holding back whenever I faced another hurdle. This culture was missing in the office. Many colleagues were anxious about their future after the takeover, yet, those challenges were not discussed in a constructive matter. Sure, many people were complaining, some louder than others, but such conversations always ended with a variant of that 'onwards and upwards' platitude. It never went any deeper. In sales, we don't tend to embrace vulnerability. We very much hang on to the belief that if we raise our hand and say we're struggling, or need help, we'll be perceived as weak.

Sales might be the 'department of habits', but it's the 'department of people', too. For all the challenges that come with our profession, and all the ways we can learn how to overcome them, more than anything else, our job is about people. People make our jobs so fun and exciting. They broaden our horizons and push us to higher levels. The most obvious way to point out this simple truth is to look at the origin of the word that sits at the heart of sales: *compete*. The root of the word compete is the Latin Con Petire, which means 'to seek together'. As psychologist Mihalyi Csikszentmihalyi says in *Flow*, 'What each person seeks is to actualize her potential, and this task is made easier when others force us to do our best'. Just like there would be no setbacks if it weren't for others, there would also be no purpose, no mastery, no planning or progress. The inherent drive to compete pushes us to be better. We need people to push us to excel, just like we need people to support us to. We can't just rely on ourselves.

I've been lucky enough to have experienced firsthand how the people around me have pushed me to become better. In sales, people can broaden our lives and help us to succeed in similar waves. But when you're in knee deep, that's sometimes easy to overlook. I hope these next suggestions will help you find the significance of the people around you.

Perseverance Promotors

1. Shape your support team

Consciously create and maintain a network of people who you can help, and who can help you. At the start of each quarter, sit down and think about who you would like to have in your support team. You don't have to ask them formally. Often a modus operandi based on an informal give-and-take works just fine. In terms of tangible support, you could involve your sales enablement team, your manager, or your peers sitting next to you. Informational support can come from outside your (direct) organisation. These could be sales coaches, network organisations and friends, preferably those who have sales roles at different companies. For emotional and companionship support, you'll want someone who's closer to you, and who understands you, more than the inherent challenges from work. Below are a few examples to help you determine what network you'd like to cultivate around you.

2. Find a sales buddy

A great source of tangible and informational support can be a 'sales buddy'. This is someone in your company who is familiar with the specifics of your challenge. See if you can team up with a new joiner, or better yet, with someone who's been there for a while. Unfortunately, that's not always practical. The guy who sits next to you slugging away at a different territory might take his competitiveness a bit too far and see it as a threat to help you get to your target. If you can't convince him of the shortsightedness of such an attitude, look farther afield.

In international companies, leverage a sales buddy overseas with the same role, the same target, and the same challenges. During SKO, network with the guys and girls in Europe, the USA, South America or APAC and find someone with whom you click. Agree to check in once every two weeks to compare notes. These could be practical tips around where to find a great example for a presentation you're preparing. Maybe you want to test your new pitch in a role play, or get some feedback on how to best position yourself against a competitor. Unless you're able to develop a close relationship on a personal level, international sales buddies are not always the best for emotional and companionship support. It's easy to vent your frustration with someone who doesn't sit right next to you, but not always the most productive way to develop a relationship over the phone. Be careful to not make it a 'whine session'.

3. Go cross-functional

If you're an SC, it's easy to limit yourself to others in the solution consulting team. Same for AE, SDRs, or CSMs. In reality, while they don't have the exact same role, your colleagues from other teams will understand many of your work specific challenges. When I was a sales rep, I enjoyed mentoring CSMs on how to present proposals, up-sell, or get ready for a negotiation. They're often less 'salesy' and always appreciate a helping hand. In turn, they provided me with invaluable support by looking at my challenges from a different angle.

4. Find a mentor or coach

A good mentor or coach can help provide new approaches to your challenges and bring clarity to your thinking. For most of my sales career, especially during my years as a sales rep, I've had weekly or bi-weekly check-ins with my coach. I never was able to get the company to pay for it, but am 100 percent convinced that I closed more deals because of my coach.

Be careful to pick a mentor or coach who suits your challenges. There are many life coaches who could be of value with generic challenges and struggles, but who have no idea what it is like to be in sales. Sales brings a particular set of challenges, and there is huge value in getting support from someone who's been there before you. They might not have had exactly the same role, but should at least have had experience in selling products of a similar nature. I struggle to take advice on how to persevere at selling from people who have never sold anything; there are so many nuances in our profession that bad advice can have really poor consequences. Find someone who can go beyond what you can find in self-help books and see if they can provide practical tips to help you persevere.

5. Look beyond sales

At the same time, be careful not to become too narrow-minded. There's value in going outside your own tribe. People with different motivations tend to look at problems differently. Now and then, have lunch with one of the project managers or technical support specialists, and you'll see that they can have a refreshingly different view on your challenges. You won't necessarily take advice from them on how to sell, but you are likely to get value from the different views they will bring to the table.

6. Open up to your manager

It's not easy to be vulnerable within your own team. In reality, however, everyone has periods of struggle and low confidence, including your manager. See if you can create an open relationship by asking for help. Chances are your manager is more than willing to get involved and can offer constructive ideas. If you don't think you can get the relationship with your manager to a point where you can ask for help, get support from a sales coach, or get closer to your sales buddy.

7. Show your gratitude

However short your deal cycle or small your deal, make a habit of calling the key people at your newly-won client, to *thank them for their business.* Although it should be an automatic act based on common decency, I encounter sales cultures where it's a forgotten custom. It's amazing what such simple appreciation can do, not just for the person at the receiving end, but for the one expressing appreciation. As we saw with the Count your Blessings exercise in Chapter 7, gratitude is scientifically proven to increase well-being. It can be a real motivation builder, so don't pass on the chance to say thank you.

8. Laugh

Earlier, you read that putting on a happy face can trick the brain to reduce stress levels. It goes without saying, however, that there's nothing better than the real thing. The jokes that Barney kept feeding me calmed me down when things didn't go well. The work environment doesn't always lend itself to see the funny side of life, but that's only more reason to put some effort into finding it. A bit of humour can take away a lot of tension. Several companies I have worked with have implemented the Friday afternoon trivia hour. They are entertaining get-togethers that lead to a lot of laughter, which helps release the stress built up during the week.

I've never tried it, but there's a group in my neighbourhood that gets together once a month for laugh therapy. It's a joy to hear them laugh, even after you realise they're doing it quite deliberately. I can imagine it provides a relief and helps boost their mood.

9. Accept mistakes

Trust is needed to strengthen relations within your team and with your customers. Sales professionals sometimes make it hard to build such trust by refusing to admit they made a mistake. They blame others instead. Always be honest to yourself and 'fess up' to your team members and clients if you dropped the ball. You'll come to see that people will appreciate you for your honesty and will be more willing to offer to help out.

10. Help others

Remember John, Richard and Rob, the brick layers from Chapter 3 who worked on an elderly home? Their intrinsic motivation level differed widely. John came to his job with the sole purpose to lay bricks. Richard had a broader perspective and wanted to build a wall. Rob's mission was to provide elderly people with an environment of safety and enjoyment. While my initial reaction, after my accident, was to *Get My Old Life Back,* the experience profoundly changed my inner drivers. I now am motivated by helping other people become better at selling. I coach SaaS sales teams and have never enjoyed my work more. I am surprised at how much joy I get from helping others. I've come across more trauma survivors in recent years and see that it is not uncommon for them to go through similar career shifts that have intrinsic motivation at their core.

The accident has shifted my True North

Fortunately, you don't need an accident to try a similar shift in your daily work. That presentation that you're nailing? See if you can help new joiners in your team perfect their pitch. Join them in their meetings, and help them find their feet. Hear someone struggling on the phone with a prospect? Take them for lunch and ask if you can help. Think sales enablement is not doing a good job? Offer to help and take on a module at the next boot camp.

Perseverance Destroyers

1. Don't let your partner bear the brunt

There will be moments at work where you'll be biting your tongue. Be careful not to take that pent-up frustration home and vent on your partner or close friend. As you look for emotional support, 'spread the load' of such venting to others. Maybe your coach or sales buddy can play that role. I tend to call a couple of friends whenever I am desperate to get things off my chest. That doesn't mean that Elvira is fully spared, but I make a very deliberate attempt to not dump it all on her.

2. Don't pretend like nothing happened

When someone shows vulnerability, offer a helping hand. The compassion of others increased my ability to persevere. It also led to deepened relationships. I've noticed that of all the professions in my network, it's sales people who find it most uncomfortable to discuss topics that could potentially be upsetting. Some people opt out. This is not only a clumsy way to avoid uncomfortable situations where someone might need mental support, it is also a missed opportunity to improve perseverance levels of the team, rather than just the individuals.

As a manager, if you find someone in your team struggling or even crying, don't view them as an emotional wreck. They are displaying in a physical way that they are dealing with stress or disappointment. Others' mechanisms could be an angry face, silence, or a walk-out. Everybody deals differently with the stresses that built up at work. In these cases, pretending that nothing happened is an approach that will only lead to more friction later, *so do* address it. Take your colleague out for a walk, or step into a room and let them calm down first. Crying typically lasts

5–6 minutes before a sense of well-being overtakes. Show compassion to the difficulties being experienced and try to steer towards a solution with questions that are specific. 'What are you struggling with? What are you trying to accomplish?' These questions allow for a more solution-oriented discussion than a question like 'What's going on?'[48]

Also, make sure you don't leave things open-ended but confirm the specific actions agreed. Not doing so could potentially create an unproductive loop where inaction leads to the trigger of stress recurring, which leads to crying, which leads to inaction ...

If the struggle from one of your colleagues is unrelated to work, that doesn't mean it shouldn't be addressed. Particularly with big impact events like sickness or death in the family, it's important to show empathy. This doesn't mean you have to play the role of a shrink, though. During my recovery, I obtained a huge amount of energy from emails, text messages and cards simply saying 'thinking of you'. Knowing that I wasn't on my own provided enough emotional support to keep me going.

3.   Don't create boys' clubs

In many companies, sales is still a male-dominated profession. In 2014, LinkedIn found that just 39 percent of all sales roles were filled by females. Among sales leaders, women represented only 19 percent.[49] I haven't been able to find more recent numbers, but I know from my daily interactions with sales teams that women are indeed very much underrepresented. This could be because their bosses tend to be male with a (unconscious) biased notion as to what makes a great sales professional. Whether deliberate or not, job descriptions seem to confirm this bias with words like 'hunter', 'aggressive', 'determined', 'work hard, play hard', 'rock star', 'sales warrior', and so on.

In San Francisco, the Women in Sales Everywhere team (WISE) organises events to help create a healthier balance. Check out their blog with excellent tips specifically for women in sales.[50] Europe is lucky enough to have the Woman in Sales Awards (WISA) that celebrate the accomplishments of women in sales roles.[51] Do a bit of Googling to see if there are similar initiatives in your neck of the woods.

4. Don't ignore others

People in sales often aren't comfortable talking about bad news or opening up in conversations that could expose their vulnerability, or that of the other party. That doesn't mean you should ignore someone in your team who seems to be struggling. A simple 'how are you doing?' could suffice. Offer to help, or simply lend an ear. Often, when someone is asked to articulate the problem, the solution becomes much clearer. It is one of the main benefits I get from my coach, who, with one simple question, can get me completely unstuck. I'm doing all the work, but he knows what kind of questions will get me to solution mode.

5. Don't squander SKO

It pains me to see 'cliquish' sales teams during global SKO or other internal networking events, who only socialise with the people from their local office. It's such a valuable time to network and find international sales buddies, yet it's often such a missed opportunity. Do your homework before you attend; decide who you want to meet, and network just like you would on any other sales event. Don't fly home until you have met at least ten new people. Go home richer.

6. Don't let your competitiveness kill the team spirit

Remember the origins of 'to compete' were *to seek together*. Sales people tend to be competitive, which is good until it hampers collaboration in the team. It's no fun being the only one who made target; ensure you pull your friends over the finish line as well. If you're that one guy or girl who wants to win at all cost, you'll be struggling all by yourself when things look bleak.

7. Don't think you're the only one struggling

Like all people, sales professionals have their insecurities. Sales professionals also question their own abilities. They wonder if they're good enough and doubt if they'll ever achieve what's expected of them.

Struggling with your ability to stay motivated and persevere is not a weakness. It's just one of the challenges that come with our demanding jobs. Everyone struggles with these challenges. Even that amazing rep who always seems to land the biggest deals. Whatever face we put on, whatever air of confidence we gather, we all have periods where we can't see how we can possibly succeed. Knowing that you are not alone should reduce the mental barrier to ask for help.

8. Don't give up

Now that technological progress has become much more accessible, it is harder for companies to develop products that truly have a long term USP. Whenever your company launches a new feature, your competitor will follow promptly, particularly in SaaS. You shouldn't wait for product development to come up with crystal clear USPs that make prospects fall over themselves to sign up with you. You're better served to develop *your own* long-term USP: *your ability to persevere as a sales professional.* If you can master the many practices and skills I have shared with you better than the person who is hired in the same role at your competitor, you're more likely to win the deal. If you manage to stay motivated when things don't go your way and keep going at it with a smile on your face, more business will come your way.

Whenever the weight of setbacks becomes unbearable, it can be tempting to look for greener grass and start looking for a job elsewhere. While there are always valid reasons to resign, you're guaranteed to encounter setbacks and challenges in your new role, too. Are you sure you're not taking the easy way out? Are you leaving for the right reasons? The best way to assess that is to write them down into two columns: negative and positive reasons. Examples of negative reasons are 'Our product sucks', 'We're too expensive', 'I don't like my manager', 'They never give me enough leads' and so on. Positive ones could be 'I'm genuinely excited about the product from this new company', 'This new role is more aligned with my True North', or 'These new responsibilities really accelerate my path towards my career vision'. Give the reasons a rating from 1 being 'mildly important', 2 being 'important' and 3 being 'very important'. Add up the weighted numbers in each column.

If your negative reasons outweigh the positive ones, be careful. The question is not so much whether these reasons are correct, rather, it's the negative mindset they bring. When you are in a negative space, you are less likely to make the right long-term decision. If, on the contrary, you're mostly seeing positive reasons, go for it. Never make such an important decision in isolation and articulate your reasoning with your wider support network to keep yourself honest. Ask for their opinions and be open to changing yours. Not giving up when things look bleak will create a level of satisfaction that will stay with you forever. Persevering makes your life richer and more fulfilling, so don't throw away the opportunity.

A final word

'Why, in God's name, would you want to strap yourself to a kite again?' Dr Tom asked.

It was six months after my accident and I was having a check-up with the man who screwed my pelvis back together. He had been studying the X-rays jammed to the clips of the light box on the wall, and slowly turned around. I couldn't decide what to make of the look in his eyes – it was somewhere between fascination and frustration. Over his shoulder, I could see the five long screws scattered around the messy sea of grey tones that was my pelvis. They stood out as long, contrasting white lines.

'Why would you want to tie yourself to a big kite? That's how you ended up here in the first place,' he pointed out while throwing his arms in the air. Maybe I should not have told him about that last step in my SMART plan. 'Haven't you learned how dangerous these extreme sports are?' No ... I definitely shouldn't have told him. He turned around and started pointing at the screws with an old school fountain pen. 'I am not sure if your pelvis can handle the force. Let alone the falls.'

He kept talking but I stopped listening. Then, before I knew it, he whisked me out of the door, told his assistant something about what billing code to apply, and closed the door without shaking hands.

***

Back then, I was still in the early stages of my journey to find out what motivates people to persevere. I wasn't able to answer his questions, beyond a weak 'but I like it'. I wouldn't have had the framework to put my motivation, nor his point of view, into perspective. I was merely following my gut.

Now, I see that the focus kitesurfing gave me played a huge role in my ability to come out stronger. Taking it away would have been detrimental. Dr Tom didn't know about all the things I would be learning about my brain, and the effort I put into my exercises to stay motivated and pain free. He didn't know how previous setbacks, like the session with Max, had nearly dragged me under and made me lose perspective.

He hadn't seen my SMART plan and didn't know the role the roundabout had played in my rehabilitation. Sure, he would have had the technical know-how to determine whether my goal was even remotely *attainable*, but he wouldn't have understood the *relevance* of it. Dr Tom had never kitesurfed and would never understand how important the sense of *autonomy* and *mastery* was for my *motivation to persevere*. He wouldn't have appreciated how much the *appraisal* of that progress of kitesurfing would push me to keep going. And he had no idea of the *support network* that had formed around me. He only saw the downside, quite literally, in those X-rays.

There was no point asking him as he didn't know what sat behind my motivation to persevere. That was up to me to discover.

Five years later, at the exact spot where the accident happened

What about you?

I hope that sharing the lessons learned from my journey can help you stay motivated to find joy in your work. I hope the practical ideas help you to persevere whenever you find yourself facing challenges in sales.

As a starting point, I suggest you select just a few new habits you want to work on this quarter. Pick the chapters that resonated most, and quickly review the Perseverance Promotors and Destroyers. Decide which ones you want to make your own, and set yourself a goal to work on, say, five of them. Write them down, print them out, hang them up. Use the examples, exercises, models and printouts in the workbook (get it from www.franklodewick.com/books) to develop these habits. Slowly incorporate them into your day-to-day practices, and see which ones make most sense for you.

Once you're comfortable with your new way of working, find a couple more to add on to your skill set. I've deliberately listed over a hundred suggestions with the expectation that you'll be able to find at least a dozen that will work for you. But even if you just find one new habit that makes it easier to persevere, I'm grateful that I have helped you.

If you have feedback, ideas or suggestions that can help build perseverance for you and your colleagues, do send me an email (enquire@franklodewick.com).

About the author

When Frank finished his MBA in the USA in 1994, one of his professors offended him by suggesting he'd go into sales. 'Whatever you want to do in life, you'll need to be able to convince others', he said. 'You need to know how to handle people with other interests and understand how you can get them on your side. Whether it's your colleague whose help you need, your manager who needs to be convinced that you deserve a raise, the CEO who needs to approve your expansion plan, or even a shareholder who needs to put money into your exciting new venture. Whatever you do, wherever in the world, *getting people to buy into your ideas* is key to your success, and happiness. And there's no better place than to start in sales.'

Now, 25 years later, Frank is not only thankful he took that advice, he has dedicated his entire career to the exciting profession that sales turned out to be. Following his first sales roles in Amsterdam, he spent five years in Singapore, travelling the region to close deals with companies in Indonesia, the Philippines, Thailand, India, Pakistan and Malaysia. His sales career then took him to Sydney, Australia, where he still resides with his wife. He has closed nearly $100 million in deals for hi-tech businesses ranging from pre-IPO start-ups to the big corporate end of town.

Throughout his career, Frank noticed how poorly prepared he and his colleagues were for the many challenges that were thrown at them. A life-threatening kitesurfing accident was the catalyst for Frank to change things. As an author, keynote speaker, and sales coach, he now supports sales professionals to close more deals, but to also 'enjoy the ride' and stay healthier and happier.

Work with Frank

Frank's clients are SaaS sales teams that are keen to increase their sales success, and need more than another sales training. Through workshops, ongoing reviews, and 1:1 sessions, Frank gets embedded in sales teams and works side by side with the account executives, sales development reps, solutions consultants, customer success managers, and their front line sales managers to drive change. Engagements range from one-off workshops, to multi-month engagements of multiple days per week.

Frank can also bring a fresh bout of inspiration through his speaking engagements at sales kick offs, or in smaller settings, for example a quarterly business review. His unique angle on what it takes to persevere in sales can be the catalyst for change in sales teams that want to push themselves to become better.

If you are keen to explore how Frank can help you, please check out www.franklodewick.com, send an email to enquire@franklodewick.com, or reach out on LinkedIn: https://www. linkedin.com/in/franklodewick/.

References

Amabile, T. (2011). *The progress principle: Using small wins to ignite joy, engagement, and creativity at work.* Harvard Business Review Press.

Brown, B. (2012) *Daring Greatly: How the Courage to Be Vulnerable Transforms the Way We Live, Love, Parent, and Lead.* Avery.

Chamine, S. (2012). *Positive intelligence: Why only 20% of teams and individuals achieve their true potential and how you can achieve yours.* Greenleaf Book Group Press.

Csikszentmihalyi, M. (2008). *Flow: The psychology of optimal experince.* Harper Perennial Modern Classics.

Duckworth, A. (2017). *Grit: The power of passion and perserverance.* London: Ebury Publishing.

Friedman, M., & Rosenman, R. H. (1974). *Type A behavior and your heart.* New York: Knopf.

Huffington, A. (2017). *The sleep revolution: Transforming your life, one night at a time.* Ebury Publishing.

Kerridge, T. (2017). *Dopamine diet: My low-carb, stay-happy way to lose weight.* Absolute Press.

Loehr, J. (2005). *The power of full engagment: Managing energy, not time, is the key to high performance and personal renewal.* Free Press.

McLeod, L. E. (2012). *Selling with noble purpose: How to drive revenue and do work that makes you proud.* Wiley.

Oettingen, G. (2015). *Rethinking positive thinking: Inside the new science of motivation.* Current.

Pink, D. (2011). *Drive: The surprising truth about what motivates us.* Riverhead Books.

Sandberg, S., & Grant, A. (2017). *Option B: Facing adversity, building resilience, and finding joy.* London: Ebury Publishing.

Sinek, S. (2011). *Start with why: How great leaders inspire everyone to take action.* Penguin Press.

Stengel, J. (2011). *Grow: How ideals power growth and profit at the world's greatest companies.* Crown Business.

Yousafzai, M. (2013). *I am Malala: The girl who stood up for education and was shot by the Taliban.* Little, Brown and Company.

Endnotes

1 https://journals.lww.com/ccmjournal/Abstract/2016/09000/Depressive_Symptoms_After_Critical_Illness___A.14.aspx

2 https://www.bls.gov/cps/cpsaat17.htm

3 https://blog.hubspot.com/news-trends/how-salespeople-learn

4 https://www.salesforce.com/story-of-sales/

5 https://journals.plos.org/plosone/article?id=10.1371/journal.pone.0120644

6 https://www.hubspot.com/sales-close-rate

7 https://www.forbes.com/sites/kenkrogue/2017/09/26/new-sales-trend-research-us-sales-reps-lagging-behind-european-counterparts/#1ed060e4632f

8 https://www.salesforce.com/form/conf/state-of-sales-3rd-edition/

9 https://business.linkedin.com/talent-solutions/blog/trends-and-research/2018/the-3-industries-with-the-highest-turnover-rates

10 https://www.icmi.com/resources/2016/Reducing-Attrition-in-Contact-Centers

11 https://www.forentrepreneurs.com/bridge-group-2015/

12 https://www.siriusdecisions.com/blog/itsturnovertimeforsales

13 https://www2.deloitte.com/content/dam/Deloitte/global/Documents/About-Deloitte/deloitte-2019-millennial-survey.pdf

14 https://business.linkedin.com/content/dam/business/talent-solutions/global/en_us/job-switchers/PDF/job-switchers-global-report-english.pdf

15 https://www.forbes.com/sites/christinecomaford/2016/06/18/how-leaders-can-engage-retain-top-sales-talent/#2c7123535cbb

16 https://www.stress.org/workplace-stress/

17 https://www.healthdirect.gov.au/work-related-stress

18 http://www.hse.gov.uk/statistics/causdis/stress/stress.pdf

19 https://www.amazon.com/Daily-Drucker-Insight-Motivation-Getting/dp/0060742445

20 https://hbr.org/2014/04/does-your-company-have-enough-sales-managers

21 https://hbr.org/product/managing-oneself-harvard-business-review-classics/2312E-KND-ENG

22 https://www.etui.org/Topics/Health-Safety-working-conditions/HesaMag/The-future-of-work-in-the-digital-era

23 https://www.templafy.com/blog/how-many-emails-are-sent-every-day-top-email-statistics-your-business-needs-to-know/

24 https://www.bloomberg.com/news/articles/2018-11-09/move-over-medium-skill-workers

25 https://www.saleshacker.com/salestech-landscape-2019/

26 https://www.ncbi.nlm.nih.gov/pmc/articles/PMC4035568/

27 https://www.sleepfoundation.org/articles/how-much-sleep-do-we-really-need

28 https://www.ncbi.nlm.nih.gov/pmc/articles/PMC3579000/

29 https://www.theguardian.com/business-to-business/2017/dec/04/
    clocking-off-the-companies-introducing-nap-time-to-the-workplace

30 https://www.bbc.com/news/magazine-26958079

31 http://citeseerx.ist.psu.edu/viewdoc/download?doi=
    10.1.1.832.6320&rep=rep1&type=pdf

32 https://www.ncbi.nlm.nih.gov/pmc/articles/PMC3070188/

33 https://www.independent.co.uk/news/media/tv-radio/average-
    watching-tv-briton-10-years-life-research-a8367526.html

34 https://www.ncbi.nlm.nih.gov/pubmed/19560716

35 https://famemass.com/time-spent-on-social-media/

36 https://psycnet.apa.org/doiLanding?doi=10.1037%2Fa0034415

37 https://hbr.org/2001/01/the-making-of-a-corporate-athlete

38 https://greatergood.berkeley.edu/images/application_uploads/
    Emmons-CountingBlessings.pdf

39 https://www.positiveintelligence.com/program/

40 https://www.smh.com.au/politics/federal/over-65s-flooding-the-job-market-
    and-finding-they-re-not-so-employable-20190810-p52fsc.html

41 https://hbr.org/2011/06/the-seven-personality-traits-o)

42 https://www.forbes.com/sites/christinecomaford/2016/06/18/
    how-leaders-can-engage-retain-top-sales-talent/#2c7123535cbb

43 https://www.ncbi.nlm.nih.gov/pmc/articles/PMC3654935/

44 https://www.amazon.com/Social-Support-Physical-Health-Understanding/
    dp/0300182716

45 https://www.ncbi.nlm.nih.gov/pmc/articles/PMC3683363/

46 https://www.theleader.com.au/story/4000415/
    governors-message-on-the-importance-of-mateship/

47 https://www.youtube.com/watch?v=iCvmsMzlF7o

48 https://hbr.org/2018/03/how-to-manage-an-employee-who-cries-easily

49 https://business.linkedin.com/sales-solutions/resources/sales/
    top-trends-of-women-sales-professionals

50 https://womeninsaleseverywhere.com/

51 http://wisawards.com/index.html

Notes

Notes

Notes

Lightning Source UK Ltd.
Milton Keynes UK
UKHW020242051219
354766UK00006B/183/P